WHAT'S THE MATTER
WITH LIBERALISM?

WHAT'S THE MATTER
WITH LIBERALISM?

RONALD BEINER

University of California Press
Berkeley • Los Angeles • London

University of California Press
Berkeley and Los Angeles, California

University of California Press, Ltd.
London, England

Copyright © 1992 by
The Regents of the University of California

First Paperback Printing 1995

Library of Congress Cataloging-in-Publication Data

Beiner, Ronald, 1953–
   What's the matter with liberalism? / Ronald Beiner.
     p. cm.
   Includes bibliographical references and index.
   ISBN 0-520-20335-6
   1. Liberalism. 2. Political science—Philosophy. 3. Political
ethics. 4. Civil rights. 5. Citizenship. 6. Social justice.
7. Socialism. I. Title.
JC571.B45   1992
320.5'1—dc20   91-29453

Printed in the United States of America

1 2 3 4 5 6 7 8 9

Contents

Prefatory Note

This little book was mainly put together during a time of remarkable revolutionary upheavals in Europe. The Central European revolution was hailed in the liberal, market-oriented West in a self-congratulatory mood. The self-congratulation was thought to be warranted because, first, the West had "won" a certain kind of war that had been waged in the preceding four decades, and second, because the economic dynamism of liberal societies was deemed to be the decisive mark of superiority of the West over the East in the winning of this war. One of the intentions of this book was to question whether uncritical self-congratulation was the most suitable way in which to receive the great changes in the socialist world. The appropriate questions for us have in fact already been formulated by one of the leaders of that revolution:

> The post-totalitarian system has been built on foundations laid by the historical encounter between dictatorship and the consumer society. Is it not true that the far-reaching adaptability to living a lie and the effortless spread of social auto-totality have some connection with the general unwillingness of consumption-oriented people to sacrifice some material certainties for the sake of their own spiritual and moral integrity? With their willingness to surrender higher values when faced with the trivializing temptations of modern civilization? With their vulnerability to the attractions of mass indifference? And in the end, is not the greyness and the emptiness of life in the post-totalitarian system only an inflated caricature of modern life in general? And do we not in fact stand (although in the external measures of civilization, we are far behind) as a kind of warning to the West, revealing to it its own latent tendencies?[1]

Earlier versions of chapter 1 were presented at Queen's University, the University of Toronto, and the University of Dayton; a

---

1. Václav Havel, "The Power of the Powerless," in *The Power of the Powerless*, ed. John Keane (London: Hutchinson, 1985), pp. 38–39.

version of it was published in the *Queen's Quarterly*. Earlier versions
of chapter 2 were presented at Osgoode Hall Law School and
McGill University; a version of it was published in *Law and the
Community: The End of Individualism?* edited by Allan C. Hutchinson
and Leslie Green (Toronto: Carswell, 1989). An earlier version of
chapter 3 was presented at a meeting of the American Society for
Political and Legal Philosophy, and is to be published in volume 34
of NOMOS, edited by John Chapman and William Galston. An
earlier version of chapter 4 was presented at the University of Toronto Law Faculty. An earlier version of chapter 6 was presented
at a private discussion group attended by Rebecca Comay, Dieter
Misgeld, and Graeme Nicholson. A collage of various sections of
the book, entitled "The Liberal Regime," is to be published in the
Chicago-Kent Law Review; versions of it were presented at Harvard
University and the Chicago-Kent College of Law. I am grateful for
the use of material published elsewhere, grateful to the individuals
and institutions that invited me to speak, and not least, grateful to
the audiences that received and criticized what I presented. I have
received very generous financial assistance toward the completion
of this project from the Connaught Programme in Legal Theory and
Public Policy, the Social Science and Humanities Research Council
of Canada, and the Lynde and Harry Bradley Foundation, all of
which I thankfully acknowledge. I must also express my deep appreciation for my good fortune in being able to conduct these studies in an environment so wonderfully conducive to work in political
philosophy as the University of Toronto. I owe a debt to all of my
political theory colleagues, but in the completion of this project I
have received particular help and encouragement from Joe Carens.
Huge thanks must go to Brenda Samuels, Anna Apuzzo, and Mary
Wellman for their tireless work on the manuscript. Finally, my com-
panions on this voyage of writing should not go without mention:
Ann, who dragged me to the resting-place of John Stuart Mill, aptly
enough, to write chapter 5; and Zimra, citizen of the twenty-first
century, whose claim to a better world gives a special impulse to
these reflections.

Avignon
November 1990

1

Prologue: The Theorist as Storyteller

Political philosophers in the twentieth century have on the whole been a curiously self-abnegating lot. The majority of them have deliberately abstained from the large and deep speculations on the good society and the good for humanity that characterized the great tradition of Western thought. Political philosophers, at least those of the analytical variety, have confined themselves to the modest enterprise of conceptual analysis—theoretical clarification of the concepts that figure prominently in political life. Philosophers within the Continental tradition have shown less abstinence, but where they did dare to pronounce on large, substantive questions of human nature and the essence of politics, they tended to reiterate well-established theories already on offer within the tradition. Of course, there are exceptions. But it is striking that even Jürgen Habermas, who *is* committed to offering a comprehensive theory of the rational society, can say in his book *Legitimation Crisis* that we can expect no guidance from metaphysically grounded theories of ethics or from substantive theories of human nature. And with the influence of French poststructuralism gaining ground, an even more radical renunciation of traditional philosophy is demanded, and even a minimal appeal to shared rationality is rendered suspect.

Certainly within Anglo-American modes of thought one strains to think of any serious effort to formulate an original statement of the good for humanity. There are many who will say that now this has all changed. In recent years, with the publication of John Rawls's *A Theory of Justice* and works of a similar kind, vitality has once again returned to political philosophy, which once more offers guidance on the major questions of political life. However, it seems to me that however ambitious the work of Rawls may appear, it is in fact no less self-restricting and self-effacing than other work in the analytical tradition. One of the reasons for this is the insistence

on offering a guide to practical affairs—cutting theoretical speculation down to the need for practical decisions on the immediate
questions of daily life. This is a conception of theory that Rawls
shares with most other contemporary political philosophers. Indeed, the conception of political philosophy most prevalent in the
Anglo-American world today is that of recommending policies: the
function of the philosopher is to supply clever arguments for favoring one set of policies rather than another. Cutting theory off more
sharply from immediate practice would restore to theory its freedom of speculation—something always indispensable to original
works of theory.

In many cases philosophers have failed to produce important
reflections on moral and political life not for want of ability but
because they believed it did not befit the philosopher to pronounce
on what is important and essential in human life. In other words,
they deliberately forsook such reflections on account of theoretical
scruples. They were persuaded that such "modesty" was appropriate to the philosophical vocation.

Let us compare what may be considered appropriate to a great
work of literature. The great novel or great drama often succeeds
in disclosing what it means to be a human being, what is worthy
or unworthy in human life, what is ennobling and what is degrading in human affairs; and the best literary characterizations may
present us with exemplary human types.[1] It is not surprising, indeed it is only natural, if novelists, poets, and dramatists aspire to
some major insight into human nature and the defining features of
a significant human life. Why should the philosopher now aspire
to less? Here the reply will come that the literary artist can allow
himself or herself this indulgence because his or her preoccupation
is with the world of imagination, not with the establishment of
truth, whereas the philosopher's enterprise is one of cognition and
requires that one set one's standards by the satisfaction of demon-
strable claims to propositional validity. The literary imagination, it

---

1. The point here can be rephrased as follows: "Literary interest will
always be parasitic on moral interest. In particular, you cannot create a
memorable character without thereby making a suggestion about how your
reader should act." Richard Rorty, *Contingency, Irony, and Solidarity* (Cambridge: Cambridge University Press, 1989), p. 167.

will be said, can allow itself a rich array of possibilities in conceiving human experience; philosophy, however, must discipline itself to the strict requirements of truth, and accordingly must be wary of the merest hint of extravagance. Therefore literary authors can indulge themselves in a way that philosophical authors cannot.

But is this the case? Distinguished works of literature have the force that they do because they seek to give us some unified and compelling vision of ourselves; that is, they attempt to uncover some important truth about ourselves. The work of literature, when it fulfills its highest potentialities, enters truth-claims, and the imaginative effort is at the same time a cognitive undertaking. The real achievement at which it aims is not the mere conjuring of possibilities, but the securing of a knowledge of human existence. Again, we pose our question: Why should philosophy aspire to less? Literature in this traditional and noble sense has not been abandoned; why, then, should theorists and political philosophers voluntarily abandon substantive philosophical anthropology (the philosophy of humanity, or a systematic theory of human nature)?

Let me give an example of the kind of theory that has been purposely neglected. For Aristotle it was possible to discern a set of ethical capacities having a reality on a par with our physical capacities. These are both natural and habitual. We are born with a range of native endowments, physical and ethical, but these can (and must) be developed through exercise and deployment in practice. On the basis of Aristotle's ethics, one could extrapolate an analogy between physical fitness and "ethical fitness." No one would think to assert that we are all born with identical physical endowments, or that all such endowments are identically desirable. Some are better endowed than others. There are people who have a capacity for swift running that I can never hope to emulate. But this is not simply a matter of native endowment. Muscles that are not exercised will atrophy. Capacities can be trained to a certain extent, and the point of physical fitness is to develop one's inborn capacities to their full employment. Aristotle's writings on ethics suggest a parallel with ethical life. Ethical fitness is a combination of native endowment and trained practice. Just as a muscle must be exercised in order to reach its full potential, so an ethical capacity (such as justice or prudence or capacity for friendship) must be put into practice in order to realize one's human potential as an ethical being.[2] And just as some people will always have the ability (latent or developed) physically to outrun me, so there are some people who naturally outrun others in their capacity for moral insight. Ethical fitness means exercising through habituation our natural ethical endowments, just as physical fitness consists in developing our muscles to their natural potential. Ethical life, for Aristotle, is a matter of developing our innate endowments to a state of maximal fitness. We have little difficulty in distinguishing when someone has attained a state of full physical well-being; ethical theory looks for an analogous standard of ethical well-being, and the latter standard should be no less accessible to the normal intelligence than is the former.

Physical fitness is a normative concept, no less normative than ethical fitness in our sense. In fact it would be odd to omit normative terms from the description of someone's *physical* condition; such terms arise when we say a person is overweight, out of shape, or sluggish, for example. Why shouldn't the description of a person's *ethical* condition be likewise normative? Just as we can say that it is undesirable when someone is obese, unfit, and sufficiently out of shape that he or she cannot ascend a flight of stairs without panting, so we can say with no less legitimacy that it is undesirable when individuals become so ethically unfit that they are incapable of sustaining friendships, or when they corrupt their own moral ends in order to satisfy base impulses such as stinginess or greed. The way the person of practical wisdom exercises his or her capacities for ethical insight in situations of praxis is, on this understanding, fundamentally no different from the way the person of physical strength flexes his or her muscles in the appropriate context. (Needless to say, our exemplar here is *not* Arnold Schwarzenegger!) So, in one case as in the other, it is entirely unexceptional that we can derive practical norms from the description of ordinary capacities and the situations in which they are commonly exercised.

Now this is precisely the kind of theory that contemporary philosophy regards as unfeasible. Why *should* we now abstain from such reflections? To be sure, Aristotle assumed that the students of

---

2. Cf. John Stuart Mill, *On Liberty*, ed. David Spitz (New York: W. W. Norton, 1975), p. 55: "The mental and moral, like the muscular powers, are improved only by being used."

his ethics would already be equipped by upbringing and the ethos of their community to be receptive to his characterization of ethical well-being. Contemporary philosophy makes no such assumptions. But the primary reason why such an ethical theory meets with skepticism is that it presupposes a substantive theory of human nature—an account of the virtues that conduce to an excellent human life.

As I argued earlier, literary works, even today, do not flinch from such normative claims. Let me give a specific example of how important works of literature depend upon normative truth: Italo Calvino's *Invisible Cities* is a masterpiece of storytelling about the diversity of urban living-spaces and the dissolution of this diversity. The implication is that, collectively, we are paying a fatal price for the homogenization of the human habitat. The work owes its force to the validity of this descriptive truth-claim. Either our situation is like that or it isn't, and the literary creation loses an essential dimension if it is a misdescription. I need not go so far as to claim that this kind of message exhausts the novel; I need merely establish that it accounts for an important part of the literary power of the work. The novel asserts that human beings risk losing themselves if they so reconstruct the conditions of their existence that Tokyo becomes indistinguishable from Los Angeles, that one city becomes absolutely the same as and continuous with another city, except for the name of the airport. This is not very different from the sort of claim offered by the traditional political philosopher or philosophical anthropologist. In fact, in certain respects Calvino's truth telling bears affinity with some aspects of Aristotle's theory: if certain conditions are not present or are removed, human ethical life atrophies; in particular, virtues that flourish in the polis perish in the megalopolis.

In support of my argument that works of literature assert normative and cognitive claims to validity, I will cite the testimony of Iris Murdoch, who is both novelist and philosopher:

> I think that though they are so different, philosophy and literature are both truth-seeking and truth-revealing activities. They are cognitive activities, explanations. Literature, like other arts, involves exploration, classification, discrimination, organized vision. Of course good literature does not look like "analysis" because what the imagination produces is sensuous, fused, reified, mysterious, ambiguous,

particular. Art is cognition in another mode. Think how much thought, how much truth, a Shakespeare play contains, or a great novel. It is illuminating in the case of any reflective discipline to see what kind of critical vocabulary is directed against it. Literature may be criticized in a purely formal way. But more often it is criticized for being in some sense untruthful. Words such as "sentimental," "pretentious," "self-indulgent," "trivial" and so on, impute some kind of falsehood, some failure of justice, some distortion or inade- quacy of understanding or expression. The word "fantasy" in a bad sense covers many of these typical literary faults. It may be useful to contrast "fantasy" as bad with "imagination" as good. . . . In condemning art for being "fantastic" one is condemning it for being untrue.[3]

Murdoch's point is that the imagination is itself a cognitive faculty, that the efforts of the imagination are a form of cognitive exertion, and that one immerses oneself in a literary work not simply to derive enjoyment or to be entertained, but often in order to come to a better understanding. Many philosophers today, particularly in France (poststructuralists and practitioners of deconstruction), would wish to relax the distinction between philosophy and litera- ture in order to reduce the cognitive claims of philosophy. My aim is exactly the opposite: to liken philosophy to literary activity in order to elevate the cognitive claims of literature.

Let there be no mistake about the kind of normative claims that I am ascribing to philosophy and literature. The literary work, in its evocation of exemplary types, does not offer direct practical in- junctions of the form, "Live your life thus." Rather, it recommends, "Reflect on life in the light of these truths about our common situa- tion." The case is the same with works of theory such as Aristotle's *Ethics*. It too does not contain specific practical injunctions of the form, "Live your life thus." It, too, suggests rather, "Reflect on life in the light of these truths about our common situation."

To put this point another way, so its implication will be clear: I am urging both more modesty and greater ambition on the part of theorists—more modesty with respect to specific practical recom- mendations, greater ambition in general reflection upon the nature

---

3. "Philosophy and Literature: Dialogue with Iris Murdoch," in *Men of Ideas*, ed. Bryan Magee (Oxford: Oxford University Press, 1982), pp. 235–236.

of humankind and the ends of society. I do not believe it is the place of the theorist to tell us, for instance, whether we should be opting for a unilateralist or multilateralist nuclear disarmament policy; that is a matter not for theoretical decision but for common deliberation among citizens. On the other hand, however, I believe it is within the competence of theory to inform us of the general implications of a state of affairs where the means of defense of a society's way of life is so remote from the experiences and imaginative capacities of its members that such public deliberation is rendered nearly meaningless. The anxiety of many theorists to supply answers that would be of immediate practical relevance impairs their ability to address questions of the more far-reaching kind.

What I am appealing for is a return to the sort of full-bodied philosophical anthropology that can specify the basic moral and political needs of human beings, and a repudiation of the formalistic preoccupation with rights, interests, and rational preferences. The latter have been the staple of liberal political philosophy. What we need is political philosophy that will no longer take human subjects as the supreme arbiters of their own interests and preferences, but will try to illuminate needs and desires of human life that the subjects themselves may have failed to acknowledge. This is what great literature has always achieved, and philosophers today can take assurance from their own great tradition that philosophical literature can match this achievement and give it rational grounding. This, then, is an appeal for the broad, substantive, mode of theory practiced by Plato, Aristotle, Aquinas, Hobbes, Rousseau, Kant, Hegel, Marx, and Nietzsche—each of them possessing a living literary power that is not merely accessory to their philosophical claims, but lies at their source. Tied in with this is the fact that many great works of philosophy, and especially political philosophy, have also been works of literature: Plato's *Republic*, Rousseau's *Emile*, Nietzsche's *Thus Spoke Zarathustra*. Political philosophy, at its best, can be like a story that reminds us of forgotten needs and longings; literature, after all, is the supreme embodiment of the tremendous power of memory and recollection. Just as art preserves our most cherished experiences, so philosophy restores to collective consciousness our rational needs and desires.

Let me restate these issues in a way that brings them closer to immediate political reality and at the same time highlights the

ideological context that forms their background. The widely assumed if not absolutely prevailing view within contemporary liberal society is that there is no need to adjudicate between competing
substantive conceptions of what is good. Indeed, it would be preju-
dicial to our rights and liberties as individuals to do so, for such
decisions are the prerogative of the individual consumer. Everyone
is free to determine what are his or her preferred objects of consumption, and the function of the political system is to guarantee
fundamental rights in the context of free consumer choice. Such a
system does not discriminate between competing conceptions of
what is good; it is neutral. (In this respect, Rawls's theory mirrors
contemporary ideology; society sees to it that there is fair distribution at the level of primary goods; beyond that, it is up to the
rational consumer to design his or her preferred plan of life—a
singular determination of the good.) But this neutralist presumption
is clearly false. If it does not discriminate between substantive consumer choices, it does privilege the consumer model itself, and this
is a particular conception of human life and society that is deeply
partisan and has been intensely contested, both in theory and in
practice. As a social theory it is anything but neutral in its basic
philosophic assumptions about the nature of human beings and
the purpose of social life. From republican political thought we are
familiar with the opposition between *bourgeois* and *citoyen*, most
sharply formulated in the political writings of Rousseau. To forgo
a substantive theory of the human good in favor of consumer freedom is already to exclude an entire way of life postulated upon
nonconsumerist conceptions of human fulfillment, and so to favor
a particular vision of the human good, thereby contradicting the
neutralist presumption. Thus, paradoxically, to say there is no need
to adjudicate between rival conceptions of the good is already to
yield, by default, to a particular vision of personal and political
good, namely that of consumerist liberalism.[4] To take a fairly ob-

4. A terminological clarification may help to obviate misunderstand-
ings, here and in the chapters that follow. Liberalism is generally taken to
denote (1) *a political doctrine* concerned with the hedging in of state power,
usually conceived in opposition to the claims of individuals—claims that
are conceptualized on the basis of one among a set of theories in the idiom
of utility or contract or natural rights. Liberalism as (2) *a social order* denotes
the regime of the modern bourgeoisie—regime in the sense adumbrated

vious example: if I consider the automobile to be the curse of modern society, it is not sufficient for me to opt out simply by not purchasing one; I am already, by necessity, implicated in a form of society that is subject to the imperatives of the motorized style of life, for instance, the expenditure of considerable public revenues on the construction of highways. Again: consumerism is not neutral; it favors those goods that facilitate that whole way of life.

Political philosophers in search of more concrete modes of theorizing than that available in, say, John Rawls or Robert Nozick have taken up the cause of storytelling. Alasdair MacIntyre's book *After Virtue*, where the categories of narrative and storytelling figure prominently, is one notable example of this new tendency among political philosophers. In one of the essays in Michael Oakeshott's book *On History*, entitled "The Tower of Babel," political philosophy and virtuoso storytelling merge into a perfect union of theoretical insight and narrative skill. And Judith Shklar, in the final chapter of her book *Ordinary Vices*, offers a forthright defense of storytelling as the proper vehicle of political theory. This, she tells us, "is really only a reminder of something political philosophers used to do quite normally. I mention Plato as a matter of pure reverence, but among more modern theorists, Montesquieu's *Spirit of the Laws* is one story after another, and its penetrating qualities owe much to the author's skill as a novelist."[5]

---

in the last section of chapter 5. It is primarily in this sense that I address myself to liberalism throughout this book, but my usage encompasses a third sense as well. Liberalism as (3) *a philosophical outlook* denotes the conviction of those who supply the theories upholding liberalism as a political doctrine that it is of greater theoretical urgency to affirm the bourgeois regime's political superiority to its historical and contemporary alternatives than to explore its own shortcomings. To illustrate: Jacob Burckhardt is liberal in sense 1 but antiliberal in senses 2 and 3, for his liberal antipathy to the state did not inhibit his resolve to probe theoretically what we are calling the bourgeois regime and what he called "the epoch of money-making and traffic," "our ugly, restless world." *Reflections on History*, trans. M. D. Hottinger (London: George Allen and Unwin, 1943), pp. 114, 64. As for the recent use of the term *liberal* as a weapon of rhetoric, as in George Bush's 1988 presidential campaign, meant to besmirch any impulse of decency in politics, this is theoretically null, and hardly merits further comment.

5. Judith N. Shklar, *Ordinary Vices* (Cambridge, Mass.: Belknap Press, 1984), p. 231.

Thus far I have been appealing for a more expansive conception of theory than that typical of most contemporary, and especially liberal, political philosophy. Such theory will be essentially narrative; that is, it will seek to tell true stories that help us to see our nature more clearly, and it will serve to disclose (or remind us of) possibilities of human life that are hidden from us by our immersion in the needs and preoccupations of the present. To give substance to this argument, let us turn to one particular mode of narrative in its relationship to political philosophy, namely historical narrative. I shall focus on two exemplars of narrative theory who, I would claim, point in the direction of the kind of wider theoretical horizons I have been advocating. Both Hannah Arendt and Walter Benjamin offer radical theories of historiography, or what one might call the idea of history as storytelling. Both see redemptive possibilities in the notion of historiography that serve wider theoretical purposes. The case of historical narrative may thus help to illuminate the dimensions of possibility open to theory.

Toward the end of her life, Hannah Arendt was engaged in a comprehensive inquiry into the life of the mind, which was intended to culminate in a treatise on judging.[6] Although Arendt's reflections were presented as a general account of judging as a mental faculty, what she really offers is a theory of historical judgment. Arendt was concerned with the judgment of the political spectator reflecting on what has been, a capacity of reflective judgment exemplified preeminently in the activity of the historian. An adequate theory of historical judgment, she implies, depends upon defeating the assumptions, which she associates with Hegel and Marx, that there is such a thing as progress of the human race and that all things should be measured by the criterion of success. Against such historicist assumptions, she appeals to the autonomy of the judging spectator. Autonomous judgment is identified with what she calls the backward glance of the historian (as opposed to Hegel's *Weltgeschichte* as *Weltgericht*: judgment pronounced by the

---

6. The relevant texts are collected in Hannah Arendt, *Lectures on Kant's Political Philosophy*, ed. Ronald Beiner (Chicago: University of Chicago Press, 1982). For extended commentary, see my interpretive essay in the same volume, pp. 89–156.

course of world history). Historiography redeems those who are left behind by the historical process. This conception is summed up perfectly in the famous epigram she quotes from Lucan: "The victorious cause pleased the gods, but the defeated one pleases Cato."[7]

In his intriguing "Theses on the Philosophy of History," Walter Benjamin likewise commits himself to an antihistoricist idea of historiography. In his ninth thesis, Benjamin offers the following allegorical depiction of "the angel of history":

> His face is turned toward the past. Where we perceive a chain of events, he sees one single catastrophe which keeps piling wreckage upon wreckage and hurls it in front of his feet. The angel would like to stay, awaken the dead, and make whole what has been smashed. But a storm is blowing from Paradise; it has got caught in his wings with such violence that the angel can no longer close them. This storm irresistibly propels him into the future to which his back is turned, while the pile of debris before him grows skyward. This storm is what we call progress.[8]

Like Arendt's "judging spectator," Benjamin's "historical materialist" historian seeks, above all, to keep faith with the past. Historiography or historical narrative places us in a unique relationship to the subjects of our narrative. In the kinds of situations that are of concern to Arendt and Benjamin, this activity of storytelling rescues the events and the actors from an oblivion they would otherwise suffer. The anthropological corollary of these ideas is that a human being is, by nature, an historical being—that is, a being who remembers and tries to come to terms with his or her past, a being who does not forget.

To tell a story about the conditions and styles of life in nineteenth-century Paris, as Benjamin does—brilliantly—in "Paris,

---

7. Ibid., pp. 4–5. Lucan, *Pharsalia* 1.128. The Cato referred to in Lucan's poem is not, as Arendt assumes, Cato the Elder (234–149 B.C.) but Cato the Younger (95–46 B.C.). The Hegelian conception comes from *Philosophy of Right*, para. 340, which in turn draws it from Schiller's poem "Resignation."

8. Walter Benjamin, *Illuminations*, ed. Hannah Arendt, trans. Harry Zohn (London: Fontana, 1973), pp. 259–260. For elaboration of Benjamin's concept of history, see my essay, "Walter Benjamin's Philosophy of History," *Political Theory* 12, no. 3 (August 1984): 423–434.

Capital of the Nineteenth Century," is to disclose what possibilities are being opened for us and what possibilities are being closed in modern life. To tell a story about the novelty of totalitarianism as the twentieth century's distinctive contribution to the history of the human condition, as Arendt does, is, again, a source of deep political-philosophical reflection on the possibilities open to humankind. Historical reflection of this sort at the same time enlarges the narrative possibilities of political philosophy.

In theorizing, then, we tell a story—preferably a true story. (We want to tell stories that are not only interesting or evocative but also valid, that is, true to the real nature of our experience.) Several clarifications are required here. First, in saying that we tell a story, we are not prescribing what form the narrative should take—for instance, that it should be a fictional narrative or an historical narrative or whatever. (Narrative does not necessarily mean something made up or fictional; true histories are also told in the form of a narrative.) The theory is self-prescribing as regards its mode of narrative. It *may* draw upon historical narrative (as in Marx) or fiction (as in Plato's or Nietzsche's use of myth) or some blend of different modes of narrative. But the choice of narrative mode will be internal to the kind of theory that it is, and in this sense can only be prescribed from the "inside." Second, in drawing attention to the narrative dimension of theory we are by no means dissolving the distinction between theoretical and literary activity. Theory may well incorporate fiction, depending upon what the theory is, what it is trying to do, and what modes of narrative are prescribed by its purposes (consider, for instance, the use of the "state of nature" fiction within the contractualist tradition). But it *needn't* do so, and in any case its use of fiction is certainly subordinate to the very different purposes of theory. Rather, the point of emphasizing the analogy between storytelling and theory is to make clear, first, that theory always draws power from a rhetorical structure that is not merely supplementary to its logical structure, and that the rhetorical structure (as well as the logical structure) of a theoretical text is constitutive of and internal to the compellingness of the theory; and second, that one cannot prejudge or dictate, in advance of hearing the whole story, the scope of the argument that is needed to render the theory compelling.[9] Even "straight argument" is a kind of narrative, but it is not the only legitimate kind of narrative for establishing theoretical truth. The difference between straight argument and storytelling is really a difference between argument of a more narrow scope and argument of a more expansive scope, and it is precisely this question of scope that one does not want to constrain or prejudge; it all depends on the kind of truths that one hopes to capture in one's narrative. (Hegel's *Phenomenology* is a monumental exercise in historical storytelling: it compels, not by apodictic argument, but by the way it marshals literary images of our past experience.)

What the "universality" of hermeneutics as invoked by Gadamer and others ultimately means is that we must try to interpret and make sense of the practical choices that compose our lives and our aspirations in just the same way that we try to interpret and make sense of a text. To tell a story, then, is not merely a literary undertaking; it engages all aspects of our ethical and practical being. On this account, a social and political theory may be found good or bad, plausible or implausible, coherent or incoherent, in much the same way that a textual interpretation may be found cogent or lacking in cogency. The former finding possesses no more, but also no less, rigor and rationality than the latter. Anyone who has invested energy in explicating the meanings of texts knows that this whole enterprise is governed by its own immanent standards of reason and argumentation. The same is true of those who involve themselves in decisions of practical conduct. For both, the appeal to narrative standards of rational judgment does not in any way devalue these activities but merely describes the form of reason that is proper to each. The invocation of narrative and hermeneutics may have a fashionable ring to it, but it is not very different from the teaching that Aristotle was trying to convey in book 1, chapter 3, and book 2, chapter 2, of the *Nicomachean Ethics*.

9. This is one point on which I agree with Rawls: justification of a moral theory "rests upon the entire conception." It is "a matter of the mutual support of many considerations, of everything fitting together into one coherent view." See John Rawls, *A Theory of Justice* (Oxford: Oxford University Press, 1971), p. 579.

It may be supposed, falsely, that if we tell stories we forfeit any concern with truth, and that if our concern is with truth, we cannot engage in storytelling. The object of this chapter has been to suggest that these are false alternatives, and that the presumed dilemma has an exit: narrative is also truth-seeking, and the narrative dimension of our quest for truth is not irrelevant to its validity. Having established the cognitive claims of narrative, one can then speak of character, community, and ethical life with the richness and concreteness that these topics demand. To offer the image of the theorist as a storyteller is therefore not to urge a *modest* conception of the theorist's task, but to solicit greater boldness, more expansive ambitions, on the part of the theorist. To tell a story is not a modest undertaking, but engages with the grand questions of human nature and human destiny.

2

Liberalism

Since the publication of Alasdair MacIntyre's *After Virtue*, Michael Sandel's *Liberalism and the Limits of Justice*, Michael Walzer's *Spheres of Justice*, and Charles Taylor's writings on "atomism," there has arisen a quite stimulating controversy over the deficiencies or otherwise of contemporary liberalism. This altercation has, on the whole, been a friendly affair as academic controversies go, for the protagonists on both sides of the argument tend to be what I think one can fairly label liberal social democrats.[1] What this amounts to, so we are told, is a debate between liberals and so-called communitarians. Perhaps in reaction to the ascendant individualism of the Reagan years, it has become fashionable to argue that the problem of liberalism as a philosophy of social life is that it lacks the conceptual resources to appreciate the constitutive communal attachments that give the lie to an individualist self-understanding. If that is the case, the solution to the deficiencies of liberalism lies in embracing, once again, the joys of family, neighborhood, and ethnic or national existence that individualism endangers. But does this analysis penetrate deeply enough into the sources of liberal and postliberal malaise? In what follows, I wish to explore the question of whether the very character of the communitarian "solution," far from resolving the discontents of liberalism, perhaps confirms at a more funda-

1. The meaning of this label is nicely summarized by Richard Rorty in "Thugs and Theorists," *Political Theory* 15, no. 4 (November 1987): 565–567. Amy Gutmann certainly exaggerates the antiliberalism of critics like Sandel and Taylor when she ends an article by urging them to "improve" liberal justice rather than "replace" it—presumably with something militantly illiberal. "Communitarian Critics of Liberalism," *Philosophy and Public Affairs* 14, no. 3 (1985): 322; cf. p. 32 n. 52. Far from being revolutionaries rushing to dismantle the liberal social order, it might be thought that Sandel and Taylor err on the side of being too modest in their critique of liberalism rather than on that of being overbold.

mental level the really intractable dilemma at the heart of the liberal dispensation.

THE ANTILIBERAL CHALLENGE

To begin, let me quickly summarize the main lines of communitarian argument.[2] Sandel, in his justly celebrated book, argues that the fatal flaw of liberal theory is an incoherent theory of the self. The liberal vision of the individual as the autonomous chooser of his or her own purposes presupposes that the chooser is sufficiently sovereign over, and therefore distanced from, the choices that compose his or her identity that none of them must be regarded as binding. However, this conception of the self is incoherent, for a self that is as open-ended as the liberal conception requires would be not so much free as identityless. Only a "thickly constituted self" shaped in its very being by traditions, attachments, and more or less irrevocable moral commitments can actually make choices that count.

Walzer, in *Spheres of Justice*, argues that we cannot talk about justice (which is what liberal discourse is centrally about) without an appropriate awareness of the sorts of goods that a particular

2. Michael Sandel, *Liberalism and the Limits of Justice* (Cambridge: Cambridge University Press, 1982); Michael Walzer, *Spheres of Justice: A Defense of Pluralism and Equality* (New York: Basic Books, 1983); Alasdair MacIntyre, *After Virtue* (Notre Dame, Ind.: University of Notre Dame Press, 1981); Charles Taylor, "Atomism," in *Powers, Possessions, and Freedom*, ed. Alkis Kontos (Toronto: University of Toronto Press, 1979), pp. 39–61. A recent article questions whether Walzer belongs in the communitarian camp: "Michael Walzer is sometimes categorized as a communitarian, but does not clearly fit the designation." Patrick Neal and David Paris, "Liberalism and the Communitarian Critique: A Guide for the Perplexed," *Canadian Journal of Political Science* 23, no. 3 (September 1990): 419n. I find this statement most puzzling since, for reasons set out in this chapter, Walzer seems to me the most consistently communitarian of these authors; indeed, as I suggest later, perhaps he is the only one to whom the communitarian label properly applies.

It is surprising that commentators on the liberal-communitarian debate have not drawn attention to its religious dimension. It is hard to appreciate the full contours of the debate without being aware of the degree to which it involves a Jewish-Catholic challenge to the "Protestantism" of contemporary Kantianism (even if some of the spearheads of this Kantian revival are themselves non-Protestant).

society distributes among its members. But these goods are not merely given, they are themselves socially constituted by shared experiences, communal meanings, and traditions of self-understanding that evolve through history. Therefore liberal justice cannot presume to maintain neutrality toward ends and goods at the disposal of individuals, for the precise ends and goods at stake are made available to individuals through a process of communal self-definition that is *not* at the disposal of individuals.

According to MacIntyre's arguments in *After Virtue*, which develops insights of a very profound Aristotelian and Hegelian kind, possibilities of virtue and moral character are not simply contingent on individual choice but are historically embodied, reflecting more encompassing realities. That is, they require some manner of sociological account. Every moral theory, he argues, presupposes a sociological and historical story that fills out the conditions of possibility of a given range of moral experiences, such as the virtues to which one aspires within a certain culture.

Taylor's "Atomism" essay argues that even the extreme libertarian acquires his or her uncompromising passion for individual autonomy by virtue of participating in a civilization that has learned, over the course of many centuries, to put a premium upon such aspirations. Abstracted from such a global social-historical context, the very desire for command of one's individual destiny would be inaccessible, void of meaning. Therefore, precisely those aspirations that define the atomist perspective are the expression of a debt to one's society, and in turn the source of social obligations, that the libertarian himself or herself overlooks.

These critiques of liberal individualism are perfectly valid, as far as they go. But do they penetrate to what is really problematical about liberal theory and practice? And do they offer a satisfying exit from the deepest quandaries of liberalism?

THE ANTI-ANTILIBERAL REJOINDER

The ensuing debate between critics of individualist liberalism and the critics' own critics has made clear, I think, that there are a variety of ways in which defenders of liberalism can incorporate communitarian insights without relinquishing the central tenets of liberal social philosophy. First of all, it is open to the liberal simply to concede that liberal ideals are historically generated, the product of a particular, specifically modern culture and of a shared liberal tradition. Many liberal theorists, including Rawls in his more recent writings, have quite happily embraced this more historicized, and therefore less individualistic, rendering of their liberal commitments. It is all too easy for the defender of liberalism to reply to the communitarian critique as Amy Gutmann does: "The unencumbered self is . . . the encumbrance of our modern social condition."[3] As I noted, Rawls himself, of course, has increasingly resorted to this line of defense: justice as fairness "is the most reasonable doctrine *for us*. We can find no better charter for *our* social world."[4]

In this respect, some communitarian arguments serve merely to help liberal theory give a better or clearer account of itself. For instance, if, as Taylor argues, the very awareness or perception of oneself as an individual choice maker is itself socially constituted, this means that membership in a liberal society is in fact less individualist than may appear from its own theoretical self-understanding. But as soon as this fact is recognized, the critique of liberal individualism is defused or loses a significant measure of its force. It is only against the most extreme type of rights theorist, like Nozick, that Taylor's atomism thesis can retain any critical bite at all. Any other liberal can readily circumvent Taylor's critique by allowing, or even insisting, that conceptions of individual rights, liberty, and autonomy are by necessity socially constituted. It is not surprising that liberal theory has moved in this direction in response to Taylor and Sandel. But of course the best versions of liberalism have never been guilty of the atomistic fallacy. It seems clear that classic liberals like Tocqueville, J. S. Mill, and T. H. Green were no less distressed than contemporary communitarians by the prospect of modern atomism. Merely to convict Nozick of an atomistic self-misunderstanding hardly suffices as a serious challenge to liberalism as a theory of society.

I find it puzzling that Taylor's "Atomism" essay has been identified by many as a source of communitarian theory, since Taylor

3. Gutmann, "Communitarian Critics of Liberalism," p. 316.
4. John Rawls, "Kantian Constructivism in Moral Theory: The Dewey Lectures," *The Journal of Philosophy* 77, no. 9 (September 1980): 519; my italics.

nowhere in that essay challenges the commitments of most liberals; he limits himself to the modest task of showing how the liberal aspiration to autonomy presupposes certain cultural and political conditions—again, not something that appears remotely controversial or provocative. As a matter of fact, it is difficult to conceive Taylor's "Atomism" essay as a critique of liberalism at all, since no sane liberal would deny the claims Taylor makes in that essay. Taylor's argument is really addressed to what he calls the "ultra-liberal,"[5] who also would have to be insane to admit to being an atomist.

Is it possible for a liberal such as Rawls to recast his liberalism within a communitarian framework? In order better to appreciate with what ease the liberal can deflect the communitarian challenge, let us consider a line of thought suggested by Rawls himself. Toward the end of *A Theory of Justice* Rawls conjures up the picture of a society in which his principles of justice themselves furnish the substantive basis of shared membership in the society.[6] Let us suspend skepticism and suppose that this proposal were actually realized in exactly the way that Rawls imagines to be possible. In that case, the liberal vision of the just society that Rawls describes would be a communitarian theory. It would describe a society founded on the shared communal attachment to a particular set of moral commitments. Allegiance to these principles would be constitutive of the identity of its members. Such a theory would fully satisfy the demand for "constitutive community." But it would not be any less a liberal theory. Indeed, precisely these principles express our established identity because they alone are consistent with the pluralistic conditions of a liberal society, whereby different individuals

5. Taylor, "Atomism," p. 48. Taylor's substantive communitarianism is expressed in "Alternative Futures," in *Constitutionalism, Citizenship and Society*, ed. A. Cairns and C. Williams (Toronto: University of Toronto Press, 1985), pp. 183–229; the argument of "Atomism," by contrast, is not positively communitarian, merely antiatomist.

6. John Rawls, *A Theory of Justice* (Oxford: Oxford University Press, 1971), §§ 79, 96; e.g., "To appreciate something as ours, we must have a certain allegiance to it. What binds a society's efforts into one social union is the mutual recognition and acceptance of the principles of justice; it is this general affirmation which extends the ties of identification over the whole community. . . . Individual and group accomplishments are no longer seen as just so many separate personal goods" (pp. 571–572).

find their constitutive identity in different, and perhaps conflicting, subgroups. It is exactly this that Rawls intends in referring to his idea of a well-ordered society as "a social union of social unions."[7]

Rawls in fact goes further. He not only claims that it is possible for there to be a society in which there is a constitutive commitment to these principles; he claims that this is actually the case in liberal society. In *A Theory of Justice* he declares that "a common understanding of justice makes a constitutional democracy" (on express analogy with Aristotle's notion that the polis is founded upon a common understanding of justice).[8] That is, existing liberal democracy *already* embodies a concrete community of understanding, and furthermore this community of understanding can be enhanced and given added substance insofar as its underlying shared conception of justice can be supplied with a more explicit articulation (which is just what Rawls aims to do).

What is shaping up now is something of a convergence between communitarian liberals, who are no less conscious than Walzer or Sandel of how ideals of life are socially constituted,[9] and on the other side, liberal communitarians, who, it appears, were never all that remote from liberalism to begin with. Perhaps this convergence is less surprising than the original debate would have suggested, since of course all of the protagonists, as noted at the outset, are good social democrats whose disagreements at the level of meta-ethics in no way disturbed their basic consensus on the level of policy. Here, it strikes me, MacIntyre's critique of liberalism opens up deeper possibilities of reflection than the liberalism/communitarianism debate could permit.

THE LIBERAL DISPENSATION:
AN ETHOSLESS ETHOS

What is liberalism? And what is the relation between liberal theory and liberal practice? Some communitarians seem to assume that the

7. Ibid., pp. 527, 529.
8. Ibid., p. 243.
9. See, for instance, Ronald Dworkin, "Liberal Community," *California Law Review* 77, no. 3 (May 1989): 479–504; other semicommunitarian liberals that may be mentioned are Joseph Raz and Will Kymlicka. Dworkin in the article cited assumes, as liberals typically assume, that the only alternative

practices of liberal society are the "expression" or "embodiment" of ways of thinking articulated in liberal theory, so that if the major failing of liberal theory is excessive individualism, this must provide the key to understanding the correlative failings of liberal practice. (Perhaps, too, the correction of liberal theory's errors will herald a better practice.) The questionableness of this presumption has been highlighted in a very acute way in a recent essay by Bernard Yack.[10] We may be burdened with a bunch of rotten theories intended to justify what are really a set of wonderful practices and institutions, or, equally, we may be presented with wonderful theories matched up against a rotten liberal reality. Richard Rorty has argued the same point: "Communitarians . . . often speak as if political institutions were no better than philosophical foundations."[11] In reply, Rorty draws upon Dewey and the "political not metaphysical" Rawls to contend that "liberal democracy can get along without philosophical presuppositions."[12] But clearly this point can cut in two opposite directions: if liberal practices and institutions are distinct from their supposed philosophical foundations, liberal practice may be either more or less sound than the liberal philosophy that is the target of communitarian critics. And even if we could come up with a perfectly satisfactory formulation of liberal theory, this in itself would certainly not put to an end our worries about liberal society itself.

Rorty celebrates the historicized Rawls who views the principles of justice as limited in their validity to "we liberals."[13] He says that

---

to liberalism is illiberalism, and that therefore the communitarians, as critics of liberalism, are defenders of illiberalism. But of course the communitarians Dworkin has in mind, for instance Sandel and Taylor, are no more committed to the persecution of homosexuals than he is.

10. Bernard Yack, "Does Liberal Practice 'Live Down' to Liberal Theory? Liberalism and Its Communitarian Critics," in *Community in America: The Challenge of 'Habits of the Heart,'* ed. Charles H. Reynolds and Ralph V. Norman (Berkeley: University of California Press, 1988), pp. 147–169.

11. Richard Rorty, "The Priority of Democracy to Philosophy," in *The Virginia Statute for Religious Freedom,* ed. Merrill Peterson and Robert Vaughan (Madison: University of Wisconsin Press, 1988), p. 260.

12. Ibid., p. 261.

13. Ibid., p. 278 n. 22: "The only 'theory of the person' we get is a sociological description of the inhabitants of contemporary liberal democracies."

on the basis of Rawls's later writings we must learn to reread *A Theory of Justice* as no longer "committed to a philosophical account of the human self, but only to an historical-sociological description of the way we live now."[14] But this of course invites the further challenge: Does this redescription of the Rawlsian enterprise exonerate the theory, or does it indict "the way we live now"? Perhaps it is even the case that liberal practice is in far worse shape than either liberals *or* communitarians imagine.

Rorty is quite right, in my view, that one doesn't need a public philosophy "to hold a free society together."[15] But it certainly doesn't follow from this that there are *no* conditions necessary for the social cohesion of a liberal society. The "glue . . . required to hold a community together"[16] is ethos, not shared metaphysics. So while the absence of an adequate philosophy may well not be fatal to liberal society, it cannot necessarily be assumed that liberal society is therefore in good health. Aristotle's most powerful insight is that in every society, moral life is based upon ethos, that is, character formation according to socially bred customs and habit. (One finds the same insight in many modern political thinkers, including Montesquieu, Rousseau, Hegel, Nietzsche, and Heidegger.) Every society has an ethos. One that didn't would not just fail to be a moral community, it would fail to be a society at all. So liberal society does have an ethos. Under the liberal dispensation, the ethos is—lack of ethos; individuals in this society are habituated to being insufficiently habituated. That is the liberal paradox. Incoherent as it may appear, it goes to the core of what liberalism is and what it attempts to be.

The starting point for an understanding of liberalism is the notion that there is a distinctive liberal way of life, characterized by the aspiration to increase and enhance the prerogatives of the individual; by maximal mobility in all directions, throughout every dimension of social life (in and out of particular communities, in and out of socioeconomic classes, and so on); and by a tendency to turn all areas of human activity into matters of consumer preference; a way of life based on progress, growth, and technological dyna-

14. Ibid., p. 265.
15. Ibid., p. 264.
16. Ibid., p. 260.

mism. The fact that nonliberal societies in the developed world share some features of this way of life shows that Eastern and Western societies are closer cousins than they have generally been willing to acknowledge. In particular, both types of societies are expressions of the modern drive toward universal "freedom" and mastery, as evidenced in the furious rivalry for high-technological supremacy, both civilian and military.

This liberal mode of existence is marked by tendencies toward pluralistic fragmentation, but paradoxically it is also marked by tendencies toward universalism and even homogenization. It is important to see why these two seemingly opposing tendencies are compatible—why indeed they are two sides of the same coin. The distinctiveness of liberalism is not, I think, refuted by its tendency to invade and overrun other ways of life, for the dialectic of liberal existence encompasses both diversity and sameness, pluralism and uniformity, privatization and planetarization. The official ideology of liberal society, endlessly expounded by liberal theorists, is of course diversity—the rich multiplicity of different conceptions of the good or of the ends of life. But when one actually surveys the liberal reality, what one sees is more and more sameness—of tastes, of clichéd perceptions of the world, of the glum ennui with which one reconciles oneself to the monolithic routines of our world. Needless to say, it is all too common for a rhetoric of robust individuality to obscure a reality of dreary conformism.[17] Such is liberalism, with its shopping mall culture—where one has hundreds of shops to choose from, all of which sell the same junk. This dialectic of superficial pluralism and underlying conformity is nicely summarized by George Grant: "As for pluralism, differences in the technological state are able to exist only in private activities: how we eat; how we mate; how we practise ceremonies. Some like pizza, some like steaks; some like girls, some like boys; some like synagogue, some like the mass. But we all do it in churches,

---

17. Cf. Allan Bloom, *The Closing of the American Mind* (New York: Simon and Schuster, 1987), p. 247. See also Robert N. Bellah, Richard Madsen, William M. Sullivan, Ann Swidler, and Steven M. Tipton, *Habits of the Heart: Individualism and Commitment in American Life* (Berkeley: University of California Press, 1985), pp. 147–149, 162. It is in respect of this central insight that, despite their very different angles of vision, both of these books are Tocquevillean.

motels, restaurants indistinguishable from the Atlantic to the Pacific."[18]

Another deep paradox of the modern liberal dispensation is that while it enforces a highly contracted vision of the dignity and uniqueness of the individual within his or her particular subgroup, it simultaneously offers a collective way of life ("Americanism") that is rapidly expanding to encircle the globe. (The Europeans are even naming themselves after the United States!) North America is history's great experiment in a cosmopolitan way of life. Thus far, this civilization has obviously been an enormous practical success, for its efforts to export its own brand of rootless cosmopolitanism to every other part of the Earth have met with little resistance.[19] What is more difficult to judge is whether this grand experiment can be considered a moral success. Perhaps the great conservatives and romantics of the late eighteenth and early nineteenth centuries were closer to the mark when they anticipated with deep consternation a world such as ours, in which the businesspeople of every nation speak English, every written word is recorded on computer discs, and everyone's kids, from Paris to Peking, are fed on hamburgers from McDonald's.

Liberalism, no less than socialism, feudalism, or any other social order, is a global dispensation—that is, a way of life that excludes other ways of life. It does no good for the liberal to say that the liberal state is neutral between the diverse life-choices of individuals. Is it neutral about continual growth and higher productivity? Is it neutral about scientific progress? Is it neutral about the market as a means of maximizing consumer choices? The fact that all of this supposedly enhances the prerogatives of individuals in the design of their life-options is what actually defines this dispensation rather than showing that there is none.

If it is true, as I believe it is, that all social theory is addressed to the question of what is good, and if, as Walzer argues, all politically relevant goods are communal goods (including even salvation as a social good), then it follows that liberalism itself is unavoidably a

18. George Grant, *Technology and Empire* (Toronto: Anansi, 1969), p. 26.
19. A recent public opinion poll in the Soviet Union reported that 65 percent of the respondents preferred the American lifestyle over other possibilities. The Asian-Japanese lifestyle came in second at 23 percent.

communitarian theory. It makes available a determinate set of social goods that excludes rival goods. The task of social theory is to weigh and compare the worth of these different goods. However, as we shall now go on to see, even those defenders of liberalism who discount the deontological pretensions of recent liberal theory stop well short of rising to this challenge.

My argument is that liberalism itself instantiates one particular vision of the good, namely, that choice in itself is the highest good. This comes into view when we look at what liberals tend to get exercised about, such as restrictions on pornography. Amy Gutmann takes Sandel to task for entertaining the prospect of a communitarian ban on pornography within a local community (as if this were somewhat comparable to witch burning in Salem).[20] This illiberalism, she argues, underestimates the complexity of our diverse aspirations toward the good. But what claim of good can be made on behalf of the consumers of hard-core smut, except that of choice itself? In fact the liberal invocation of the language of rights in this instance merely serves as a device to avoid having to give an account at the level of what is good. Gutmann argues that the liberal need not be committed to an absolute priority of right to good (as Rawls seems to be in *A Theory of Justice*); liberalism is merely an acknowledgment of the rich articulation of possible conceptions of the good. But this stance is betrayed by the pornography example, where the presumption of a putative good that is supposedly being upheld (cloaked by the slogan "right of free speech") cannot sustain even minimal scrutiny. Here the notion that there is a *good* at stake, rather than the pure *right* of a sovereign individual, turns out to be hollow. In this case at least, the appeal to rights, such as the right of free speech, betokens the absence of a good.

According to Richard Rorty, writing in defense of Rawls, political philosophy ought to recommend that citizens of a democratic polity forsake a quest for "the good independently defined" not "because a capacity for choice is the essence of personhood" but simply "because *we*—we modern inheritors of the traditions of religious tolerance and constitutional government—put liberty ahead of perfec-

---

20. Gutmann, "Communitarian Critics of Liberalism," pp. 318–319, 321.

tion."[21] Yet it may surely be asked *why* we put liberty first—unless we do believe that "choice is the essence of personhood." As always, the liberal surreptitiously inserts the tacit philosophical anthropology, the underhandedly concealed conception of "the good independently defined." For of course it would be impossible for us to make sense of why we put liberty ahead of perfection if we disregarded the fact that we had already defined liberty (meaning freedom of choice) as the good.[22]

Rorty states that a liberal social order is one which, for the sake of political freedom, is willing to content itself with producing human beings that are "bland, calculating, petty and unheroic."[23] But this is an acknowledgment of precisely that global or collective decision at the level of philosophical anthropology that liberals generally, and very implausibly, disavow. Far from liberalism allowing us to abstain on the question of how human beings should be, it represents one particular answer: The human good reposes on public justice and private perfection, rather than on the public pursuit of perfection. To say, as liberals are committed to saying, that justice is to be preferred to perfection is to choose a particular way of being human as a member of a particular social order, within a global destiny of a particular kind.

Here the liberal will typically counter that sharing in an established way of life, whether high or low, is unobjectionable provided that it is not imposed by the state. After all, liberalism is principally a doctrine of the limitation of state power. But here again, all kinds of important questions are begged. Liberals stubbornly adhere to the view that the state alone poses a threat to the freedom of otherwise self-governing individuals. If we can merely secure the neutrality of the state with respect to diverse opposing ends of life then, it is assumed, the individual is sufficiently free and self-determining. But of course the very fact of life in society (any society) puts this in question. How can we know, prior to substantive inquiry into the whole fabric of life within a given society, whether individ-

21. Rorty, "Priority of Democracy to Philosophy," p. 265.

22. Taylor, "Atomism," p. 48, where it is argued that even the "ultraliberal" (e.g., Nozick) smuggles in a normative standard of "self-realization."

23. Rorty, "Priority of Democracy to Philosophy," p. 269.

uals are self-determining or are brainwashed, manipulated in subtle and incalculable ways, and locked into forms of false consciousness by social forces (aside from the coercive powers of the state). It is unclear why the state alone should be conceived as threatening the autonomy of its citizens—an autonomy that may turn out to be highly illusory. In fact the state might be needed to render individuals *more* autonomous—for instance, by removing or inhibiting the power of other social forces to captivate and bewitch individuals without directly coercing them.[24] The general liberal assumption that state coercion is the exclusive threat to individual freedom presumes that individuals are as a matter of course free. However, as Taylor argues in "Atomism," autonomy is not a given but an achievement—something that is very much a function of the general culture and historical evolution of the society that shapes our identity. Even if the state is or tries to be neutral (which is likely to prove impossible), the wider social order in which the individual is nourished is not. Liberal neutralism is therefore a mirage. It is hard to see why the state is constrained to be neutral (whatever that might mean) if social life as a whole is and must be strongly partial toward a particular way of life.

As soon as one begins to examine the content of the common good of a liberal social order, one sees much that is admirable but also much that is dismaying: The suburbs in which more and more of us live are a spiritual wasteland; our city cores are a disgrace; our children are culturally illiterate; much of the energies of our society go into producing and consuming goods that no reasonable person would choose to produce or consume.[25] All of these considerations, and others of a like kind, are relevant to the evaluation of liberalism

24. For an argument of this kind, see, for example, Jennifer Nedelsky, "Reconceiving Autonomy: Sources, Thoughts and Possibilities," in *Law and the Community*, ed. Á. C. Hutchinson and L. J. M. Green (Toronto: Carswell, 1989), pp. 219–252. Relevant here is Matthew Arnold's opposition of Humboldtian practice (statist) to Humboldtian theory (antistatist); see *Culture and Anarchy*, ed. J. Dover Wilson (Cambridge: Cambridge University Press, 1960), pp. 126–127.

25. Consider, for instance, the estimated three million women in the United States who have felt obliged to equip themselves with cosmetic breast implants, one-quarter of which, it now turns out, may be carcinogenic.

as a substantive way of life. Unfortunately, none of them are even up for consideration within the horizon of liberal theory as it has been articulated within the last twenty years.

WHY I AM NOT A COMMUNITARIAN

The ultimate challenge that faces liberalism is whether it yields the intellectual resources to pass judgment on individuals—and indeed whole societies of individuals—who exercise their presumed autonomy by opting for ways of life that are banal, empty, and stultifying. If we go by Dworkin's definition of liberalism ("political decisions must be, so far as is possible, independent of any particular conception of the good life, or of what gives value to life"[26]), it is clear that liberalism *on principle* offers no such intellectual resources. It denies itself the possibility of such critical judgment on account of its guiding conception of what is morally and politically right. Now with the decisive challenge to liberalism framed in these terms, we can see that the communitarian critique does not necessarily provide much help in exposing what is wrong with liberalism. We can easily imagine a warm sense of community based on mutual participation in the decrepit ways of life opted for by our postulated autonomous individuals. In fact these individuals may actually draw their constitutive identity from communal membership in these very ways of life (e.g., one's identity as a yuppie, or as the citizen of a condo community). It may even be possible to describe liberal society in precisely this way. But if so, the communitarian criterion is satisfied much too easily. We can see this, for instance, in the case of Walzer's communitarianism in *Spheres of Justice*. On his view, the only standard of critical judgment is the internal standard of whether a concrete community remains true to the traditions, practices, and shared understandings that compose its communal identity. But if we conceive liberal society as a

---

26. Ronald Dworkin, "Liberalism," in *Public and Private Morality*, ed. Stuart Hampshire (Cambridge: Cambridge University Press, 1978), p. 127; cf. p. 142. To judge by *Considerations on Representative Government*, ed. C. V. Shields (New York: Bobbs-Merrill, 1958), pp. 25–28, the criticism here offered against Dworkin could not be made against John Stuart Mill, nor could it be made against Tocqueville and various other great figures of the liberal tradition.

community dedicated to a relentlessly pluralistic way of life, then that society, on Walzer's account, would be obliged only to pursue consistently the moral incoherence to which it had historically committed itself. What is absent here is any independent, external standard that sheds light on whether identity-constituting communities confer worth upon their members beyond the bare fact of possessing something shared. The mere presence of community furnishes no such standard, and therefore fails to make good the default of liberalism. The pluralistic communitarian, in common with the pluralistic liberal, abstains from specifying the content of the good life for individuals or communities. In his clear avowal of pluralism, Walzer himself acknowledges that, for all his credentials as a communitarian, he remains a liberal first—which, again, confirms that communitarianism can be consistent with a fundamental allegiance to liberalism.[27]

The question I am raising is this: Is lack of community the central deficiency of liberalism? Or is a certain experience of community part and parcel of liberalism? At the moment, there are millions of North Americans passionately committed to a shared vision of a Christian evangelical community. Is their communitarian commitment in itself an answer to the ills of liberal individualism, or is it rather an expression of those ills? Surely, communitarianism of this sort is the consequence, not the cure, of the moral emptiness of liberal culture. If this is what the situated self looks like, then, as liberal countercritics argue, by all means give us back the "disencumbered self"! This is the standard liberal rebuttal of community, and to be sure there is much truth in the liberal's case that there is nothing intrinsically good in the experience of community as such. But the liberal rebuttal fails to recognize how deeply implicated the liberal and the communitarian are in each other's dilemmas.

There are at least two ways in which one can embrace community consistent with a commitment to liberalism. First, one can base

27. What is confusing about the liberal/communitarian taxonomy comes out clearly in the fact that Rorty, who is a defender of Rawlsian liberalism, is actually more of a communitarian than critics of liberalism like Taylor and Sandel (though not more of a communitarian than Walzer). See Richard Rorty, *Contingency, Irony, and Solidarity* (Cambridge: Cambridge University Press, 1989), chap. 3.

communitarianism *on* liberalism. Here we may recall the account given earlier of Rawls: Rawlsian community can in theory be constitutive, except that, owing to the thinness of the theory, the kinds of selves that it would constitute might tend to live vapid, atrophied lives. Alternatively, one can view the attachment to a particular ethnic or civic community as itself an expression of liberal autonomy: I choose to live in this neighborhood, with these neighbors who share my "values"; or I choose to become a Zionist within a community of Zionists dedicated to affirming our shared identity. Or even: I choose to become a Jew—like Sammy Davis, Jr.! Now liberal society on the whole embodies both of these kinds of communitarianism without ceasing to be liberal. Indeed, this kind of communitarianism defines liberalism. That's what liberalism is.

Much of the initial force of the communitarian critique was directed against the privileging, central to deontological liberalism, of right over good. To this it was possible to counter that what underlies liberal philosophy is not so much a repudiation of the good in favor of the right, as an acknowledgment of the plurality of goods to which citizens of liberal society are committed (as defenders of liberalism like Gutmann and Galston[28] have suggested). But if this statement of the problem is accurate, it is not clear whether the communitarian option surmounts the problem or compounds it. For, as Walzer, Taylor, and Sandel each in their own way recognize, the affirmation of community is at the same time an affirmation of pluralism. These theories exalt not just community but communities, the blossoming of which may result in a further impetus to the centrifugal tendencies of liberal society.[29] MacIntyre puts his finger on the basic problem, in a way that places him in contradistinction to other commonly cited communitarians, when he refers to "the great pluralist mishmash of the shared pub-

---

28. William Galston, "Defending Liberalism," *American Political Science Review* 76 (1982): 621–629.

29. Cf. Bloom, *Closing of the American Mind*, pp. 192–193: "The 'new ethnicity' or 'roots' is just another manifestation of the concern with particularity, evidence not only of the real problems of community in modern mass societies but also of the superficiality of the response to it. . . . The blessing given the whole notion of cultural diversity in the United States by the cultural movement has contributed to the intensification and legitimization of group politics."

lic life of liberal societies."[30] This is the real predicament, one which does not admit of a communitarian solution, for the withdrawal into particularistic communities merely confirms what defines the problem in the first place.

Here the communitarian is landed in a quandary that exactly matches that of the liberal. If what is required is a truly national community, the communitarian promise would seem to be a hopeless one, for clearly no modern industrial state can sustain this sort of community without stoking up the very hazardous fires of nationalism. On the other hand, if what is sought is the autonomy of local communities as such, there is no assurance that this will not give further momentum to the relativization of tastes and morals that mandated liberal neutralism in the first place. So the appeal to community, far from resolving the quandaries of liberalism, merely confirms them in another guise.

The same problem may also be formulated from a slightly different perspective. One of the main stumbling blocks of liberalism, at least in its official professions, is its formalism. To uphold the prerogatives of the autonomous, choice-making individual means that, politically speaking, one abstains from judgment about the substantive character of these choices. One can exercise one's autonomy just as well by choosing X as by choosing Y—whatever X and Y happen to be. But the communitarian affirmation is beset by the same formalism.[31] To affirm community as such is to abstain from judgment about the substantive attributes of a given community. Communal autonomy, like individual autonomy, abstracts from judgments of substance. It is this formalism that renders the language of communitarianism so confusing and that prompts disquiet both among liberals and among many critics of liberalism.

30. Alasdair MacIntyre, "Does Applied Ethics Rest on a Mistake?" *Monist* 67, no. 4 (October 1984): 511.

31. This may be illustrated by the pornography issue debated by Sandel and Gutmann. Sandel defends the prerogative of any local community "to ban pornographic bookstores, on the grounds that pornography offends its way of life." "Morality and the Liberal Ideal," *New Republic*, 7 May 1984, p. 17. But suppose we are presented with a local community whose way of life is not violated but buttressed by pornography; such a possibility is not entirely fanciful. By itself, the appeal to community can as easily sanction the desirability of pornography as its undesirability. Here again, the

As I stated at the beginning of this section, the basic question is whether liberal philosophy can furnish the intellectual resources to investigate whether the way of life in which we all today participate is fundamentally satisfying. Once again, if we accept Dworkin's definition of liberalism, the answer to this question must be no. Liberals and communitarians are both wrong here. Liberals are wrong because we are not essentially choosers, autonomous agents, or framers of our own individual destiny, but members of an established dispensation. Communitarians are wrong because the fact that liberalism offers a constituted identity (for instance, that of autonomous consumers) within a larger social dispensation fails to redeem liberalism. And here, needless to say, it is a question not so much of the failings of liberalism as a social philosophy, but of liberalism as a way of life.

The liberal way of life, upheld by a particular dispensation, a particular ethos, is one where the liberal self draws its constitutive identity from its capacity to choose autonomously how and where it will work, who it will marry, where it will live, how and where it will seek means of leisure, where it will drive in its car; in short, what it will be. This is a way of life centered on choice, mobility, and maximal personal freedom.[32] Now is this a vision of human life that any of the communitarians can straightforwardly repudiate?[33] Or to which they can suggest, by way of contrast, a convincing alternative? And if not, isn't the appeal to existing or possible or imaginary communities rather pointless? *Of course* the liberal

---

communitarian ideal points toward not the repudiation of pluralist liberalism but the confirmation of it.

32. For an excellent statement by Walzer of the decisiveness of the question of mobility, and of the limited extent to which communitarians can repudiate this central feature of modern life (in respect of which liberal societies form merely the vanguard of a global movement), see "The Communitarian Critique of Liberalism," *Political Theory* 18, no. 1 (February 1990): 6–23, especially pp. 11–13.

33. Gutmann, "Communitarian Critics of Liberalism," pp. 317, 320, observes that Sandel's communitarianism is more qualified than appears at first glance. This is hardly surprising. By contrast, Stephen Holmes suggests that "a balanced and fair assessment of their thought" requires that communitarians be seen as cagey and irresolute rehabilitators of fascism. "The Permanent Structure of Antiliberal Thought," in *Liberalism and the Moral Life*, ed. Nancy L. Rosenblum (Cambridge: Harvard University Press, 1989), pp. 228, 234.

dispensation undermines traditional communal attachments. How could it be otherwise?

REPUBLICAN COMMUNITY

It strikes me that the very label "communitarian" has introduced an unfortunate and wholly unnecessary degree of confusion into recent debates about liberalism. It suggests, misleadingly, that the major failing of liberalism is that it deprives its citizens of the satisfactions of communal life, as if the latter were an end in itself. I do not believe that this is the true concern of the communitarians themselves, and in the remainder of this chapter I want to urge that their own case would be both strengthened and clarified by forgoing the communitarian label.

In order to alleviate some of these confusions, it may be helpful to avail ourselves of a distinction drawn by Robert Paul Wolff in *The Poverty of Liberalism* between "affective community" and "rational community." Wolff defines affective community as "the reciprocal consciousness of a shared culture."[34] Rational community, by contrast, is defined as "that reciprocity of consciousness which is achieved and sustained by equals who discourse together publicly for the specific purpose of social decision and action."[35] Specifically, we need Wolff's distinction (or one like it) to render more precise whether what we are after is the raptures of *Gemeinschaft* or a more effective sense that citizens in a democratic society inhabit a shared world of political concerns that affect all in common, and that should be addressed in common. It is clear that the latter is what is decisive for theorists like Taylor, MacIntyre, and Sandel, who are better described as republican than as communitarian thinkers.[36] It is clear as well that the same problem was no less

34. Robert Paul Wolff, *The Poverty of Liberalism* (Boston: Beacon Press, 1968), p. 187.

35. Ibid., p. 192.

36. In "Alternative Futures," pp. 213–214, Taylor very usefully distinguishes between republican and communitarian concerns. Elsewhere, however, communitarians, no less than their critics, conflate the two, or treat them as synonymous. See, for instance, Sandel, "The Political Theory of the Procedural Republic," in *The Rule of Law: Ideal or Ideology*, ed. A. C. Hutchinson and P. Monahan (Toronto: Carswell, 1987), pp. 85, 92.

important for classical liberal philosophers like Tocqueville and
J. S. Mill. In this context, one might be quite struck to discover that
a certain sort of liberal individualism (for instance, that articulated
by Mill) is in fact remarkably compatible with civic republican concerns. The basic point is this: If our world succumbs to nuclear
or ecological catastrophe, we all suffer the same fate; if injustice,
inequality, and political oppression run rampant in our world, we
are all diminished as human beings; if the absence of a common
culture leads to a new, postliterate barbarism, we are all the worse
for it. The minimum notion of community required to cope with
these grave political realities is the sense that our fate, for good or
ill, is a shared one, from which no one can sensibly retreat into a
private domain of either pleasures of consumption or burdens of
conscience. The great mistake of liberalism is to pretend that modernity forces us to regard private morality as reigning supreme
and public morality as limited to the business of negotiating "successful accommodation" between ourselves as rational individuals.[37] The problem with liberalism is not that it deprives us of the
delights of communal attachments, whether national, ethnic, sec-
tarian, or whatever, but that it tends to cause us to forget that our
destiny in this dangerous world of ours is a collective destiny, and
that the perils of insufficient citizenship are likewise shared.

The problem is not lack of *Gemeinschaft*. Often, modern societies
succumb to *too much* ethnic, linguistic, cultural-national particularism—naturally, in the context of a more general social fragmentation. Modern societies, of course, are hardly impervious to the
curse of nationalism, or to outbursts of ethnic chauvinism. What
is the problem then? Typically, we find ourselves barbarized by
an empty public culture, intimidated by colossal bureaucracies,
numbed into passivity by the absence of opportunities for meaningful deliberation, inflated by absurd habits of consumption, deflated
by the Leviathans that surround us, and stripped of dignity by a
way of living that far exceeds a human scale. We live in societies
that embark upon the grandest and most hubristic collective
projects, while granting their citizens only the feeblest opportunities for an effective say over the disposal of their own destiny. To

37. Rorty, "Priority of Democracy to Philosophy," p. 264.

speak of autonomous moral agency and the ethical prerogatives of free, choice-making individuals in this context is a grotesque insult.

To my mind, the only communitarianism that allows us to escape the pluralist quandary that I have described is the idea of a community of discourse, where the very possibility of public talk about a world we share confers an experience of substantive citizenship. According to this conception, it is the public world itself as a locus of shared concern that rescues us from the fragmentation and moral anarchy of a liberal-pluralist universe. In other words, it is the "republican" ideal developed most notably among recent theorists by Hannah Arendt and Jürgen Habermas that offers a genuine alternative to liberalism. In particular, we may recall Hannah Arendt's brilliant account in *The Human Condition* of what it means to lose a shared world and how, as modernity gathers pace, public objects become dissolved in subjectivity. However, as that account intimates, the experiences that render republican community possible have been so deeply attenuated by liberalism that the very idea of a community of this kind is barely intelligible. Indeed, even to conceive of richer possibilities of citizenship has become so difficult for us that it is questionable whether pluralism as we know it today can be surpassed without revolutionary upheavals in the character of our world. It is not for nothing that MacIntyre concludes his book with a cry of despair, suggesting that moralists alive to the dimensions of our crisis retreat to some contemporary version of medieval monasteries in order to wait out the dark ages that have already commenced. What makes MacIntyre unique among commonly cited communitarians is that for him the problem is not merely individualism or liberalism but modernity as such.[38] Therefore he includes even Marxism within the scope of his critique.

---

38. By contrast, Taylor, like Habermas, seeks a redemptive potentiality within modernity itself; see "Alternative Futures," pp. 206, 222–223. In order to locate this potentiality, Taylor has to argue that civic republican aspirations are already significantly present in contemporary liberal society, and that therefore the flourishing of republican citizenship requires no major change of direction within our civilization but merely the accentuation of certain strains already operative, or at least latent, in the modern identity. Ibid., pp. 194, 223; "The Diversity of Goods," in *Utilitarianism and Beyond*, ed. A. Sen and B. Williams (Cambridge: Cambridge University Press, 1982), p. 143. This claim is not terribly persuasive.

The problem with liberalism is not that it exalts the idea of what is right to the exclusion of notions of the good, for (however strenuously this is disavowed by liberal theorists) liberal society in fact instantiates a subterranean yet tacitly shared conception of the good, or a set of such conceptions. And the problem is not that it treats individuals in complete abstraction from community, for (whether liberal theorists are aware of it or not) liberal society, like every other society, offers a community of experience that identifies its members as inhabitants of the same social order.[39] Nor is the problem that the liberal self is ahistorical and lacking in tradition, for liberal individualism itself constitutes a considerable tradition.[40] The problem is quite simply that the liberal good, as defined by the bourgeois civilization of the last few centuries, is not good enough, and that liberal community defeats the possibility of a sense of meaningful collective purpose.

The communitarian insight, properly understood, reveals not merely conceptual errors or oversights in liberal theory but, more concretely, deficiencies in the character-building capacities of liberal culture (the liberal ethos). Allan Bloom shares this insight with communitarian radicals like Sandel and MacIntyre, perhaps against his will, when he writes that "a young person today . . . begins *de novo*, without the givens or imperatives that he would have had only yesterday. His country demands little of him and provides well for him, his religion is a matter of absolutely free choice and . . . so are his sexual involvements. He can now choose, but he finds he no longer has a sufficient motive for choice that is more than whim, that is binding."[41] MacIntyre points toward a similar predicament, with an intention that is at once radical and conservative, when he observes:

> One of the crucial failures of the Enlightenment ideology has been in respect of the kind of ground for protest and rebellion and the kind of hope that it offers to those systematically excluded from the practices and the institutions which make the good life possible. For

39. For elaboration of these points, see Yack, "Does Liberal Practice 'Live Down' to Liberal Theory?"

40. See Alasdair MacIntyre, *Whose Justice? Which Rationality?* (Notre Dame, Ind.: University of Notre Dame Press, 1988), chap. 17.

41. Bloom, *Closing of the American Mind*, p. 109.

it has fatally infected much of modern protest and rebellion with the idiom of abstract universality. And so it has not focused upon the tasks of creating practices and institutions which will actually enable the children of the hitherto deprived and the hitherto arbitrarily excluded to learn how to read Greek and to play baseball or cricket and to listen to and to play string quartets and to value excellence in all these areas. It has instead encouraged them to pursue fictions of rights and of equality so that everybody in the end will have equal right to an education that it is worth nobody's while to have.[42]

What the communitarian is getting at is not that liberal autonomy is a bad thing, but that without the "thick" attachments provided by the kind of ethos that builds meaningful character, free choice between abstractly posited alternatives hardly seems worth the bother.[43]

Liberalism at its best is characterized by certain great virtues that no society ought to wish to forfeit. But it should be possible to acknowledge this without paying the intellectual price that liberal theorists do when they make their peace with modernity. Nietzsche, in one of his last letters, wrote a century ago to Jacob Burckhardt, like himself one of the towering nineteenth-century critics of modernity: "I pay twenty-five francs, with service, make my own tea, and do my own shopping, suffer from torn boots, and thank heaven every moment for the *old* world, for which human beings have not been simple and quiet enough."[44] Nietzsche, perhaps philosophy's greatest enemy of liberal civilization, was able to observe, even in the last century, the relentless draining away of dignity and nobility in the frenzied new world that was arising before his eyes. His forebodings have been uncannily borne out by the experience of the past hundred years.

42. Alasdair MacIntyre, "Bernstein's Distorting Mirrors," *Soundings* 67, no. 1 (1984): 40.

43. Will Kymlicka speaks of "the freedom to choose which of the culture's narratives to adopt as the most valuable for me." "Liberalism, Individualism, and Minority Rights," in *Law and the Community*, ed. Hutchinson and Green, p. 190 n. 21; the context is a criticism of MacIntyre. But if we all exercise this freedom to pick and choose among possible cultural memberships, it is difficult to see how *any* particular culture can continue to sustain itself. This precisely is the quandary of liberal community.

44. *Selected Letters of Friedrich Nietzsche*, ed. Christopher Middleton (Chicago: University of Chicago Press, 1969), p. 347.

The defender of liberal modernity will of course reply that we are no more likely to be able to turn the clock back on the pluralism, dynamism, and scale of modern societies than we are likely to recapture the *Gemeinschaft* of preliberal societies. Both the communitarian and the republican visions are therefore equally mired in nostalgia (worse, nostalgia for societies that never actually existed!). Liberal pluralism is our fate, and it would require either ignorance of or blindness to historical realities to yearn for some radically different dispensation. To this inevitable rejoinder I reply that it would be depressing indeed to think that the only possible function of theoretical reflection is to resign us to our historical fate; it would also be a betrayal of the traditional vocation of theory, which is to offer critical reflection on the given state of affairs. It seems highly improbable that Plato and Aristotle conceived with any seriousness the possibility of arresting the decline of the polis by their theoretical exertions, yet that did not deter them from assuming a critical posture toward their own society. Nor should we be deterred from surveying the discontents of our civilization.

3

Moral Vocabularies

> The student of politics must obviously have some knowledge of the workings of the soul, just as the man who is to heal eyes must know something about the whole body. In fact, knowledge is all the more important for the former, inasmuch as politics is better and more valuable than medicine, and cultivated physicians devote much time and trouble to gain knowledge about the body. Thus, the student of politics must study the soul.
>
> Aristotle, *Nicomachean Ethics*

Talk of "virtue" immediately strikes the modern ear as somehow illiberal, certainly antiquated, perhaps perverse. It must surely be galling to liberal moralists that this old-fashioned language is back in vogue to some extent; in any case, the liberal will inevitably see in all this Aristotelian talk something vaguely threatening to the much more familiar liberal notions of rights, autonomy, value pluralism, the privacy of moral conscience, and the protection of moral diversity. In this chapter, I want to offer some account of why this older moral language is in some measure back in favor; to examine why liberals would be (with good reason) inclined to see it as subversive of the prevailing moral language; to consider some of the ways in which ancient moral thought may perhaps be more coherent than the established moral categories of modern liberalism; and finally, to argue that it truly matters which mode of moral discourse we opt for. My thesis, basically, is that the moral self-understanding of liberalism would be notably strengthened, both theoretically and practically, if it were to shift from a Kantian discourse of rights and individual autonomy to an Aristotelian discourse of virtues and character formation.

Adapted by permission of New York University Press from *Virtue*, NOMOS XXXIV, edited by John W. Chapman and William A. Galston. Copyright © 1992 by New York University.

THE PREVAILING VOCABULARY

Before I can embark on a sketch of an alternative moral vocabulary, it will be necessary to state briefly a few standard objections to some main terms of liberal discourse—values, rights, and individual autonomy—with which I am dissatisfied. I will later consider typical liberal objections to my preferred moral vocabulary.

VALUES

One of the chief theoretical advantages of an Aristotelian moral language is that it allows one to speak of moral and political phenomena without ever having to resort to the reductive notion of "values," whether individual or collective. For some reason, liberals tend to have difficulty appreciating why avoidance of this unfortunate language constitutes a theoretical advantage, or indeed why the ubiquity of this language within liberal society is a pathological feature of modern moral experience. Whether the captives of this vocabulary are aware of it or not, what it suggests is that value originates not in what is admirable or worthy of being cherished in the world, but in the idiosyncrasies of our own inner life. It is an intrinsically subjectivizing vocabulary.[1] It has the effect of canceling

---

1. It is a common strategy of liberals to deny that their commitment to political liberalism in any way entails a moral skepticism concerning the ranking of superior and inferior forms of life; the liberal commitment merely affirms the illegitimacy of the imposition of any such ranking through the agency of the state. Nonetheless, the subjectivizing tendency of liberal philosophy usually shows through. For instance, John Rawls in his discussion of "the principle of perfection" in *A Theory of Justice* (§ 50) states that "the freedom and well-being of individuals, when measured by the excellence of their activities and works, is vastly different in value. . . . Comparisons of intrinsic value can obviously be made." Yet a few pages later he argues for the exclusion of perfectionist criteria as political principles—that is, for the rejection of notions of excellence as applied to the determination of public policy—on grounds that this would involve our being "influenced by subtle aesthetic preferences and personal feelings of propriety." *A Theory of Justice* (Oxford: Oxford University Press, 1971), pp. 328, 331. For a particularly ingenious attempt at reconciling liberalism and perfectionism, see Will Kymlicka, "Liberalism and Communitarianism," *Canadian Journal of Philosophy* 18, no. 2 (June 1988): 181–204.

out the claims to real validity anchored in the world; it is a self-defeating moral language. Talk of values implies that we do not find goodness in the good things there in the world, but confer value from our own subjectivity.

The language of value is inseparable from the notion of an exhaustive dichotomy between facts and values, where it is presumed that the world consists of evaluatively neutral facts that we then inject with value on the basis of our own prejudices and proclivities. However, the dichotomous conception of a world of facts charged with value from without, at the initiative of value-dispensing subjects, is unfortunately unequal to the way we actually experience the world commonsensically. We experience a world that is already a repository of good, not one that depends parasitically upon us for any value it can manage to borrow or scrounge.[2] The Aristotelian language of virtue is incalculably superior to the modern language in retaining this truth of common-sense experience.

Liberals assume that the language of values is neutral, but this is merely one among numerous instances of a spurious liberal neutralism. The discourse of values, intended to be neutral, is already predisposed toward a particular way of experiencing and thinking about moral and political phenomena.[3]

RIGHTS

According to Amy Gutmann, "most prominent political philosophers are now rights theorists."[4] This is certainly a striking pronouncement about the development of contemporary theory. It seems fairly clear that this development mirrors in some important

2. An excellent guide here is E. J. Bond, *Reason and Value* (Cambridge: Cambridge University Press, 1983).

3. Heidegger hits the nail on the head in his analysis of "valuative thought" (*Wertgedanke*) in *Nietzsche*, vol. 4, *Nihilism*, ed. David Farrell Krell, trans. Frank A. Capuzzi (San Francisco: Harper & Row, 1982).

4. Amy Gutmann, "The Central Role of Rawls's Theory," *Dissent* (Summer 1989): 338. For a parallel acknowledgment of the pervasiveness of rights-based theorizing, but from the opposing side, see John Gray, "The Tyranny of Rights-Talk," *Times Literary Supplement*, 1 February 1991, pp. 7–8.

way the reality of a liberal social order; whether it is expressive of
the moral strength or moral weakness of liberal society is still an
open question. Here I would merely mention the accusation, familiar by now, that rights discourse tends to posit forms of social life
that are excessively adversarial, litigious, and geared toward modes
of self-assertion of individuals or collectivities. It is an interesting
question whether the latter features of liberal public culture are
the outcome of the prevailing moral language, or (perhaps more
plausibly) whether the resort to the language of rights as the dominant moral and political vocabulary is merely a symptomatic
expression of these features. As Alasdair MacIntyre says, "since in
modern society the accommodation of one set of wills to the purpose of another continually requires the frustration of one group's
purposes by those of another, it is unsurprising that the concept of
rights, understood as claims against the inroads of marauding others in situations where shared allegiances to goods that are goods of
the whole community have been attenuated or abandoned, should
become a socially central concept."[5] In order to see why this might
be so, consider an argument between two individuals of differing
political persuasions concerning whether it would be *good* for the
society as a whole if the state were to make available a certain social
service (say, universal state-funded daycare). Now imagine how
the tone of the debate would be altered if it suddenly turned into
a contest between the *right* of one of the parties to receive the service
in question and the *right* of the other party not to be burdened by
the higher taxes necessary to supply the service. I will defer until
the next chapter a more detailed elaboration of this argument; for
now, I will simply admit my sympathy for this general line of critique.

INDIVIDUAL AUTONOMY

In *A Theory of Justice*, John Rawls makes much of the ideal of designing for oneself a "rational plan of life." It might indeed be possible

---

5. Alasdair MacIntyre, "Rights, Practices and Marxism," *Analyse &
Kritik* 7 (1985): 239. Cf. George F. Will, *Statecraft as Soulcraft* (New York:
Simon & Schuster, 1983), p. 160: the expression of all social issues in the

for a few rare artists or intellectuals to contrive a plan of life of their own design. But the great majority of individuals in any society are simply socialized to given roles that may be fulfilling or banal depending upon the organized practices of the society in question. Activities and choices are ranked by any given society, and so the liberal model of unlimited individual choice with respect to "life-styles" is disingenuous. The very term *lifestyles* betrays the fatuous-ness of this vision, for of course the lifestyles from which one makes one's selection are all carefully prepackaged, or rather they form a prepackaged set, and this belies the apparent pluralism of self-designed options. This is the nub of truth in MacIntyre's statement, which might otherwise seem a gross simplification, that liberal society is in essence a society of aesthetes, managers, and therapists.[6] MacIntyre surely did not overlook that many individuals within liberal society have, and avail themselves of, the opportunity to pursue vocations other than these. It should be sobering for contemporary liberals that one of the greatest of modern liberals, Max Weber, conceded to Nietzsche that modern society was evolving in the direction of a culture ruled by "specialists without spirit, sensualists without heart."[7]

Rawls's example of an individual who exercises rational autonomy by maximizing his resources for a life devoted to counting "blades of grass in various geometrically shaped areas"[8] undoubtedly expresses a ludicrously truncated understanding of practical reason. But even on a less absurd account of rationality, it is not clear that the exercise of individual autonomy ought to loom as large as it does in the preoccupations of modern liberals. My suspicion is that the actual substance of autonomy and diversity in liberal society is in inverse ratio to the vigor and enthusiasm with which liberals celebrate it as the characteristic strength of a modern pluralistic society. It would indeed be excellent if liberalism made avail-

language of individual rights "raises the general level of truculence in civic relations."

6. Alasdair MacIntyre, *After Virtue* (Notre Dame, Ind.: University of Notre Dame Press, 1981), p. 29.

7. Max Weber, *The Protestant Ethic and the Spirit of Capitalism*, trans. Talcott Parsons (New York: Scribner's, 1958), p. 182.

8. Rawls, *Theory of Justice*, pp. 432–433.

able the genuine pluralism it promises; as it is, much of what is so extravagantly advertised turns out to be hollow. What is worse, the rhetoric of pluralism serves to squelch a concrete examination of social practices that would validate or invalidate the claim of wondrous diversity.

But of course these challenges to liberal theory are all very familiar, and should not be belabored. In any case, perhaps they apply more to the popular idiom of liberal culture than to the most refined statements of liberal philosophy. Yet the point is that it should be the task of theory to challenge the popular idiom, rather than to rationalize it and help it to feel content with itself. Relative to this standard, I do not think contemporary liberal social theory has been doing as good a job as it might of fulfilling its philosophical mandate.

ANOTHER VOCABULARY

Having considered, at an exceedingly swift pace, some leading terms of liberal discourse, let us now proceed, no less swiftly, with the alternative vocabulary. What is neo-Aristotelianism? Its basic conception is that moral reason consists not in a set of moral principles, apprehended and defined through procedures of detached rationality, but in the concrete embodiment of certain human capacities in a moral subject that knows those capacities to be constitutive of a consummately desirable life. The characteristic Aristotelian themes are encapsulated in the Greek word *ethos*, which encompasses character formation, that is, habituation to good character, as well as the kinds of social milieus that engender good character and proper habituation. Clearly this whole conception of virtues understood as realized capacities that tend to the perfection or completion of the human organism rests upon the postulate of a human good that is simply there, not freely designed; it forms a rational standard for moral judgment. The content of this human good is not grasped by reason alone, but rises to self-consciousness in the embodied praxis of a moral agent who makes good choices and is pleased by activities that confer worthy pleasures. The standard liberal challenge to Aristotelian moral reflection is that the very notion of an objective human telos evinces an ethical and political monism that does violence to modern experiences of pluralism, diversity of goals and aspirations, and moral conflict. Much of what follows is an attempt to respond in various ways to this liberal challenge. Among the most controversial of neo-Aristotelian theses are the notion of a summum bonum; the unity of the virtues; prudence as the ruling virtue; and politics as an architectonic science. Some brief observations on each of these may help to clarify both the liberal critique and the outline of an Aristotelian rejoinder.

SUMMUM BONUM

The central thought of Aristotelian ethical theory is that human activities, for all their unquestioned diversity, are nonetheless governed from within; there is a center to human action; there are patterns of coherence in human existence. The proper unit of moral analysis is "the happy life." It should be clear that this entails no monistic principle in the understanding of ethical life. An appropriate analogy might be the variety of forms of artistic activity. All artistic activities, in some fashion or other, strive after "the beautiful work." It would be ludicrous to employ aesthetic theory to dictate a single binding route to the creation of beauty. On the other hand, it would be equally crazy to suggest that there are no standards whatever in the evaluation of relative success or failure in the realization of the beautiful work. There are intelligible standards of judgment governing those works already belonging to the canon of great art, and there are also intelligible standards of judgment governing the enlargement or expansion of the canon by new works of genius. The truth lies neither in some kind of monistic algorithm nor in a concession to orderless diversity. Rather, it is a matter of embodied judgment. The same is surely true of ethical practice. We neither seek to impose a single pattern of the happy life by the fiat of reason, nor deny the existence of patterns of coherence, forms of ethical order that are not of our own making. Furthermore, these practices are, inescapably, situated within a social dimension that is also subject to embodied judgment. There is nothing strange or farfetched about these claims; they seem perfectly in accord with average everyday experience.

The starting point of Aristotle's analysis in the *Nicomachean Ethics* is not the affirmation of a latent or attainable moral consensus, but the fact of moral disagreement: different individuals conceive differently the nature of the good. But can one make sense of this disagreement if one jettisons the claim that there *is* a "nature of the good"? Can one really deny that all human beings seek to live well, and care about whether their judgments as practical agents are conducive to their living well? Moreover, they cannot help but care about whether the social context in which they live promotes or hinders the living of a complete and satisfying life. The fact that different agents disagree substantively in their actual judgments does not contradict these Aristotelian claims. If we all set off in pursuit of an elusive fox, we may disagree about how to hunt our quarry, what routes to take, and what strategies to pursue. But our quarry is the same. Moreover, at the end of the day, our quarry may finally have eluded us; but this does not prove that we have not shared in a common quest. This is true also of ethics. That we are never in possession of a final moral certainty does not prove that we do not participate in a shared moral quest; nor does the variety and mutual opposition of our choices negate the existence of a shared human telos.

I have trouble seeing what it means to accuse Aristotelians of failing to perceive moral conflict. Of course there are conflicts in moral belief and moral perception. How could anyone fail to be aware of that? The point, however, is what moral conflict or differences in moral perception are *about*. If we disagree morally, what is the object of our disagreement? If our ends are simply different in an ultimate and absolute sense, are we really talking about disagreement, or about something more like the habitation of separate moral universes? The latter, it seems to me, is basically unintelligible. When Aristotle, at the beginning of the *Ethics*,[9] speaks of a single end—*telos* in the singular—shared by all human beings, he is referring to the fact that all human beings share an interest in living well and cannot help being concerned with whether their judgments in this regard are suitable to their constitution as human beings. It seems nonsense to call this monism. It may indeed be monism in the culpable sense to insist, as Aristotle does in book 10 of the *Ethics*, that anyone who does not live the contemplative life falls short of being a full human being. But this does not apply to

9. All references to "the *Ethics*" are to the *Nicomachean Ethics*.

the very idea of a human telos, and, as Aristotle argued, it is not clear that one can think coherently about ethical life at all without the supposition of such a telos.

It is striking that even philosophers who are in strong sympathy with Aristotle find it difficult to embrace the doctrine of the summum bonum. In a searching analysis, William Galston concludes, in light of Aquinas's restatement of the Aristotelian argument, that the idea of a highest good "is fundamentally hypothetical" and depends on unproven assumptions concerning the essential unity of human nature.[10] And Stuart Hampshire, in an essay *defending* Aristotelian ethics, writes: "We cannot suppose that there must be some one form of life, called 'the good for man,' identifiable a priori, merely because it is a condition of conclusiveness in practical reasoning that there should be such a norm."[11] An Aristotelian answer to these challenges might go something like this. There is no theoretical proof that human nature can find fulfillment, or can unify its diverse strivings, in a virtuous life. At best, we can locate moral exemplars who embody a relative unity and finality. To be sure, *eudaimonia* in the exhaustive sense implies the life of a god, and this is out of reach. Still, the relative success of the practical exemplar in shaping a life that is full and happy serves to reassure us that our strivings both for the satisfactions of praxis and for the satisfactions of *theoria* have a direction that is not merely contingent or arbitrary. Even this more modest achievement of contentment can supply a standard by which to judge critically the lesser achievements of individual lives and social ways of life.

Aristotelian intuitions of ethical order are supported by very commonplace moral experiences. We know that there are some individuals—like Christina Onassis, to cite an extreme instance—whose lives are nothing but a frustrating succession of desires, where the obtaining of desire $x + 1$ confers no more satisfaction than the obtaining of desire x. By Hobbes's account, in *Leviathan*,

10. William A. Galston, *Kant and the Problem of History* (Chicago: University of Chicago Press, 1975), p. 135.

11. Stuart Hampshire, "Ethics: A Defense of Aristotle," in *Freedom of Mind and Other Essays* (Oxford: Clarendon Press, 1972), p. 79. This essay offers a very powerful statement of the surpassing strengths of the Aristotelian approach to moral theory, without neglecting its possible weaknesses.

chapter 11, this is the inescapable fate of all human beings, however they choose to live their individual lives. But this is simply not the case. We know, as a matter of common experience, that there are individuals whose lives are not simply a futile succession of desires, where a new desire arises the instant that its predecessor desire has been satisfied. There *are* individuals whose desires and strivings have been organized into a stable order. But we also know that a distressingly high proportion of individuals in our society live lives that are a watered-down or less dramatic version of Christina Onassis's life. Therefore the Aristotelian ideal of a life that is not mere restless striving furnishes a critical standard for the judgment of a society that tends to breed such individuals.

Unity of the Virtues

This doctrine is less ambitious than it looks at first glance, especially if it is regarded, as it must be, in conjunction with the thesis of the primacy of prudence as the ruling virtue. A virtue would not be a virtue, in the sense of an excellence productive of an excellent life, if it were seen in isolation, separate from the moral quality of a person's life as a whole. A virtue is defined as a moral attribute conducive to eudaimonia, and eudaimonia is a global property of a life viewed as a whole. It hardly makes sense to say that someone is courageous but lacks the moral insight to judge suitable occasions for the exercise of courage, or that someone is generous but lacks the moral insight to judge suitable occasions for the exercise of generosity. If we lack knowledge of how to concretize our experience of the virtues, we cannot practice them; and if we cannot practice the virtues we do not have them. The virtues come into play as virtues within the organized conduct of a moral life whose center of gravity is prudence. Therefore it is entirely reasonable that Aristotle, in book 6, chapter 13, of the *Ethics*, rejects as inadequate the argument "that the virtues exist independently of one another."

MacIntyre, for one, rejects Aristotle's thesis of the unity of the virtues. At issue is whether, for instance, an otherwise immoral Nazi can possess, say, the virtue of courage (as MacIntyre holds), or whether (as argued by P. T. Geach), what we normally call courage is in this case not really courage, or, if we insist on calling it courage, that it is in this instance not a virtue.[12] To my mind, there is more to be said for Geach's view here than MacIntyre allows. But apart from this case of courage in its relation to the other virtues, Geach too, as it happens, denies the unity of the virtues.[13] I would be inclined to say, in answer to MacIntyre *and* Geach, that Aristotle's ethical theory is not a theory of the separate human virtues, but a theory of general human flourishing, and that it is concerned with the virtues and with their mutual relation only insofar as they bear upon the possibility of general human flourishing. So while it is true that one may be an honest man and yet a coward, or a fearless man and yet a fool, one has to affirm some kind of unity of the virtues in order for the theory of the virtues to have the relevance for the problem of eudaimonia that Aristotle intended it to have.

PRUDENCE

As we have seen, what distinguishes Aristotelian moral theory is a preoccupation with virtues embodied in character. Character is understood as something abiding, so that the felicity or infelicity of the agent's choices is not fortuitous but flows from an organized pattern of life, the lifelong sway of a rational principle. Therefore to speak in an Aristotelian way about the virtues requires a central reference to the capacity for making good judgments, having the fortitude to put those good judgments into action, and doing so not merely episodically but on the basis of enduring dispositions that are deeply entrenched in one's character. This is the virtue of prudence (*phronesis*), and as we saw in the preceding section, it is what lends intelligibility to the doctrine of the unity of the virtues. As Aristotle says, "in the case of those virtues which entitle a man to be called good in an unqualified sense . . . as soon as he possesses this single virtue of practical wisdom, he will also possess all the rest" (*Nicomachean Ethics*, book 6, chapter 13).

12. MacIntyre, *After Virtue*, pp. 167–168; Peter Geach, *The Virtues* (Cambridge: Cambridge University Press, 1977), pp. 159–162. See also Philippa Foot, *Virtues and Vices* (Oxford: Basil Blackwell, 1978), pp. 14–17.

13. Geach, *The Virtues*, pp. 162–168. See also Bernard Williams, *Ethics and the Limits of Philosophy* (Cambridge: Harvard University Press, 1985), pp. 36–37, 43, 153.

The doctrine of the unity of the virtues does not imply that this unity finds its concrete realization always in an identical fashion, or that the virtues are organized into a unity identically in every virtuous human being. Nor does the doctrine presuppose that the achievement of this unity in an exemplary life represents a seamless harmony. Indeed, Aristotle did not think, any more than any of us today thinks, or any more than Isaiah Berlin thinks, that even the happiest and most well-constituted individual will be able to reconcile every one of his or her leading goals and aspirations. Rather, the idea of the happy life is that over the course of a lifetime one will be able to fit one's various purposes into a pattern that makes sense and achieves a reasonable coherence. If Aristotelian ethics were as harmony seeking and blind to competing goals as the pluralists charge, not only would prudence not be the central virtue, prudence would be superfluous. Prudence occupies the center of Aristotelian ethical thought precisely because the adjudication of alternative possibilities in a concrete situation requires an exemplary performance on the part of the moral agent. And Aristotle gives us no reason to doubt that each such performance will be unique. Again, Aristotelian teleology does not imply that one individual who has achieved, or approximated to, eudaimonia will turn out identical to every other individual who has done so. It does not imply virtue clones! What *is* implied is that there is a distinction, and one not of our own invention, between a well-turned-out human being and a poorly turned-out human being. And here the pluralist who renounces teleological categories is much more out of accord with common sense than is the Aristotelian.

Thrift is a virtue and stinginess is a vice, but where is one to draw the line between thrift and stinginess? The whole thrust of Aristotle's doctrine of prudence is to suggest that a merely theoretical drawing of the line would be abstract to the point of uselessness; an answer of any meaningful substance would have to be determined at the level of context-bound judgment. A theory of the virtues simply tells us what we already know, such as that there is a distinction between thrift as a virtue and stinginess as a vice; it does little to guide conduct. The difficulty of judgment in practice does not impugn the reality of the analytical distinction; on the other hand, being able to distinguish analytically between the virtue and the vice does not make it any easier to resolve the problem of practical choice. And indeed, practical judgment is what really counts here, governed as it is by the contingencies of the situation, the distinctive moral dispositions of the agent, and the larger context of moral life that informs these particularities of character and circumstance. The privileged status of prudence among the virtues underlines the strictly limited practical helpfulness of a mere theory of the various virtues.[14]

The Preeminence of Politics

For a canonical statement of the liberal repudiation of Aristotelian "civic humanism," one may consult section 7 of Rawls's essay "The Priority of Right and Ideas of the Good."[15] Rawls, along with other liberals, assumes that politics represents merely one among many sectors of social life, and that it would be metaphysically extravagant to privilege one among many possible outlets of social interaction. I am not persuaded that Aristotle has in any way been refuted in his conception that the political relationship encompasses and orders the multitude of lesser social relationships and that the former denominates the whole in relation to which the latter stand as parts. But I hope that my reasons for trying to hold the Aristotelian fort on this point will become apparent in later stages of my argument. For now, I would simply suggest that a life lived in ignorance of or indifference toward the larger forces shaping one's destiny in the modern world—ignorance and indifference that seems to afflict the majority of citizens in even the most liberal and most democratic of modern societies, or perhaps especially in those societies—may without absurdity be claimed to be a less than properly human existence; and that a society that abides such ignorance and indifference is failing in its responsibility to nurture properly human capacities.

To summarize: For the Aristotelian, moral life is ordered, not episodic or haphazard. The central purpose of a society, understood as a moral community, is not the maximization of autonomy,

14. This Aristotelian theme of the limits of theory is pursued at greater length in chapter 7.

15. John Rawls, "The Priority of Right and Ideas of the Good," *Philosophy & Public Affairs* 17, no. 4 (Fall 1988): 272–273.

or protection of the broadest scope for the design of self-elected plans of life, but the cultivation of virtue, interpreted as excellence or as a variety of excellences, moral and intellectual. The last of these theses is set in sharp relief in the following statement by Alasdair MacIntyre: "The good life for man is the life spent in seeking for the good life for man, and the virtues necessary for the seeking are those which will enable us to understand what more and what else the good life for man is."[16] This passage makes clear that it is not a question of prescribing a single commanding excellence, but a finite (and not indefinite) set of excellences by which one judges the moral and political achievement, or moral and political deficiency, of a given society. Clearly, none of the above discussions are anywhere near adequate to a full defense of Aristotle; at most, they suggest why an Aristotelian account (even with respect to its most controversial claims) is not obviously implausible, and they merely gesture in the direction of a fuller argument as to its plausibility.

MORE ARISTOTLE

In order to probe a bit more deeply some of the most problematical aspects of Aristotelian ethical theory, let us examine in greater detail Galston's thorough interrogation of the argument of the *Nicomachean Ethics* in chapter 4 of his book on Kant. It should be noted that Galston's critique is of the devil's advocate variety, constructed as it were in the light of Kantian preoccupations. At the outset of Galston's critique he writes that he will let himself be "implicitly guided by . . . the major premises of Kantian morality,"[17] and at the conclusion of the critique he writes that his purpose has not been to demonstrate "the superiority of Kantian ethics to those of Aristotle," since the former are no more free of difficulties than the latter.[18] What we shall try to explore in dialogue with Galston's critique is whether Aristotle's reflections on ethical life form, or are intended to form, a moral system. This is what the very notion of a summum bonum seems to suggest. However, if Aristotle's ethics

16. MacIntyre, *After Virtue*, p. 204.
17. Galson, *Kant and the Problem of History*, p. 133.
18. Ibid., pp. 188–189.

is seen as a strict "science of ends," governed by a strict, and readily discernible, ethical hierarchy, the Aristotelian will be drawn into a dual trap. On the one side, the liberal pluralist will protest that the very systematicness of Aristotelian ethics convicts it of monism or inattention to moral complexity. On the other side, critics will show how the system succumbs (as it inevitably will) to various tensions and antinomies. My strategy will be to defend Aristotle on both fronts by arguing that Aristotle's intentions are misunderstood if viewed through the prism of the more systematic Aristotelianism of Aquinas.[19]

One of Galston's arguments is that there is a tension between happiness and morality in Aristotle that Kant alone succeeds in dissolving by liberating morality from its subordinate relation to happiness. The source of the tension may be glimpsed in the fact that Aristotle's theory of the virtues is set within, and delimited at both ends by, a larger theory of the good—which suggests that moral reflection and moral action do not exhaust the broader question of the good, and that they form a part, but only a part, of the more comprehensive inquiry.[20] It follows that the realization of any particular moral virtue stands in an uncertain relation to the realization of the highest good for human beings, which is not exhausted by the ensemble of moral virtues. For Kant, as for Aristotle, the conjunction of morality and happiness

19. For instance, in his doctrine of prudence, Aquinas, precisely by resolving the ambiguity in Aristotle as to whether phronesis appoints ends or merely selects means, actually diminishes the status of prudence. In consequence, phronesis cannot loom as large in Aquinas's moral theory as it does in Aristotle's ethics, despite the fact that the doctrine of prudence is intended by Aquinas to be faithfully Aristotelian. The doctrine is more categorical but less Aristotelian. See St. Thomas Aquinas, *Summa Theologiae*, vol. 36, *Prudence*, ed. Thomas Gilby, O.P. (London: Eyre & Spottiswoode, 1974), p. 23 (2a2ae, question 47, article 6). Chapter 5 of Geach's book *The Virtues* should offer a sufficient illustration of the difference between Thomist prudence and Aristotelian prudence.

20. As I understand the structure of the *Ethics*, the theory of the good, interspersed with various digressions, is composed of the following passages: 1094a1–1094b12; 1095a14–1095a30; 1095b13–1096a10; 1097a15–1098a19; 1098b7–1102a4; 1176a30–1179a33. The theory of the virtues, or more strictly, the theory of excellences of character, runs from 1102a5 to 1176a29. Read like this, the theory of the virtues represents almost a kind of large digression!

constitutes a summum bonum for human beings; but for Kant morality must not be pursued with a view to the achievement of this summum bonum, and the imperativeness of morality is in no way affected by the prospects of its achievement. The Stoics also dissolved the tension, but only by means of a highly implausible identification of happiness and morality that even Aristotle would certainly have rejected.[21] (In the words of Marcus Aurelius: "Every action in accord with nature should be regarded as a delight."[22]) As Galston points out, the tension is manifest in the very first virtue treated in Aristotle's theory of the virtues, namely courage; for this Aristotelian virtue is typically exercised by human beings in situations of peril that threaten rather than promote their securing of the comprehensive good.[23] From the Kantian point of view, Aristotelian ethics renders morality all too contingent upon a summum bonum that in turn may or may not be supported by a fickle, if not hostile, nature. Again from the Kantian perspective, the harmony of virtue and happiness can only be saved by the anthropomorphic optimism of Aristotelian cosmology.[24]

What answer can the Aristotelian or neo-Aristotelian give to this modern critique? For one thing, the Kantian challenge to Aristotle—as Galston emphasizes—rests upon the antiteleological premises of modern science, which until recently have been generally assumed to be more theoretically decisive than they perhaps are. (A modest resurrection of teleological categories was the object of Charles Taylor's book *The Explanation of Behaviour* [1964]; a more ambitious resuscitation of teleology is attempted in Hans Jonas's book *The Phenomenon of Life* [1966]). In any case, it is not clear that ethical teleology is as wedded to cosmological teleology as Galston (in common with many other readers of Aristotle) supposes.[25] Of course, one of the most familiar objections to Aristotelian practical philosophy is that it depends upon a set of metaphysical and cosmological doctrines that are today highly implausible, or even unin-

21. Galston, *Kant and the Problem of History*, pp. 178, 183.
22. Marcus Aurelius, *Meditations*, book 10, section 33.
23. Galston, *Kant and the Problem of History*, pp. 157–158.
24. Ibid., pp. 189–190.
25. Ibid., pp. 161–162, 168, 172.

telligible.[26] Stoic ethical theory is indeed so dependent, with frequent appeals to the rational structure of the universe, the moral intentions of the gods, and cosmic providence. In Aristotle, by contrast, the whole stress is on the inner structure of the virtues, with only minimal reference to metaphysical or cosmological assumptions. (In this respect, I think Leo Strauss is correct to emphasize the opposition between natural law, e.g., the Stoics, and natural right, e.g., Aristotle.[27]) What is striking is the autonomy of the ethical world in relation to cosmological doctrines. In fact, if anything the emphasis in Aristotle (for instance, in book 6, chapter 7, of the *Ethics*) is on the contrasts between the eternity of the cosmos and the transience and mutability of everything human, the transcendent order of the former and the relative contingency of the latter, and so on.

To return once again to the issue of the tension between virtue and happiness, the problem is often merely one of perspective, with Aristotle's position being misconstrued by being viewed against the backdrop of more extreme alternatives. For instance, both the Stoics and Kant adopt the more radical Socratic position that the just person is happy, regardless of the fate that person suffers in the external world; Aristotle rejects it. Aristotle does not embrace the position of Eudoxus, affirming pleasure as the good, but he appears to approximate to a Eudoxian position relative to

26. This thesis of the dependence of Aristotelian ethics on Aristotelian cosmology is affirmed by, among many others, Leo Strauss. See Strauss, *Natural Right and History* (Chicago: University of Chicago Press, 1953), pp. 7–8; "Letter to Helmut Kuhn," *Independent Journal of Philosophy* 2 (1978): 24; *The Rebirth of Classical Political Rationalism*, ed. Thomas L. Pangle (Chicago: University of Chicago Press, 1989), p. 34. Strauss avows that, much as he would wish to embrace Aristotelianism, he is debarred by the incredibility of Aristotelian cosmology. Although MacIntyre seems also to be committed to this thesis in *After Virtue*, p. 183, he adopts a radically different line in "Bernstein's Distorting Mirrors," *Soundings* 67, no. 1 (1984): 38–39. For further discussion of this question, see my presentation of Gadamer's Aristotelianism in "Do We Need a Philosophical Ethics?" *The Philosophical Forum* 20, no. 3 (Spring 1989): 231–232; and Charles Taylor's account of his own Aristotelianism in relation to MacIntyre's, in "Justice after Virtue," in *Kritische Methode und Zukunft der Anthropologie*, ed. Michael Benedikt and Rudolf Burger (Vienna: Wilhelm Braunmuller, 1985), p. 24.

27. Leo Strauss, *Studies in Platonic Political Philosophy* (Chicago: University of Chicago Press, 1983), pp. 140–141.

the more radical position of Socrates and the orthodox Socratics. (Plato may or may not be counted among these orthodox Socratics.) Perhaps the tension would appear less intractable if *arete* were translated by "excellence" rather than by the misleading term "virtue." In fact one would avoid multiple confusions in the reading of Aristotle if one were to avoid altogether the terms "virtue," which "sounds" Kantian, and "happiness," which "sounds" utilitarian.[28] The advantage of rendering *arete* and *aretai* as "excellence" and "excellences," and *eudaimonia* as "well-being," is that it becomes more difficult even to state the Kantian problem of virtue versus happiness; that this appears as a problem shows that we are already within a horizon of Kantian premises (though this would seem to have the curious consequence that the moral horizon of Socrates in book 2 of *The Republic* would have to be seen as closer to Kant's than to Aristotle's).

Another of Galston's critical arguments is that Aristotle's account of virtue is deficient or incomplete relative to Aquinas's because Aristotle presupposes a science governing the apprehension of the good (corresponding to the function of nous in theoretical science) that would supply ends for phronesis as a science of means. Aquinas, with his concept of synderesis, supplies this faculty for the apprehension of ends; Aristotle should do likewise, but fails to. He thereby implicitly concedes the missing element in his moral theory; the foundations are lacking a crucial pillar.[29] But this misstates the character of phronesis, and it fails to convey the outstanding modesty of the theory as a whole. Phronesis is not a science of means that waits upon a theoretical or quasi-theoretical apprehension of ends supplied by some other faculty; it is itself the capacity for defining the ends through the effort to embody them in the concrete exigencies of particular situations.[30] Hans-Georg Gadamer has given a brilliant explication of how the contribution of phronesis to articulating the nature of the good is much more decisive than

28. Similar points are made by Martha Nussbaum in *The Fragility of Goodness* (Cambridge: Cambridge University Press, 1986), p. 6n. Inexplicably, though, she employs the very un-Aristotelian language of value (ibid., p. 7n.).

29. Galston, *Kant and the Problem of History*, pp. 153–157, 173, 186–187.

30. Cf. Hampshire, *Freedom of Mind*, p. 59.

Aristotle himself sometimes implies, and of how, correspondingly, the provision of a science of ends, theoretically defined, is indeed superfluous.[31] Gadamer writes: "The idea of the good lies beyond the scope of any science. . . . We cannot conceptualize the idea of the good. . . . The theoretical man remains subordinated to phronesis."[32] The core of Aristotle's thought is that we can only test our notions of what our ends are through a living engagement with choice of means—understanding of the end (happiness or the good) as mediated by deliberation upon means in a specific situation—and this can only be brought to pass in the exemplary performances of a person of practical wisdom, not in theoretical apprehension of any kind.

Let us address one further major challenge to Aristotelianism to which Galston draws attention. Near the beginning of the *Ethics*, Aristotle argues that human life would be a senseless anarchy unless it were ordered in the direction of a highest good. He goes on to say that this highest good is easy to name (eudaimonia), but that its content is highly controversial. Yet by book 10 it appears that the controversy concerning the content of the highest good has been settled; it is the contemplative life: theoria.[33] But what constitutes the highness of this highest good? Aristotle lists several considerations; the main one is the sublime object of theoria, which is infinitely more stable and worthy of contemplation than the paltry objects of prudence. Yet it would seem that modern natural science has rendered it highly implausible that inanimate planets possess an ontologically higher status than animate things on this planet, especially human beings. This seems to impugn the whole project of locating a highest good, as Hobbes, among others, suggests.

31. Hans-Georg Gadamer, *Truth and Method* (New York: Seabury Press, 1975), p. 525 n. 225. More generally, see *Truth and Method*, pp. 278–289, 489–490; Gadamer, *Reason in the Age of Science*, trans. F. G. Lawrence (Cambridge, Mass.: MIT Press, 1981), pp. 133–134; and Gadamer, *The Idea of the Good in Platonic-Aristotelian Philosophy*, trans. P. C. Smith (New Haven: Yale University Press, 1986), chap. 6.

32. "Gadamer on Strauss: An Interview," *Interpretation* 12, no. 11 (January 1984): 12.

33. The problem of whether book 10, chapters 6–8, of the *Ethics* is consistent or inconsistent with the broader intent of Aristotle's ethical theory is posed very sharply in Nussbaum, *Fragility of Goodness*, pp. 373–377.

However, a closer look at the account in book 10 raises questions about whether theoria is as straightforwardly privileged over praxis as it appears at first glance, and as it especially appears relative to Kant; and therefore, also, whether it is so easy to dismiss the idea of a moral hierarchy with the contemplative life at its summit. As Galston himself shows, theoria such as human beings experience it carries us no closer to eudaimonia in the pure sense than does the corresponding experience of striving for moral completeness in the domain of praxis.[34] Gods enjoy bliss, but human beings can merely grope in the direction of full contentment; and though theoria can offer us intimations of divine understanding, it can likewise offer us no more than intimations of divine happiness. If this is the case, then theoria and arete are actually closer in rank than the initial assertion of the superiority of theoria in book 10 suggests. When the practical virtues are judged relative to the standard of happiness conferred by theoria, the practical life is held up to a standard that even philosophy fails grossly to satisfy.

Theoria *is* privileged in relation to the life of politics (pursuit of honor) and the life of pleasure. But it is not so clear that theoria is absolutely privileged in relation to the moral life in general; more likely, theoria, as well as the moral life, stands in a relation of part to whole to the full human life. Theoria is more sufficient than pursuit of honor or pursuit of pleasure. But is it fully self-sufficient? The virtuous person who is cut down in his or her prime is judged to fall short of happiness. But what about the contemplative person who theorizes or philosophizes very intensely in his or her twenties, and is also cut down in his or her prime, or suffers horrible misfortune? Does not the latter fall short of proper happiness in just the same way that the person of virtue does?[35] The fact that the summum bonum presents itself to us as an object of interminable aspiration confirms that it cannot be fully identified with either the contemplative life or the practical life. The priority assigned to the contemplative life is itself a part of the practical life, and therefore itself subject to the comprehensive arbitration of phronesis. As I argued earlier, a quest is intelligible only in relation to a definite

34. Galston, *Kant and the Problem of History*, pp. 137–138, 174.
35. Cf. *Nicomachean Ethics*, book 10, chap. 7: 1177b24–26.

object. The highest good is our target, even if our arrow falls short; just as, in the life of theory, truth is our object, even if it continually eludes us (for otherwise how could we make sense of the very activity?). This principle applies as much to the practical life as to the contemplative life, and as much to the contemplative life as to the practical life. All of these supposed tensions in Aristotle— between virtue and happiness, nobility and pleasure, moral praxis and theoria—have to be seen not as posing an either/or, but rather in a relation of part to whole. A life of virtue without contentment is incomplete, but so is a life of theoretical contemplation without moral excellence. It is impossible to offer a perfect theory that resolves all tensions and gaps in moral experience, and Aristotle had no hope or expectation of articulating a moral teaching that did so. On the contrary, the great strength of Aristotle's ethics is its wonderful sensitivity to the complexity and multidimensionality of human ethical experience. That is why the liberals' charge of monism against Aristotle is so grotesque.

THE NEUTRAL STATE

Let us now proceed to some more directly political challenges to Aristotelianism. The liberal argument is that liberal political institutions are required in order to cope with inexorable moral diversity and otherwise intractable conflicts of moral aspiration. This argument has been ably articulated in various versions by, among others, John Rawls, Thomas Nagel, Richard Rorty, Stuart Hampshire, and, of course, Sir Isaiah Berlin. However, does this argument really stand up to rational scrutiny? How much moral diversity is there in liberal societies? Is there, perhaps, as much sharing in aspirations as divergence in aspirations in these societies? Does attention to the unity or identity at the core of liberal society's way of life perhaps bring us closer to a real insight into liberal reality (as opposed to the promises of liberal theory)? Aristotle's notion of an architectonic ranking of activities may strike us as bizarre, or at any rate historically outdated. But there are ruling practices in modern societies, and in liberal societies no less.

Critics of liberalism might argue that the liberal social and political order offers an ideology of pluralism (or a rhetoric of pluralism) to mask its organization of social life according to a distinct and

overarching vision of communal life. Thus the profession of pluralism serves as a cover for the privileging of a singular understanding
of the dominant human end—say, the maximization of individual
autonomy and choice making.[36] Interestingly enough, some liberals have now begun to concede the force of this line of attack and
have sought to restate the grounds of their liberalism so as to defuse
it. For instance, Charles Larmore has recently argued that the commitment to maximizing autonomy is still expressive of a controversial conception of what is good (which is true), and that therefore
it cannot be the raison d'être of the liberal state conceived as a set
of public institutions founded on the ideal of political neutrality
toward controversial conceptions of the good.[37] From this point of
view, the liberalism of Kant, J. S. Mill, and the pre-1980 John Rawls
is still too metaphysically ambitious.[38] According to Larmore, the
aim of political liberalism is not to foster any positive ideal of liberal
personality, but simply the negative goal of averting conflict and
moral stalemate. Larmore bases his ideal of liberal neutrality on a
conception of "equal respect." Moreover, he insists that this conception depends on no classical liberal assumptions about the desirability of autonomy, which he rejects because they are ineliminably
controversial (i.e., nonneutral).[39] Yet why should I "respect" a view
of life that is servile, conformist, and unreflective? How can we
know that different views of life are respectworthy in advance of
examining the substance of these views of life? If Larmore is right
that classical liberal arguments are in violation of the neutrality
principle, would it not make more sense for the liberal to renounce

36. See, for instance, Strauss, *Studies in Platonic Political Philosophy*, p.
149: "by virtue of being an -ism, pluralism is a monism."

37. Charles E. Larmore, *Patterns of Moral Complexity* (Cambridge: Cambridge University Press, 1987). In "The Priority of Right and Ideas of the
Good," Rawls voices strong sympathy and support for Larmore's reformu-
lation of political liberalism.

38. On Rawls, see Larmore, *Patterns of Moral Complexity*, pp. 125–126,
174–175 nn. 67 and 68. In "Justice as Fairness: Political Not Metaphysical,"
Philosophy & Public Affairs 14, no. 3 (Summer 1985): 245–247, and again in
"The Priority of Right and Ideas of the Good," pp. 267–268, Rawls states
explicitly that his concern is not autonomy as such. But it would seem that
here Rawls's drive for metaphysical parsimony, like Larmore's, has gotten
the better of the inner impulses of his own liberalism.

39. Larmore, *Patterns of Moral Complexity*, p. 65.

the neutrality principle rather than to renounce the arguments on behalf of autonomy and voluntary agency?[40]

It is often suggested that the application of premodern moral categories to our modern situation amounts to an impotent moralism.[41] It is an accusation that is central to Larmore's theory of liberalism. Larmore's book warrants further examination because it tries to offer a conceptualization of liberalism that is at the furthest extremity from Aristotelian ways of thinking about ethics and politics. If Larmore is right about what is theoretically attractive in the liberal state, then all the central Aristotelian categories that I am concerned to revive are beyond redemption. The central endeavor of Larmore, as well as a host of other liberals, is to jettison the Kantian or Millian visions of autonomous personhood or romantic self-development, and to construe liberal society instead according to the unromantic image of a modus vivendi where individuals agree to disagree at the political level so they can localize their pursuit of individual and group purposes that are unshared. Pluralism, on this revised understanding, is no longer a noble moral aspiration, a shared moral commitment; instead, it becomes merely the exigency of mutual political accommodation. Liberalism thus responds to its moralistic critics by becoming even less moralistic, more hardheaded.

Larmore subscribes to the standard pluralist critique of Aristotle as a monist that I have tried to rebut throughout this chapter.[42] But perhaps it is the case that while Aristotle himself is not a monist, contemporary theorists become Aristotelians on account of their yearning for monism. This is, indeed, Larmore's understanding of

---

40. The former alternative is the one opted for by William Galston in his defense of liberalism. See, especially, "Defending Liberalism," *American Political Science Review* 76 (1982): 621–629.

41. For Larmore's critique of "Aristotle's whole/part model of society," see *Patterns of Moral Complexity*, pp. 39, 96–99, 103–104, 106–107, 168–169 n. 21, 170–171 nn. 33 and 34. For similar assertions as to the obsolescence of the classical Aristotelian framework of social theory on the part of Larmore's mentor, Niklas Luhmann, see *The Differentiation of Society*, trans. S. Holmes and C. Larmore (New York: Columbia University Press, 1982), pp. 223, 229, 251, 257, 343, 391 n. 7, 392 n. 10; and for commentary, pp. xv–xvii, xx. For a very helpful filling in of the "Luhmannesque" background of Larmore's argument, see the introduction to *The Differentiation of Society*, coauthored by Larmore and Stephen Holmes.

42. Larmore, *Patterns of Moral Complexity*, pp. xii, 10, 34–35, 37–38.

MacIntyre.[43] Here we may recall the encapsulation of MacIntyre's Aristotelianism cited earlier: "The good life for man is the life spent in seeking the good life for man." Is this dogmatic monism? Yet Larmore has trouble making sense of how an antipluralist like Mac-Intyre can be committed to an open-ended teleology like this.[44] Perhaps the difficulty lies not in the coherence of MacIntyre's enterprise but rather in the monism/pluralism distinction adopted by Larmore. Perhaps these categories fail to capture the point of Mac-Intyre's critique of modern experience. Is there, after all, only one way to challenge modern pluralism—namely, by proposing a dogmatic moral hierarchy? Is it not the point of MacIntyre's challenge to direct attention at the ways in which we pursue moral conflict, and the language in which we articulate our nonidentical aspirations? Larmore is puzzled by MacIntyre's Aristotelianism because he simply imputes to MacIntyre a romantic yearning to abolish moral conflict that MacIntyre himself never for one moment embraces. Surely there are possibilities of rational disagreement that transcend the "self-assertive shrillness" that characterizes much moral argument today.[45] And that, surely, is the point of MacIntyre's challenge to contemporary moral pluralism.

43. Ibid., pp. 35–37.

44. Ibid., pp. 36–39. The curious thing about Larmore's quarrel with MacIntyre is that Larmore and MacIntyre actually agree that Aristotle is a monist, and that monism of this kind is to be avoided. Hampshire, another ambivalent Aristotelian, agrees too; see *Morality and Conflict* (Oxford: Basil Blackwell, 1983), pp. 1, 140–141, 144, 148. So Larmore concludes that Mac-Intyre is, despite his using Aristotle as a club with which to batter modernity, in fact "a pluralist malgré lui" (*Patterns of Moral Complexity*, p. 39). But the fact that certain Aristotelians and anti-Aristotelians can agree on this does not prove that they are right about Aristotle. Indeed, Larmore himself concedes ignorance "of any passage where Aristotle explicitly rules out the possibility of moral conflict"—with the exception of a single passage of dubious authorship. Ibid., pp. 159–160 n. 39. For a challenge to MacIntyre's account of Aristotle, see Hans-Georg Gadamer, "Gibt es auf Erden ein Maß," *Philosophische Rundschau* 32, no. 1/2 1–7, especially pp. 4–5. A further paradox of Larmore's polemic against neo-Aristotelianism is that MacIntyre (at least in *After Virtue*) emphasizes the dependence of Aristotle's ethics upon cosmology, whereas Larmore, closer to my own reading of Aristotle, downplays it. *Patterns of Moral Complexity*, pp. 32–33, 159 nn. 20 and 25. See note 26 above.

45. MacIntyre, *After Virtue*, p. 68.

As I mentioned earlier, the leading accusation leveled by liberals against their critics is one of impotent moralism. Surely, though, it is a gross trivialization of the Aristotelian challenge to characterize it as the product of a hankering after imaginary experiences of community. Someone like MacIntyre is making claims about the historical properties of the liberal state (its capacities to socialize its members to humanly worthwhile practices, its vulnerability to social crises, its power to elicit sacrifices from citizens, and so on) that may or may not be empirically valid, and that deserve to be taken seriously as such. Conversely, the central puzzle in Larmore's defense of liberalism is the notion (verging on blind assumption) that it will be possible to sustain within the private domain character formation, constitutive attachments, socialization into substantial ways of life, *Sittlichkeit*—all of which he affirms—within the horizon of a public philosophy of neutrality or agnosticism concerning the relative superiority of different conceptions of the good life. How can we be habituated to social roles, forms of virtue, and enduring moral character within local sectors of social life when the official philosophy of the society is morally agnostic? Larmore is quick to dismiss the "organic model of society" as historically obsolete, but he fails to ask why Aristotelians might be anxious about the fostering of *Sittlichkeit* within a liberal social order (apart from the question-begging assertion that they are driven merely by sentimental romanticism). The confrontation here is not between idealistic longings on one side and undeluded realism on the other, but rather between two competing empirical characterizations of liberal society. Empirically, the evidence is not sufficient either to validate the worst fears of the critics of liberalism or to rule out these fears entirely.

While Larmore will charge Aristotelians like MacIntyre with being blind to the advantages of modern pluralism over ancient monism, someone like MacIntyre can counter that liberals are blind to the monistic tendencies in liberal society itself. From an Aristotelian perspective, the most implausible feature of this liberal philosophy is its claim that there are no ordering principles that bind together and shape a liberal social and political community. In the words of John Rawls, social-contract theory assumes "that society as a whole has no ends or ordering of ends in the sense that associations and individuals do."[46] The distinctive advantage of this theory, he says, is that it offers "a moral conception that can take appropriate account of social values without falling into organicism."[47] Larmore no doubt would say that it is *because* society as a whole has no ends or ordering of ends that the neutralist conception of a modus vivendi to reconcile conflicting ends is required. But liberal society itself is more organic and less neutral than liberals profess. One may apply to Larmore himself the dictum that he applies to utilitarianism, namely that "a lack of neutrality, a commitment to some disputed view about the good life, may lie concealed in what appears to be a purely formal principle."[48] For instance, Larmore admits that modern liberal states cannot fail to interest themselves in the efficiency or inefficiency of their prevailing economic practices, but he, very curiously, denies that this violates the neutrality stipulation.[49] Unfortunately, he nowhere explains how one can maintain a full commitment to maximal economic growth (as all modern liberal states do) without forgoing the claim to neutrality between conflicting substantive ends. Surely the modern state has taken sides in a very clear way in what is one of the most considerable controversies concerning the good life for human beings.

It is not surprising that Larmore bases his modus vivendi theory of liberalism on the toleration doctrines of Bodin, Locke, and Bayle.[50] The question, however, is whether this model, geared to the avoidance of religious wars, is suitable for political disagree-

---

46. John Rawls, "The Basic Structure as Subject," *American Philosophical Quarterly* 14, no. 2 (April 1977): 162.

47. Ibid., p. 165.

48. Larmore, *Patterns of Moral Complexity*, p. 48.

49. Ibid., pp. 45–46. A compelling reason why the liberal state cannot afford to be neutral about the vitality of its capitalist (or semicapitalist) economy is suggested by C. B. Macpherson in "Do We Need a Theory of the State?" *Archives européennes de sociologie* 18, no. 2 (1977): 234: "Given a state's commitment to capitalist enterprise as the mainspring of the economy, the holders of state office must in their own interest maintain and support the accumulation process because the state's revenue, and hence the power of the state's officers, depends on it"; cf. p. 242: "The state in a capitalist society cannot be a neutral uncle: it must serve the interests of capital."

50. Larmore, *Patterns of Moral Complexity*, pp. 76, 130.

ments that do not presuppose incompatible religious visions of personal salvation.[51] It is reasonably clear why Catholics and Protestants in Belfast, or Christians and Muslims in Beirut, must establish a modus vivendi; it is much less clear why, say, citizens supporting and opposing state controls on environmental pollution should (or could) revert to a neutral modus vivendi. What would it mean to say that the liberal state must aim to be neutral between those whose view of the good subordinates the pursuit of profit to concern for ecological well-being, and those whose view of the good subordinates ecological well-being to concern for profit? One way or the other, the state will inevitably be forced to establish a moral hierarchy, vindicating once again the common-sense Aristotelian understanding of politics. Larmore's neutrality thesis is pitched at such an abstract level of generality that he is never obliged to specify how the neutrality doctrine can be rendered meaningful outside of the classical liberal context of life-and-death religious combat.

It is at least intelligible why one would invoke the language of neutrality in reference to the claims of religious absolutism, although even in this case it is highly questionable whether the absence of a public theology in the liberal state constitutes political neutrality, for such a regime is hardly neutral toward theocratic politics. The notion of neutrality is all the more suspect when applied to the broader range of social and economic policy. For instance, it is difficult even to know what Larmore means when he suggests that state intervention in regulating the distribution of wealth "must be neutral with regard to the interests of rich and poor."[52] Who actually imagines that such neutrality is, even in principle, attainable? Can we have, say, a neutral political order

---

51. On issues such as abortion there are opposed points of view grounded in fundamentally different moral and religious commitments that will either be abated by an agreement to disagree (modus vivendi, mutual accommodation, liberal civility and tolerance) or proceed with unremitting hostility and anger. But why should this be posited as the appropriate model of all political disagreement? Or rather, doesn't the fact that this suggests itself as an appropriate model of political disagreement in general raise doubts about the political soundness of liberal society? For an argument similar to Larmore's, to which I would raise a similar challenge, see Thomas Nagel, "Moral Conflict and Political Legitimacy," *Philosophy & Public Affairs* 16, no. 3 (Summer 1987): 215–240.

52. Larmore, *Patterns of Moral Complexity*, p. 129.

that accommodates both a libertarian and a socialist? Surely it is impossible to design institutions that will make both equally happy or equally unhappy (unless we opt for a dictatorship equally oppressive of liberty and equality). In general, the very enterprise of designing political institutions, or even conceiving what constitutes a political institution, will be weighted to one side or the other. Even in a case such as policy toward abortion—where there is, admittedly, the need for a modus vivendi—it is very unclear what neutrality might signify. What would count as a neutral policy in a conflict where one side sees abortion as such as evil and the other side sees it as an inalienable prerogative of women?[53] In such a case, one could only approach a resolution by changing the moral fabric of the terms in which the issue is debated, not by pretending to a spurious neutrality.

Another version of the neutrality thesis has recently been formulated by Will Kymlicka.[54] Kymlicka, too, argues vigorously for the traditional liberal distinction between state and society: state neutrality versus social nonneutrality; the renunciation of "state perfectionism" versus the acceptance of individual perfectionism as this unfolds within civil society. But contrary to Kymlicka's argument, the fact is that the liberal state is part and parcel of liberal society. The liberal state is no more neutral toward moral ends and cultural aspirations than is liberal society. It is surely no coincidence that the liberal state is governed by the same principles of bureaucratic social organization, technocratic management, and the pursuit of higher productivity that drive liberal society. In short, the liberal dichotomy of state and society raises more questions than it answers.[55]

The questioning of Larmore's philosophy of liberalism may be pressed on two distinct fronts. First, one may ask whether, as

53. Cf. William A. Galston, "Pluralism and Social Unity," *Ethics* 99, no. 4 (July 1989): 720–721. Galston cites the same example to argue toward the same conclusion. See also Michael J. Sandel, "Moral Argument and Liberal Toleration: Abortion and Homosexuality," *California Law Review* 77, no. 3 (May 1989): pp. 531–533.

54. Will Kymlicka, "Liberal Individualism and Liberal Neutrality," *Ethics* 99, no. 4 (July 1989): 883–905, especially pp. 893–898.

55. For a discussion of the breakdown of the classic state-society distinction from the late nineteenth century onwards, see Jürgen Habermas, *The Structural Transformation of the Public Sphere*, trans. Thomas Burger (Cambridge, Mass.: MIT Press, 1989), sections 16 and 17.

an empirical matter, the liberal state is (or could be) neutral. Second, one may ask whether, even if empirically the state falls short of neutrality, neutrality itself is a coherent political ideal, something to which we should aspire. Having posed some questions on the first front, let us now direct some attention to the second.

AGAINST NEUTRALISM

In accordance with Larmore's neutrality principle, the liberal state ought to be uncompromisingly neutral between on the one hand a conception of the good life centered on the principle of doing as little as one can get away with and endeavoring to get others to subsidize one's indolence, and on the other hand a conception of the good life centered on notions of effort, conscientious work, and pride in what one does. It should be neutral between a conception of the good life geared toward the attainment of chemical euphoria at every opportunity and a conception of the good life focused on ideas of social responsibility. (I allow that the formulation of these examples is not neutral.) It should not require a very sophisticated moral reflection to see that this provides a recipe not for principled liberal statesmanship but for the moral self-destruction of the liberal state. To the extent that the state comes to understand itself in these terms, it brings down upon itself just this kind of self-vitiating calamity.

In one place Larmore suggests that the account of liberalism in the famous "race of devils" passage in Kant's *Perpetual Peace* is superior to the standard Kantian account of liberalism, based on the protection and promotion of autonomy, because the former account makes the fewest possible moral demands upon members of the state (and therefore does not prejudice the individual's choice of his or her own personal ideal—which may have nothing to do with the pursuit of autonomy).[56] Now it may be the case that citizens of the liberal state simply *are* devils, and that it would be a moralistic fantasy to hope to transform them into something other

56. Larmore, *Patterns of Moral Complexity*, p. 83. The passage from Kant is in *On History*, ed. Lewis White Beck (Indianapolis: Bobbs-Merrill, 1963), p. 112.

than devils, but surely it cannot be a matter of indifference to the state whether its citizens are or are not devils; and it would be extraordinary to regard a state that was indifferent to whether they were devils or not as on principle morally superior to a state that was not indifferent to this issue, on grounds of the imperative of liberal neutralism. On this minimalist rendering of liberalism, liberal statesmen would be left simply having to pray that citizens do not adopt those conceptions of the good life that would render the state morally uninhabitable.

In a very revealing passage, one that is most remarkable in a treatise mainly devoted to the moral definition of political community, Larmore rules out as "next to impermissible" the violation of deontological duties involving, say, harm to the innocent "for the sake of some particularistic commitment."[57] But of course participation in a political community is a particularistic commitment that quite commonly entails the overriding of such duties (such as when citizens are enlisted in wars to defend the political community, and when this cannot be done short of conducting all-out war involving the killing of innocent civilians). That the example of citizenship as a particularistic commitment does not occur to Larmore in this context is a symptom of the poverty of his account of what is required to hold a political society together.[58] By Larmore's reckoning, the only alternative to the neutral state is the reactionary "organic" model of political society, which he assigns to all critics of liberalism, whether conservative or radical.[59] Larmore is disdainful of MacIntyre's challenge that "from an Aristotelian point of view a modern liberal political society can appear only as a collection of citizens of nowhere who have banded together

57. Larmore, *Patterns of Moral Complexity*, p. 144; cf. p. 148.
58. Cf. John Dunn, *Western Political Theory in the Face of the Future* (Cambridge: Cambridge University Press, 1979), p. 71: "If nationalism as a political force is in some ways a reactionary and irrationalist sentiment in the modern world, its insistence on the moral claims of the community upon its members . . . is in many ways a less superstitious political vision than the intuitive political consciousness of most capitalist democracies today"; and Will, *Statecraft as Soulcraft*, p. 94: "Liberal, bourgeois, democratic—in a word, Lockean—societies have more complex prerequisites than they seem to think. . . . The aim is not to make society inhospitable to pluralism, but to make pluralism safe for society."
59. Larmore, *Patterns of Moral Complexity*, pp. 119, 126.

for their common protection.''[60] However, MacIntyre here is not simply giving expression to romanticist fancy; he is posing a problem that the neutralist conception of political community has not begun to address, indeed abstains in principle from addressing.

As we have seen, on Larmore's view the liberal political order does not seek to furnish institutions or practices expressive of a certain vision of human life, philosophical anthropology, or metaphysical conception of personality; it merely offers a neutral modus vivendi between individuals whose philosophies of life cannot be otherwise reconciled. And as we noted earlier, Rawls too has increasingly seen his enterprise in these terms. In fact, in the latest statement of his views, "The Priority of Right and Ideas of the Good," Rawls's position fully converges with that of Larmore. It is not the function of political liberalism to promote autonomy or individuality since this is merely another controversial moral-philosophical ideal to be avoided. Rather, the conception takes its point of departure from the historical circumstances that pluralism is simply a fact—a sociological given. Notwithstanding differences of terminology, it is clear that Rawls's vision of liberalism is also a neutralist vision.[61]

60. Ibid., p. 175 n. 71. The quotation is from MacIntyre, *After Virtue*, p. 147.

61. Rawls states that he prefers to avoid the terminology of neutrality because of the tendency to confuse "neutrality of aim" (what the state intends) and "neutrality of effect" (what actually results). "The Priority of Right and Ideas of the Good," p. 263. Likewise, Rawls says he is unhappy with a modus vivendi terminology because it tends to imply an instrumentalist relation to the political community, rather than "a moral conception affirmed on moral grounds" (ibid., p. 274). But despite these terminological preferences, Rawls's liberal doctrine is, no less than Larmore's, a neutralist doctrine. The heart of political liberalism, he says, is "the fact of pluralism" (ibid., pp. 259, 275). Cf. Larmore, "Political Liberalism," *Political Theory* 18, no. 3 (August 1990): 358–359 n. 14.

I must confess that Rawls's distinction between neutrality of aim and neutrality of effect (affirmed also by Larmore, "Political Liberalism," p. 358 n. 4) makes little sense to me. How could one vindicate a claim to neutral intent if the social reality of a liberal world instantiates results that are systematically unneutral? For instance, are we to suppose that the state aims at evenhandedness (even if in practice it falls short) when it invests massive resources in the training of technocrats as compared with the nurturing of poets?

Although Larmore is insistent throughout that the chief aim of his neutralist political philosophy is the repudiation of any architectonic political morality, it should be fairly obvious that his political philosophy does contain a moral ranking, and must contain one. It ranks the virtue of tolerance (or decency, or civility) above other virtues, as all liberal political philosophies cannot help doing.[62] Even liberal philosophy, as anti-Aristotelian as it tries to be, fits within an Aristotelian metaethic of ranking of excellences, or hierarchies of virtue.[63] But why should it be imagined, as Larmore clearly assumes, that the avoidance of a forthright moral ranking (especially one with metaphysical sanction) actually strengthens rather than weakens liberal philosophy?[64] Not the least of the puzzles generated by recent developments in liberal theory is the question of exactly why metaphysical economy should be considered the outstanding criterion of philosophical progress. The great classic liberals, like Kant, were more honest in acknowledging that one could not pursue moral theory very far at all without committing oneself to a fairly ambitious philosophical anthropology (although Kant himself generally, but not always, concealed his philosophical anthropology by presenting his theory as a theory of moral agency for all rational agents, not necessarily limited to the class of human beings).[65] Perhaps we can await the return to a philosophically

62. For a more candid acknowledgment that liberalism involves a moral ranking, albeit a negative ranking of vices to be avoided rather than a positive ranking of virtues to be sought, see Judith N. Shklar's excellent book, *Ordinary Vices* (Cambridge, Mass.: Belknap Press, 1984). Of course, Shklar's orientation to the "table of vices" is compatible with the inverse ranking of vices yielding a corresponding ranking of virtues, with the virtue of tolerance at the summit.

63. Cf. Hampshire, *Morality and Conflict*, p. 19; and Hampshire, *Freedom of Mind*, p. 85.

64. Larmore, *Patterns of Moral Complexity*, pp. 66, 92. For another liberal writer's insistence on metaphysical parsimony, see Bruce A. Ackerman, *Social Justice in the Liberal State* (New Haven: Yale University Press, 1980), pp. 355–357, 361.

65. Cf. Taylor, "Justice after Virtue," pp. 33–34. On the other hand, one has good reason to take very seriously Kant's own belief that the addressees of his moral system are not just human beings but all rational beings (where the former are simply a subset of the latter). In an appendix to *Universal Natural History and Theory of the Heavens*, he writes: "I am of the opinion that while it is not at all necessary to assert that all planets must be inhabited, equally it would be an absurdity [to hold that all or

more inspiring phase of liberalism when liberal philosophers at last lay aside Occam's razor.[66]

What does the celebration of modern pluralism come to? Before we can render our ultimate verdict, we must try once again to clarify the classical (antipluralist) position that the pluralists repudiate. Does it mean, as the pluralists suggest, that all differences in the ends, projects, and aspirations of unique human beings are considered aberrations from a fixed norm? (In Larmore's formulation, "a wish to live life as a whole animated by a single dominant purpose, and a hope for an existence uncompromised by moral loss and unriven by unsettleable conflict."[67]) For instance, I choose to become a violinist, raise a family, and pursue the middle-class dream; my neighbor decides to forgo the cares of family life and devote his life to the priesthood, and he departs for Central America, where all his energies will henceforth be spent on alleviating the hardships of the poor. Does the Aristotelian commitment to the idea of a human telos entail that at least one of these lives is misguided, and that the two cannot both be legitimate ways to live, since the human good is unitary and these two lives pursue incompatible paths of fulfillment? Aristotelianism would then involve obliviousness to the brute fact of human diversity. Clearly, such obliviousness would be absurd. From the fact that Aristotle expressly criticized

---

indeed most of them are uninhabited]"; "most of the planets are certainly inhabited." *Kants Werke* (Akademie-Textausgabe), vol. 1 (Berlin: Walter de Gruyter, 1968), pp. 352, 354. In his *Lectures on Ethics*, trans. Louis Infield (New York: Harper & Row, 1963), p. 113, Kant refers to God's "infinite universe which contains many worlds peopled with rational creatures."

66. Ronald Dworkin goes part of the way toward addressing this challenge in "Foundations of Liberal Equality," in *The Tanner Lectures on Human Values*, vol. 11, ed. Grethe B. Peterson (Salt Lake City: University of Utah Press, 1990), pp. 1–119. As he acknowledges on p. 7 n. 2, this involves at least to some extent distancing himself from his own earlier neutralist conception. However Dworkin falls short of the challenge in the measure to which his liberalism is still a neutralist conception.

67. Larmore, *Patterns of Moral Complexity*, p. 152. Cf. Hampshire, *Morality and Conflict*, p. 140: "As moral philosophers we must be looking for the perfect specimen of humanity, without defect, lacking nothing that contributes to the ideal whole person and the ideal whole life. The idea of the human good, presented in this framework, implies that any falling-away, any comparative failure in total achievement, will be a defect and a vice, a form of incompleteness."

Plato for trying to reduce all goods to a singular Good, one may gather that Aristotle too regarded it as absurd.[68] What, then, is the Aristotelian after? Let us consider a second set of alternatives. Imagine a child raised in a loving environment, with supportive parents, ample educational facilities, and opportunities to develop his or her highest capacities (playing the violin, helping those in need, etc.). Now imagine the same child being raised in a ghetto, without adequate parental care, starved of cultural or intellectual nourishment to stimulate his or her curiosity, surrounded by dope pushers, and so on. Here the Aristotelian language of human flourishing commands great power. It seems to me that the liberal vocabulary of rights, liberties, and autonomy-maximizing diversity can hardly do justice to this situation. (Indeed, if diversity as such is what we yearn for, as liberalism suggests, then why should not life in the ghetto be considered one of Mill's "experiments of living"?[69]) Far more apt are the naturalistic Aristotelian metaphors of the plant that thrives in favorable conditions and withers or is stultified when it suffers certain definable kinds of deprivation. Admittedly, what constitutes proper care of a fern will kill a cactus, and vice versa; but Aristotle makes full allowance for differences of this kind. A healthy plant is a healthy plant, even if different plants require different conditions for maximum healthiness; so too for the notion of a flourishing human being.[70] Moreover, one need not choose

68. For a contrary account, emphasizing Aristotle's underlying residual Platonism, see Hampshire, *Morality and Conflict*, pp. 151–153.

69. John Stuart Mill, *On Liberty*, ed. David Spitz (New York: W. W. Norton, 1975), p. 54.

70. Conditions of botanical flourishing and conditions of human flourishing may stand in a less remote relation to each other than one might think. I recently came across a report describing an experiment involving the comparison of plants, otherwise similarly conditioned, placed in front of speakers playing classical music on the one hand, and heavy metal and hard rock on the other. The results of the experiment showed consistently that "the plants listening to classical music grow at a 45 degree angle toward the speakers, and they develop very healthy root systems with many more branches and hairs than a normal plant," whereas "the plants listening to rock music either die or their growth is dramatically retarded. Those that survive end up with poor, sparse root systems." "A Spoonful of Music," *Toronto Star*, 15 January 1990, p. C1. Examination of the "root systems" of regular human listeners to heavy metal music may, I suspect, yield similar conclusions.

such extreme examples in order for Aristotelian language to prove itself. If we compare the musically gifted child whose talents are encouraged with the one deprived of help or instruction, it is reasonable to speak of the frustration or consummation, stunting or flourishing, of aspects of the human telos. And the same applies, more generally, to possibilities of moral life as such. As I learn to behave decently, act generously, choose wisely, and make good judgments, I build capacities, develop forms of human potential, and help to realize human nature at its best; this once again warrants the naturalistic metaphors of a flourishing versus a truncated existence.

Why does the pluralist oppose this particular way of speaking about the human condition? What is objectionable about a teleological moral vocabulary? It strikes me that the pluralist's fears of monism or dogmatic naturalism are misplaced. Needless to say, it is not difficult to read Aristotle as advancing a neat hierarchy, with philosophers at the top, Athenian aristocrats next to the top, and everyone else judged as grossly inferior. But certainly neo-Aristotelians can avail themselves of the considerable strengths of a teleological moral language without such crude dogmatizing. A reasonable pluralism, it seems to me, maintains that there are a variety of possible ways of life, of which the way of life of modern liberal society is one; and confronted with this plurality one can compare and criticize various strengths and weaknesses of these different alternatives. An unreasonable pluralism maintains that the supreme advantage of liberalism is that it supplies a neutral political framework for the coexistence of opposing ways of life, as if it furnished a kind of meta–way of life, and were for that reason elevated above the standards of social criticism applicable to non-pluralistic societies.[71]

---

71. Am I saying that the efforts of liberal theorists fall short of the mark because liberal practice fails to measure up to liberal principles? Or am I saying that they fall short because liberal principles are not the right principles? I am saying that liberal practice fails to measure up to liberal principles *because* liberal principles, as they have been articulated by the leading contemporary philosophers of liberalism, don't make sense. To clarify this point, three questions must be distinguished: First, *is* the liberal state as it actually exists in fact neutral? If not, *can* it be rendered neutral? And finally, is neutrality *desirable*? The principles don't make sense because, if my argu-

I fear that what the celebration of pluralism comes to is a complacency concerning the moral adequacy of existing liberal society. Furthermore, there is much that is distressing in contemporary liberal societies that must be overlooked or forgotten in order to sustain such complacency. Every liberal society, even the most generous and just, accommodates large masses of human beings with their capacities stunted, aptitudes truncated, and possibilities of human nature unconsummated. The *question* of the human good, posed relentlessly by the Aristotelian even if, as for MacIntyre, the answer is recognized to be rather elusive, renders ethical complacency impossible to maintain. This raises my final theme in this chapter; that of conflicting conceptions of the place of theory, a problem that perhaps more than any other puts the Aristotelians and their critics very much at odds.

MODERNITY

Clearly, a neo-Aristotelian strategy of theorizing must involve the disengagement of the Aristotelian metaethic from some of the historically contingent contents of Aristotle's own ethical thinking (e.g., the compatibility of justice with the institution of slavery, historically specific features of the description of megalopsychia, the moral superiority of the philosopher, and so on).[72] But, it may be countered, if Aristotelianism is detachable from a set of specific ethical ideals to which Aristotle himself was in fact committed, what moral guidance can we hope to secure from this reversion to ancient ethics? My answer is that what Aristotle makes available to us above all is a certain moral vocabulary, a language in which to discuss and debate our ethical and political concerns, and that in the realm of morals and politics, vocabulary matters. It matters, for instance, that J. S. Mill appropriates Aristotle to the vocabulary of utility, rather than allowing his own thought to be subsumed within the Aristotelian vocabulary.[73] It matters that we speak the

---

ments in this chapter have weight, clear-minded reflection compels a negative answer to all three of these questions.

72. These are examples brought up by Hampshire in *Morality and Conflict*, pp. 130, 149, 153.

73. Mill, *On Liberty*, p. 25.

language of rights, interests, and preferences rather than the language of virtues, character formation, and telos. Electing to speak in terms of ends rather than values, virtues rather than rights, judgments rather than preferences, would make a difference, not just theoretically but also practically. It matters politically whether we are under the sway of a political discourse that privileges Kantian notions of the fortressing of individual rights, or one that privileges Aristotelian notions of the socialized building of character.[74]

Liberals often denounce theories deriving from alien philosophical traditions because they assume that antiliberal theorizing will immediately issue in antiliberal practice. This in turn presupposes that theory can have only one function, which is to direct practice. But the task of theory, as I see it, is not to tell us what to do but to help us understand how to reflect upon what we do, and to conceive and reconceive the theoretical idiom (the partially theorized past idioms and incompletely theorized future idioms) in which we think about diverse possibilities of social and political life. Aristotle offers little direct guidance on the living of a complete life. There are intimations of a hierarchy, but there are no prescriptions (or at least none but the sketchiest) on how to realize this hierarchy in an actual life.[75] Again, what Plato and

---

74. There is also, of course, as Judith Shklar has especially emphasized, a Kantian discourse about habituation to virtue. *Ordinary Vices*, pp. 232–236. But as Larmore rightly points out, "What is wrong in Kant's ethics is not that it has nothing to say about character, but rather that it gives an inadequate account of it." *Patterns of Moral Complexity*, p. 174 n. 60. Indeed, it is hard to see how Kant could give a coherent account of character within the framework of his moral-philosophical premises. For Kant, morality is synonymous with freedom, and freedom means unconditioned spontaneity. This is theoretically incompatible with Aristotle's (correct) understanding of the intimate relation between ethics and ethos, virtue and habit. So the problem with a Kantian virtue discourse is that it gives either a deficient or an inconsistent account of the relation between moral excellence and habituation.

75. For an energetic defense of Aristotelian ethics along these lines, see D. S. Hutchinson, *The Virtues of Aristotle* (London: Routledge & Kegan Paul, 1986), pp. 51–52, 62. As Hutchinson points out on pp. 46–47, Plato's *ergon* argument in *The Republic*, 353b–c—which Aristotle likely draws upon in *Nicomachean Ethics*, book 1, chap. 7, and book 2, chap. 6—is governed by a similar indeterminacy.

Aristotle make available to us is not so much a specific orientation prescribing the content of political choices as a distinctive moral vocabulary that may govern a range of political alternatives. (Plato and Aristotle, perhaps in common with most great theorists, stand in an immensely complex and—for us—almost infinitely elusive relation to the realm of concrete political alternatives.) One can affirm capitalism *or* socialism within a liberal vocabulary of rights and values, or one can affirm capitalism *or* socialism within a Platonic-Aristotelian vocabulary of virtues and fulfillment of a human telos. The leading question for the theorist is: On what basis does one choose between these alternative vocabularies?[76]

MacIntyre, in common with other critics of liberalism, seems to think that we need to get our philosophy right because social reality is a direct or nearly direct reflection of the adequacy or inadequacy of our philosophical beliefs. I certainly do not share this assumption. The moral language current in our society represents the most refined efforts of theorists in such a bastardized fashion that even an appreciably improved liberal philosophy offers no guarantee of reformed practices in the social reality of liberalism. What is needed is not Aristotelian theory but Aristotelian practice. (And this was Aristotle's own position, as I understand it from the *Nicomachean Ethics*.) Yet this does not mean that an Aristotelian can or should be indifferent to the liberal philosophies that supply moral categories for the liberal experience of the world; even ideological bastardization preserves something of the moral character of the doctrines that are bastardized. Reform of philosophy will not automatically induce reform of the world, but it might at least dry up some of the wells of respectable intellectual support for certain familiar kinds of nonsense—such as the liberal nonsense that antipornography statutes violate "freedom of expression," or the nonsense that indi-

76. That the decisive issue is the choice of a paradigmatic moral vocabulary can be seen from the side of liberal philosophy as well. Rawls's difference principle can be used to justify just about any social-economic policy across the spectrum of alternatives, from the policies of Margaret Thatcher at one extreme to those of Mikhail Gorbachev at the other. (Thatcher, too, could perfectly well insist that her policies would eventually secure the long-term interests of the least advantaged.) Rawls himself offers very little help in selecting specific policies.

viduals have the "right" not to be screened for AIDS, even if this right threatens the safety of others.

My major objection to Larmore's philosophy of liberalism (and kindred philosophies) is that it places intolerable constraints on the exercise of political judgment. It is not even clear what is meant by saying that neutrality concerning competing conceptions of the good life is strictly a political doctrine, limited to one specific sector of social life (the domain of state action), and that it should in no way inhibit judgment of the relative validity of extrapolitical goals and aspirations. Suppose I wish to render critical judgment on the phenomenon of endemic crack addiction in contemporary Western societies, and what it signifies with respect to global properties of these societies. Can this be anything other than a political judgment about the soundness of the way of life of entire societies? Presumably Larmore would say that this is impermissible, that it turns legitimate judgments about personal ideals into illegitimate global judgments about society regarded holistically, or that it projects an historically antiquated model of social unity upon complex, differentiated social systems. But surely this is mistaken. All judgments that really count pertain to the unifying principles of whole societies. They cannot be localized to distinct subdivisions of social life, or reduced to judgments about personal life-projects. A political judgment about crack addiction is not reducible to judgments about commercial transactions within inner-city subcultures, or the complexities of legal enforcement, or the personal aspirations of addicts. It is, inescapably, a judgment about entire constellations of social life. It is difficult to imagine how critical judgment could even get off the ground if global or holistic judgments are excluded on principle. For similar reasons, the slogan "pluralism of values," wielded by a wide phalanx of liberal theorists, represents, from my point of view, a tremendous flattening of the possibilities of critical judgment.

It can hardly come as news to anyone that a modern society is different from a premodern society, and that it would be both extremely difficult and extremely dangerous to try to transform a modern society into a premodern one. Twentieth-century experiments in this direction have certainly been sufficiently sobering to give pause to even the most naive enthusiast. I am convinced that even Rousseau, the archnostalgic according to the perspective of liberals from Constant onwards, was perfectly well aware of the inexorability of modernization and the hazardousness of attempting to reverse it. But this is not the issue. The issue is: By what theoretical standards ought we to judge a modern society?

The problem with the liberal commitment to individuality, diversity, pluralism, and toleration is certainly not that these are bad things or unworthy of concern, but that liberal individuality and pluralism are too often a phony individuality and phony pluralism. How can we know whether the individuality and diversity fostered by a society is genuine without looking at the substantive choices and forms of character cultivated by members of that society (which the liberal will regard as itself a kind of "moral intrusiveness" destructive of liberal autonomy[77])? Despite the processes of modernization and differentiation upon which the liberal insists so emphatically, every society, liberal society not excluded, has a center out of which it ranks the paradigmatic practices that define it as a society—perhaps not physically imposed from above by the state, but shaped less discernibly by the moral impulse of social life as a whole. It is this impalpable moral unity of liberal society (surely subject to ethical and political appraisal) that the theoretical partisan of liberalism in large measure fails to acknowledge.[78] It is some-

77. For a typical instance, see Nancy L. Rosenblum's critique of Michael Walzer in "Moral Membership in a Postliberal State," *World Politics* 36, no. 4 (July 1984): 581–596, especially pp. 592–593.

78. Will Kymlicka's response to my critique of liberal neutralism is based on a radical misunderstanding. "Liberal Individualism and Liberal Neutrality," *Ethics* 99, no. 4 (July 1989): 895–896 n. 29 is a response to a previously published version of chapter 2 of this book. On Kymlicka's account, the nonneutrality of activities in liberal society is not incompatible with the liberal's commitment to state neutrality; indeed, far from refuting the neutralism of the liberal, it is the very ground of the liberal imperative that the state remain neutral. This presupposes that civil society instantiates a rich diversity of moral aspirations, which is precisely what the liberal celebrates, and that this social pluralism must be protected from the threatening monism of the state. However, what I meant in asserting the nonneutrality of liberal society is that this axiom of social pluralism is largely mythical, that the activity of civil society as a whole is tilted in a certain direction (the maximization of social productivity, the organization of social life so as to enhance efficiency and technological control, the privileging of scientific over other forms of knowledge, the favoring of ways of life consistent with maximal individual mobility, etc.), and therefore that liberal society itself embodies a form of monism of which the

thing that we may still learn from book 1 of the *Nicomachean Ethics*, whose lessons turn out to be not yet obsolete after all.

---

monism of the liberal state is but one aspect. The liberal state is certainly in complicity with liberal society, even if it does not impose the liberal way of life in exactly the way that the Islamic theocracy in Iran imposes the Islamic way of life. If this claim is right, then the liberal assurance of political neutrality fails to be redeemed by the altogether different character of the social realm. For further probing of the liberal neutrality argument, see my review of D. A. J. Richards, "Toleration and the Constitution," in *University of Toronto Law Journal* 38, no. 1 (Winter 1988): 109–114.

4

The Language of Rights
and the Language of Good

In chapter 3 I made the general case that the prevailing moral language of liberalism has certain political inadequacies. In this chapter I shall focus on one specific dimension of liberal morality, namely its increasing reliance on rights discourse. Ian Scott, Attorney General of Ontario, in a speech to the Empire Club in Toronto on 9 October 1986, noted that "the language of rights has assumed new importance since the enactment of the Canadian Charter of Rights and Freedoms. The pervasiveness of the language of rights is reflected by the fact that virtually all interest groups now attempt to frame their arguments in terms of rights."[1] The Attorney General

1. Of course, the issues addressed in this chapter have lately assumed a special salience in my own polity, wrestling—as it has been since 1982—with the alternatives of an older British style of constitutional politics and a more Americanized set of political tropes and institutions. As the Attorney General observed in his address, the entrenchment of the Canadian Charter of Rights and Freedoms represents a decisive watershed, at least within Canadian political culture, in the official authorization of rights discourse. Robert Fulford, in an article in *Saturday Night*, December 1986, pp. 7–9, very acutely noted some of the paradoxes of the Charter of Rights. For instance, he pointed out that New Democratic Party leaders Tommy Douglas and David Lewis, who were early supporters of the idea of an entrenched bill of rights, would likely turn over in their graves to see the challenge to the Canadian labor movement mounted by the National Citizens' Coalition in the name of individual rights. As the charter begins to make its impact felt upon Canadian political culture, critics such as Fulford have begun to worry about whether it will lead to a more litigious public ethos, closer to the American experience. However, I think the charter, and the emphasis on individual rights that it encourages, may be not so much the cause of such changes as an expression of the view, already dominant within liberal society, that juridical relationships constitute the essence of political relationships. For more on the ever-increasing ascendency of rights consciousness within the Canadian political context, and how this complicates the problem of sustaining an experience of citizenship that is not utterly fragmented, see the contributions by Alan Cairns

went on to add that when he attended law school a generation ago, there was barely any mention of the idea of rights; now, of course, it is ubiquitous. In the course of his speech, Mr. Scott repeatedly invoked the authority of Ronald Dworkin, whose writings have done much to entrench the language of rights, at least within the academy. The Attorney General spoke of all this in celebration of it, as a major achievement of liberal society. Given this striking transformation of our political discourse—the new reality that "virtually all interest groups now attempt to frame their arguments in terms of rights"—it is incumbent on us to reconsider whether it expresses the disabilities and deficiencies of liberal society as well as its virtues and strengths.

RIGHTS TALK:
IS IT DISPENSABLE?

As noted above, it is unmistakable that our contemporary political discourse is primarily conducted in the language of rights. The way to put forward a political claim today is to assert that something is ours as a matter of right, or that we have an inviolate right to pursue a certain course of action; or conversely, that various courses of action, or various claims of others, are ruled out because they violate our basic rights.[2] Today there hardly seems to be any other way in which to contend over competing political claims. Anyone who wishes to make himself or herself heard in the political arena is virtually obliged to locate (or invent) a right of which that specific claim is an embodiment.

---

and Cynthia Williams, by Cynthia Williams, by Rainer Knopff and F. L. Morton, and by Charles Taylor, in *Constitutionalism, Citizenship and Society in Canada*, ed. Alan Cairns and Cynthia Williams, Collected Research Studies of the Royal Commission on the Economic Union and Development Prospects for Canada, vol. 33 (Toronto: University of Toronto Press, 1985), pp. 1–50, 99–131, 133–182, and 183–229, respectively.

2. In our society this manner of discourse has reached an extreme where denial of the prerogative to go shopping on Sundays is described as denial of a fundamental *right*, in the sense that it is taken to be a violation of our moral autonomy, defined in terms of living by our self-elected purposes. This is perfectly consistent with the basic assumptions of rights discourse, however much it may strike those who stand outside that discourse as a reductio ad absurdum.

The first point that I would like to insist upon is that anything that can legitimately be couched in the language of rights can be transposed without loss into the language of good. The case for this position has been stated convincingly and with great economy by William Galston in his book *Justice and the Human Good*; therefore I shall avail myself of his arguments. The core of Galston's argument is that rights, for all of our reliance upon them at the rhetorical level, have no independent force of their own. The interesting question is *why* we have the rights we claim for ourselves; but here we cannot but appeal to goods, needs, interests, and so on, which ground our putative rights. As Galston puts it, "rights as ordinarily understood cannot be central to political philosophy because they do not constitute an independent moral claim. The language of rights is at most a convenient proxy for a heterogeneous collection of familiar moral reasons."[3]

Galston's argument is that if we have rights, it is in virtue of the kind of beings that we are, the worthiness of what we do or seek, and the features of our life that support moral claims. For instance, Dworkin's liberalism as a theory of rights is founded on a notion of "equal concern and respect" that Dworkin derives from a conception of all citizens as moral agents defining their own life plans and their own visions of individual fulfillment that must be publicly respected. But as Galston points out, this is already an embryonic theory of the human good.[4] If it is our status as moral agents, or as agents who choose their own routes to happiness, that establishes our right to equal concern and respect, then it is an empirical question whether we all do in fact form reflective life plans that warrant respect. To assume dogmatically that the relevant rights extend to all is to beg the question opened up by that notion of the good from which the rights are derived. It all depends on the relationship between the rights claimed and the theory of the human good (overt or implied) from which they flow. If it is our capacity for choosing that yields such rights, the question then becomes: Do we all choose with equal intelligence and equal seriousness? And this, of course, is an empirical matter, not something that could be settled *a priori*.

3. William A. Galston, *Justice and the Human Good* (Chicago: University of Chicago Press, 1980), p. 127.
4. Ibid., p. 134.

The following passages from Galston serve to clarify the derivative character of postulated rights:

> There are two ways of arguing that human beings have rights. The first is simply to assert it, as a moral first principle: "We hold these truths to be self-evident. . . ." The defect of this strategy is that it cannot convince skeptics that rights exist or that there is any reason to take them seriously. The second is to anchor rights in certain fundamental facts. This strategy implies that the content of rights cannot be cordoned off from the characteristics of the facts that are said to underlie them.[5]

> Rights are not independent moral reasons at all, but rather an elliptical way of talking about claims based on utility, need, desert, or rationality.[6]

> To take rights seriously is to show how they are linked to fundamental human interests. But once the problem is posed in this manner, it is inevitable that some form of aggregative, teleological theory will emerge in which rights will at best enjoy a derivative theoretical status.[7]

> From a moral standpoint, there are no claims whose validity is independent of what I am or do. . . . More generally: A right is never an ultimate appeal.[8]

> To have a right is to have a valid claim; a valid claim is based solely on reasons that prevail over all competing reasons. . . . Thus, a right is not a moral reason, but rather the outcome or result of moral reasons. The language of rights is at most a convenient abbreviation. Habit and social stability may incline us to ascribe logical independence to this language, but change and extreme situations force us to deal explicitly with its underlying premises.[9]

5. Ibid., pp. 134–135.
6. Ibid., p. 135.
7. Ibid., p. 136.
8. Ibid., p. 140.
9. Ibid., pp. 140–141. In "Ethics and the Handicapped Newborn Infant," *Social Research* 52, no. 3 (Autumn 1985): 528, Helga Kuhse and Peter Singer make roughly the same point:

> To invoke the language of "rights" . . . is not always conducive to clarity of thought. Too often there is a tendency to treat rights as somehow "innate" or "natural" or "self-evident" and to use claims about rights to block any further discussion. We often make better progress in understanding moral arguments by dropping the terminology of rights and dealing directly with the underlying moral considerations by which the claims about rights are supported. . . . The expression is no more than a convenient shorthand for the moral considerations on which the right is based.

The argument, then, is that the validity of rights depends on deeper considerations, on underlying principles. When rights are challenged, we are forced to probe what underlies them. This cannot help but point us in the direction of notions of the good.

In other words, the language of rights is parasitical upon an antecedent set of conceptions of the good. But our rights-based political discourse masks this dependence, and this confinement within the language of rights gives to that political discourse an absolutist and sometimes even fanatical character to which a goods-based discourse would not be subject. This leads us to our next main topic.

GOODS TALK:
WHAT ARE THE ADVANTAGES?

My first point was that the language of rights as such is dispensable. The second point I want to develop is that it makes a difference whether we conduct our discourse in the language of rights or the language of good. To illustrate, let us turn to the problem of abortion.

The abortion debate usually proceeds as a contest between two supposed rights: on the one side, the right of a woman to dispose of her own body as she chooses—including the contents of her body, namely an unborn fetus; on the other side, the right of the fetus to maturate and to be born. The question for political deliberation and decision is: Which right takes precedence? (Or: Which is the real right?) This is a yes-or-no question; it hardly makes sense to say that both are inviolable rights. To acknowledge one as a right is to say, necessarily, that the other is not a right; to credit one is automatically to impugn the other, or to portray it as a bogus right. What would it mean to affirm both the fetus's right to inhabit the mother's womb and the mother's right to expel the fetus from her womb? Can one really imagine someone campaigning for the upholding of both rights? A "right" that may be overridden is not truly a right (this is the implied rhetoric), or at least, the admissibility of its contravention impugns its status as a right, to the point where employing this language loses its point, or ceases to have the force it is intended to have.[10]

10. If the argument presented in the first section of this chapter—that the rights idiom is simply a way of labeling moral claims that are estab-

Let us see how things stand when the same debate is conducted in the language of good. On the one side, it may be
questioned whether it is good for us as human beings that
pregnancies, processes that instantiate the sacredness of new life,
should be terminated on account of the convenience of individuals. If the disposal of one's own body is an absolute right, we
may suppose that someone may claim an entitlement to an
abortion on the sole ground that the completion of the pregnancy
would interfere with a long-planned holiday in Europe.[11] Even
if it were conceded that this was a right in some sense, one
would still have to face the further question: But is it *good*? Does
it conduce to a sustained sense of human dignity, or to human
welfare in the most comprehensive sense? On the other side, it
may be questioned whether it is good for unwanted babies to be
brought into families that lack the material and spiritual resources
to care for them. Are the rights of the fetus definitive even in a
world of dire overpopulation? Again, this opens up a way of
addressing the problem in a way that refers not to the rights of
the born or the unborn, but to the welfare of all, in a sense that
is not restricted to the utilitarian summing of preferences. But
notice a decisive shift in the recast character of the debate: it is
no longer a yes-or-no contest. It is quite possible to acknowledge
goods on both sides, whereas the acknowledgment of a right
seems to preclude the acknowledgment of an opposing right (or
at least the implicit bias of rights rhetoric carries us in that
direction). A confrontation between opposing absolutes would
immediately gain in moderation if its terms of debate were trans-

---

lished on some other basis—is a correct one, then the question of rights is
really a question of rhetoric. Thus the issue is not whether rights are absolute or are mutually exclusive, but whether describing them as such serves
or contradicts the purposes inscribed in this language.

11. In Copenhagen recently, a controversy arose over the fact that a
woman had terminated a pregnancy because the fetus was female rather
than male. A Danish member of parliament stated, very reasonably, that
within the terms of his country's abortion-on-demand laws, this reason is
no better and no worse than any other reason: "To choose against a child
because of its sex is no different from any other reason, such as having
to do with an examination or go traveling." What is less clear is whether or
not this intended defense of abortion on demand, by its frankness,
may actually serve to raise questions about the desirability of the law
itself.

posed from the language of rights to the language of good or of proper human ends.[12]

The positing of a right does not offer a set of considerations that can be weighed up against an alternative set of considerations, as the appeal to goods can. Rather, the assertion of a right seeks to put a halt to such weighing of rival considerations. In this sense, the argument between rights is not a genuine argument; it is an effort on both sides to arrest argument in a binding and definitive way. The production of a right is meant to be definitive, like a voucher that entitles one to claim final victory with no further need for argument—what Dworkin calls a trump held against the political community by the individual.[13] For this reason, political contentions conducted in the language of rights naturally incline us toward fanaticism or extremism (as the abortion debate clearly evinces).

The violation of a right, it is assumed, does violence to the bearer of the right; therefore nonobservance of our rights is taken to be intolerable in a way that nonachievement of a good is not. Thus there is a marked asymmetry in the character of a rights dispute as compared with a goods dispute. The latter lacks the unconditionality of the former. To use Kantian terms, the violation of rights is

12. Mary Ann Glendon lends support to this claim with considerations drawn from comparative law in *Abortion and Divorce in Western Law* (Cambridge: Harvard University Press, 1987). As she aptly notes, with the appeal by both prolife and prochoice activists in the United States to individual rights, "the two seemingly irrevocably opposed positions are actually locked within the same intellectual framework, a framework that appears rather rigid and impoverished when viewed from a comparative perspective" (p. 39). See also Richard Stith, "A Critique of Abortion Rights," *Democracy* 3, no. 4 (Fall 1983): 60–70.

13. See Ronald Dworkin, *Taking Rights Seriously* (London: Duckworth, 1978), p. xi; Dworkin, "Liberalism," in *Public and Private Morality*, ed. Stuart Hampshire (Cambridge: Cambridge University Press, 1978), p. 136; and Dworkin, "Rights as Trumps," in *Theories of Rights*, ed. Jeremy Waldron (Oxford: Oxford University Press, 1984), pp. 153–167. It should be added that Dworkin's case for rights derives much of its force from the fact that it was defined largely within the context of debates with utilitarians. His defense of rights would appear much less compelling than it does had it not emerged against a background of prevailing (and vulnerable) utilitarian assumptions. Dworkin himself acknowledges, in *Taking Rights Seriously*, p. xi, that his conception of rights "is, in fact, parasitic on the dominant idea of utilitarianism."

held to be prohibited, whereas the pursuit of goods is merely advised. It should be evident that there is a political advantage to debates conducted in terms of what is advisable rather than in terms of what is subject to categorical interdict. The former, but not the latter, permit considerations of better and worse, more desirable and less desirable. To say that a society that sanctions abortions with abandon is not the best society is different from saying that a society that tolerates any abortions is evil. To say that society should be sensitive to conditions in which the unborn are to enter the world is different from saying that a society that places conditions on the availability of abortions violates the inalienable rights of women.[14]

To this argument it may be objected that we can all quite easily recognize trade-offs between various rights, and that to this extent any appeal to a right is merely provisional, conditional upon the need to satisfy competing rights.[15] Yet this offers a misleading picture of the pragmatic function of rights claims. While the notion of a prima facie right, in principle vulnerable to other considerations (whether of rival rights or overriding utility), may make sense in

14. The chief worry about the *rhetoric* of the prochoice position, from my point of view, is that in a society in which everything tends to be commodified, fetuses too may come to be thought of as objects of consumer preferences. It would be naive to imagine that there is nothing to worry about in exalting the language of choice. In a social order marked by an inexorable drive to almost universal commodification, where one can not only opt to have or not have babies but can anticipate ordering them to desired specifications (sex, hair color, talents), we have good reason to be fearful of a situation where the realm of unmasterable destiny is wholly submitted to the imperatives of consumer choice. (One embryologist refers to his genetic techniques as "quality control"!) On these issues, see Hans Jonas, "Ethics and Biogenetic Art," *Social Research* 52, no. 3 (Autumn 1985): 491–504.

15. Dworkin makes this point in the title essay of *Taking Rights Seriously*, pp. 191–195, 199–204. He cites as an example the conflict between the right to free speech and the right not to be defamed. Dworkin clearly recognizes that any claim whatever can be rephrased in the language of rights, including those normally expressed in the language of common welfare and benefit, such as the "right" to political order and security. However, to avoid the self-canceling effect of phrasing all claims in the vocabulary of rights, he insists on privileging *individual* rights (such as blacks' right to equal education versus whites' right to free association) and acknowledges only these as legitimately in competition. Ibid., pp. 194, 199.

itself, it cuts against the whole rhetoric of rights, which is what concerns us here. The very reason for appealing to rights—far from reckoning on having them possibly overridden by other considerations, including other rights—is precisely in order to purchase some ultimate assurance that they will prevail. Otherwise, it would hardly make sense to conceive of them as trumps (though, admittedly, in Dworkin's usage such claims are meant to trump the prerogatives of the whole community, not to trump the rival claims of other individuals). What in fact happens in a liberal society is that each group insists upon its rights, oblivious to the parallel claims of other groups, and this cannot help but issue in a fundamentally adversarial and deeply strife-ridden climate of political debate.[16] Or, to express the point somewhat differently: from the point of view of the political or legal authorities who must arbitrate conflicting rights, different claims may well be seen as subject to balancing or supersession, as Dworkin says; but from the perspective of the parties themselves their claims are viewed as absolute and binding. It is surely the latter point of view which is decisive for the tenor of social and political life in the society. That point of view is bound to reflect the tendencies toward competitiveness and self-assertion of an aggressively pluralistic society.[17]

The essential problem here is not, as some have assumed, the intrinsic individualism of rights claims, for the same features that I have pointed to will manifest themselves where what is at stake are collective rights or the assertion of rights on behalf of groups in the society. Thus the theoretical strategy adopted by some rights

16. Cf. Edward Andrew, *Shylock's Rights: A Grammar of Lockian Claims* (Toronto: University of Toronto Press, 1988), pp. 19–20: "Rights as properties are to be conceived more as claims *against* others rather than as joint entitlements constituting a moral community. We have rights *against* others as we have duties *towards* one another. Rights as properties are option-rights rather than welfare-rights; they function to secure choice rather than direct us to what is choiceworthy." The same conceptual framework is implied in, for instance, Mikhail Gorbachev's statement, in an address to the Twenty-seventh Communist Party Congress, 25 February 1986, that "the gist of socialism is that the rights of citizens do not, and cannot, exist outside their duties."

17. As Dworkin says in *Taking Rights Seriously*, p. 184: "The concept of rights . . . has its most natural use when a political society is divided, and appeals to co-operation or a common goal are pointless."

theorists, namely to try to mitigate the putative individualism of rights claims by an appeal to group rights or communal rights,[18] is in fact of little avail. For as we saw in chapter 2 in regard to the symmetry between communal and individual pluralism, a shift from individual rights to collective rights does not necessarily offer a sufficient remedy. As even a notable champion of the idea of rights readily acknowledges, "the shift to group rights does not blunt but at most only re-expresses the criticism that individualism is inadequate as a complete theory," since the "idea of group rights makes sense only in circumstances where the group exists as an 'individual' in relation to some wider entity."[19]

To sum up my second argument: To pose a political controversy in the language of good is to open up, rather than close off, issues about which we can all debate and which we can weigh up in various ways; to resort to the invocation of rights is to preclude all debate, for the rights appealed to are meant to be nonnegotiable. One might say that what distinguishes the ethos of a goods discourse from that of a rights discourse is not some preliberal alternative to modern pluralism, but rather the pluralism of rational debate in preference to the pluralism of frenzied intemperance. Unhappily, our political world is so constituted that all parties seek to avoid reasoned discussion and are concerned only to assert their own claims. The language of rights ("verbal bludgeoning," to quote Jeremy Waldron's paraphrase of Bentham[20]) provides them with a handy means of doing just that.

To return to my initial line of reasoning: because the substance of rights is drawn from the sphere of the good, we can dispense with the whole argument over rights and revert directly to the conceptions of the good that originally ground these otherwise mysterious rights. Incidentally, in one section of his book Galston offers an Aristotelian, teleological argument for what are popularly

18. For an example of such an attempt to enlarge rights discourse by having it encompass group rights, see Denise Réaume, "Individuals, Groups, and Rights to Public Goods," *University of Toronto Law Journal* 38, no. 1 (Winter 1988): 1–27.

19. Jeremy Waldron, "Nonsense upon Stilts? A reply," in *Nonsense upon Stilts*, ed. J. Waldron (London: Methuen, 1987), p. 187. Réaume acknowledges Waldron's point on p. 24 of her article.

20. *Nonsense upon Stilts*, ed. Waldron, p. 36.

called animal rights.[21] The fact that these are usually presented today as rights gives to this position a quality of absoluteness (and at the political level, a tendency toward fanaticism) that is not to be found in Galston's Aristotelian argument. Once again, it is actually a question of more or less, not all or nothing. Animal welfare is a good, not a right; hence the more of this good we can secure, the better. But this is not to rule out the possibility that animal welfare may be overridden if necessary; it is not an absolute. The same applies in the case of human rights.[22]

Galston says that one of the main purposes of his argument is to prove that "rights to particular objects, deeds, or forms of treatment cannot be absolute or inviolate."[23] This is because rights claims depend on reasons or grounds related to considerations of human goods that are not themselves absolute. Thus Galston argues that "in certain circumstances any right, no matter how fundamental or well entrenched, may be forfeited or vanish"; it is possible to imagine circumstances in which even the right not to be tortured must be disallowed.[24] I quite happily accept the validity of this general argument. However, one cannot avoid observing here that the whole rhetorical and pragmatic appeal of "rights" consists in the belief that these do establish something absolute or inviolate. If this were accepted as fallacious, then the interest in maintaining the

21. Galston, *Justice and the Human Good*, pp. 124–126.

22. Ibid., pp. 136–410. It might be objected that the kinds of problems that I have pointed to in the language of rights do not apply to so-called human rights. However, I think it can be shown that some of the same difficulties recur even in an international or global rights discourse. For instance, Joseph Carens, in "Migration and the Welfare State," in *Democracy and the Welfare State*, ed. Amy Gutmann (Princeton: Princeton University Press, 1988), p. 226, points out that according to the U.N. Covenant on Civil and Political Rights, free mobility within a given state is a universal right of all individuals. Prohibitions in China against unrestricted mobility, intended to avoid the drastic problems of urbanization endemic in the Third World, clearly violate this right. But why should it be assumed that the rights of individuals, as formulated in the U.N. covenant, take precedence over the kinds of compelling social purposes that motivated the Chinese to restrict free mobility?

23. Galston, *Justice and the Human Good*, p. 127.

24. Ibid., p. 138. Even Dworkin admits that any right can be abridged, not only in relation to competing rights but in consideration of overwhelming utility; see *Taking Rights Seriously*, pp. 191, 195.

authority of rights in general would tend to evaporate. No longer acting as a definitive standard of judgment, incapable of being over-ridden, rights as such would cease to deliver the very advantage that accounts for their pride of place within our prevailing mode of political discourse. In short, if Galston's argument were generally accepted, the whole idea of rights would lose the grip it now exer-cises on our political life because it would no longer be able to render that which it (falsely) promises, and which confers on it its compelling appeal. We must ask ourselves why so much of our political discourse is given over to the trading back and forth of rights claims; or, to present the same question in a different guise, why all political claims in our culture tend to be treated as quasi-legal or juridical claims. To invert Galston's analysis: to say that there do not exist absolute or inviolate rights is another way of saying that we should consider dispensing with the whole lan-guage of rights, for it is simply that way of speaking about what is politically desirable that disposes us to assert claims that *are* taken as absolute and inviolate.[25]

A further drawback of the rhetoric of rights discourse is that all rights, as rights, tend to be treated as occupying an equal level, in abstraction from the heterogeneous and differentiated considera-tions that lead us to describe something as good or as advanta-geous. The attraction of this rhetoric, indeed, lies precisely in its abstractness, its lack of differentiation with regard to the substance of various entitlements (we might call it the leveling effect). In this respect, the rhetoric tends to resemble the language of values, drawn from the same cultural sources, whose unhappy effects it reinforces. ("How dare you presume to call into question my val-ues, whatever they happen to be?" "How dare you presume to

---

25. As argued above, this is a feature of collective rights as well as individual rights. Therefore the criticisms advanced against the politics of individual rights can be applied no less against a politics of group rights. For instance, consider the conflict between Israelis and Palestinians in this light: A major obstacle to Arab-Israeli peace is "the traditional obsession of both Arabs and Israelis with their 'legitimate rights,' as opposed to their legitimate interests," since ancestral or God-given rights are seen as "immutable and do not allow for compromise," whereas interests, con-nected with what is immediate and limited, "invite compromise." Thomas Friedman, *From Beirut to Jerusalem* (London: Fontana/Collins, 1990), pp. 519–520.

trespass upon my rights, whatever they happen to be?") Again, this manner of asserting claims harbors dangers of petulance and immoderation. For instance, the translation of all political claims into the homogenizing language of rights means that the "right" of Sunday shopping, or the "right" of doctors to bill their patients whatever they choose, or the "right" not to be screened for AIDS, can be asserted with as much passionate indignation as would be appropriate in the case of challenges to the freedom of speech or the freedom of religious belief. Rather than inquiring into what is actually at stake in a given argument, the very fact that a supposed right is in jeopardy introduces an extra measure of passion and intemperance into the debate, regardless of what is being debated. This problem derives from the formalism of rights discourse, in contrast to the substantive character of deliberations conducted in the language of good.

To any claim concerning rights, one can always raise the question: What constitutes the limit demarcating a defensible right from an indefensible right? (Say, the unimpugnable right to buy magazines that appeal to my private tastes versus the impugnable right to buy magazines that exploit and degrade women.) And to this question one cannot reply by a further appeal to rights, which at this point is rendered vacuous or question begging. Rather, such a challenge to any rights claim automatically compels us to inquire beyond rights. Of course, one could try to turn this into a contest between competing rights, opposing to the rights of the consumer of pornography the rights of the women which that pornography exploits and dehumanizes.[26] Then one would have an ordinary trade-off between two sets of negotiable rights. But this is simply a dodge. For the argument, if it can proceed at all, ultimately comes

---

26. Recently a prominent American feminist declared that Canada's Charter of Rights provides women with an invaluable "anti-pornography weapon." "Use Charter of Rights to Fight Pornography, U.S. Lawyer Suggests," Toronto *Globe and Mail*, 2 March 1987, p. A16. But one may ask why the charter should not appear as a no less marvelous weapon in the hands of antifeminists. And this applies to all political disputes subject to judicial resolution. The charter is of course an excellent instrument for the furtherance of one's own preferred causes—until, that is, one's political opponents avail themselves of the same instrument in the service of their own, not-so-wonderful causes. Cf. Fulford, *Saturday Night* article, p. 9.

down to the question of whether it is good (either for the consumers or for the "objects" of consumption) for sexuality to be commodified—reduced to market relations—in this way, and this is not a rights question (though it can, subsequently, be phrased in terms of rights). To couch the issue wholly in terms of rights thus obscures the fact that settlement of the competing claims must repose on a very different kind of question, namely: On grounds of what vision of human life, or in the light of what desired goods, should a society favor one set of rights over another? For instance, suppose we are obliged to arbitrate the conflict between the right to free speech and free assembly of a white racist and the right not to be harassed or victimized of a black or an Asian. How are we expected to weigh these claims simply on the basis of notions of formal equality, as Dworkin demands, without considering the substance of the needs and interests at stake, and the comparative worth of the substantive ends or purposes implied in each? To say that claim X is recognized as a right whereas claim Y is not is simply a way of expressing, within a particular political idiom or vocabulary, that such a settlement has been concluded at the level of conceptions of the good. (All societies necessarily arrive at such determinations—even liberal societies, notwithstanding liberal theorists' protestations of neutrality on the question of the good life. To imagine a society where all conceivable rights are respected is utterly incoherent.) I would assume that even the most diehard proponent of rights language would concede that simply to assert a right is not a sufficient warrant for respecting the right (though some rights theorists, like Nozick, offer little more than assertion). But this inevitably directs us to the more substantial question: What warrants rights in general? And this question carries us, willy-nilly, into the language of good.

It will be objected that there are plenty of political contexts in which the assertion of rights is perfectly legitimate and beneficial rather than harmful. I do not deny this. The ubiquity of the vocabulary of rights means that a great number of reasonable causes would be banished if we simply erased all claims that presently make appeal to rights. However, if, as I sought to show in my first argument, all legitimate rights are transposable, without loss, into the idiom of good, then we have nothing to lose with the supersession of the vocabulary of rights; whereas, as I try to make clear in my second argument, we may have much to gain.

RECAPITULATION

To conclude, let me summarize my argument, as well as briefly review the likely lines of objection or criticism that this argument will provoke. At a time when notions of individual rights have uniquely impressed themselves upon the political consciousness of my own polity, it can hardly be overlooked that much of contemporary political discourse is framed in the language of rights and entitlements.[27] This forces us to reflect not only on the philosophical status of rights but also on the question of political rhetoric, that is to say, of the fundamental terms with which we address one another as members of a particular political community.[28] This reflection suggests, first, that the appeal to rights is not self-sufficing but depends logically upon deeper moral considerations; and second, that the translation of this more primary moral language into rights discourse renders political relationships generally more adversarial than they would otherwise be. The conclusion offered is that the logical dispensability of rights language might allow us to entertain the possibility of considering it (to some extent) politically dispensable.

To this argument, two main objections will inevitably arise. First, it will be said that there are within the academic literature on rights highly sophisticated rights-based theories according to which rights

27. For similar lines of reflection applied to the Canadian context, see Philip Resnick, "State and Civil Society: The Limits of a Royal Commission," *Canadian Journal of Political Science* 20, no. 2 (June 1987):398–399, and Charles Taylor, "Alternative Futures," in *Constitutionalism, Citizenship and Society*, ed. Cairns and Williams, pp. 209 ff. While Taylor does not go so far as to recommend that all talk of rights be simply scrapped, he does make clear, I think, important limitations of a political culture in which rights, enforced by court action, are the primary locus of political contention. Certainly, we ought to be worried if rights are all that we are able to talk about politically.

28. Cf. Andrew, *Shylock's Rights*, p. 196: "The specific care of the political philosopher is political words, not political things. Thus the unique charge of political theorists is not to direct political activists but to safeguard political language."

are *not* absolute, not exclusive, and so on. This may well be so; but this reply misses the point of my argument. The notion of rights has the force that it increasingly does within our public culture because there is a certain logic contained within rights talk which connects up with certain pervasive characteristics of our pluralistic political culture, characteristics that we may celebrate for various reasons but that we may, equally, have good reason to find worrisome. Again, my principal concern is not with the concept of a right as a philosophical category (which, naturally, admits of all manner of refinements), but with the rhetoric of rights as a political phenomenon.[29]

Second, it will be objected that there are political societies where the language of rights is absent or much less pervasive than in our own society, and where political evils of various sorts are nonetheless equal to or greater (sometimes *much* greater) than those that plague the liberal West. Yet nowhere in our argument was it suggested that a displacement of political discourse away from rights talk would solve all political problems or guarantee a perfect community. But the limits and imperfections of other societies should certainly not relieve us from the effort of reflecting on the dilemmas of our own political community.

This discussion of rights has been a reconstructive exercise. That is, I have tried to imagine ways of talking about leading issues of moral and social life without employing one of the central terms of liberal political discourse. What has been the point of this somewhat fanciful thought experiment? What is to be gained by going to all the effort of reconstructing (hypothetically) a kind of language that is not likely to be altered in the real world of liberal society? Clearly, the main purpose is a heuristic one—to illustrate, through imagining an alternative political discourse, what is wrong with the

---

29. See Waldron, "Nonsense upon Stilts?" p. 196, for an admission that at least some theories of rights affirm the "image of a society of *claimers*, each preoccupied with his own grievances, with the wrongs that may or may not be done to *him*." Waldron argues persuasively that this is not inherent in the enterprise of a theory of rights as such. But what matters for my purposes is not whether a given theory does or doesn't presuppose this unattractive conception, but whether this image of society prevails in the actual practice of the rhetoric and deployment of rights claims in liberal society.

existing terms of discourse.[30] And what *is* wrong with the linguistic status quo? Well, to speak bluntly, the theorist who wishes to reflect critically on the practices and norms of a liberal social order cannot rest content with a mode of discourse modeled exclusively on the interaction of opposing lawyers fencing in a courtroom.

The problem with rights discourse is certainly not that claims registered in the name of rights are never valid moral claims. Of course they commonly are. The problem lies elsewhere. Whatever the sophisticated refinements in the theory of rights devised by philosophers, the ultimate ground of objection to the language of rights, so far as our political culture is concerned, is that it is a rather ugly vocabulary, just as the ultimate objection to the ridiculous language of values is that it is morally ugly and that it all but precludes the possibility of conversing intelligently about moral and political life. The ugliness of these vocabularies is not an aesthetic problem (as in Hegel's observation that "it is uncultured people who insist most on their rights, while noble minds look on other aspects of the thing"[31]), but a moral and political one, and the impulse to reconstruct these vocabularies, again, has a moral and political motivation.

Once again, it matters that we conduct our political arguments in terms of rights; it matters, not least, in respect of the quality of our political life. Disputes over rights tend to be conducted in terms of absolutes. As I have tried to suggest, a qualified or hedged right admits a doubt as to its status as a right. It tells us something about the fabric of our political life that we feel we can cope with political arguments only in these terms. What this in turn tells us is that, while it may be politically salutary for us to forgo the language of rights in the conduct of our political arguments, it would require a major transformation or overhaul of our political life in general before we could switch to the altered terms of debate that I have

30. For an extreme expression of the constricted theoretical imagination of some rights theorists, consider Thomas Hurka's suggestion that opponents of rights-based politics might most plausibly trace the principles that underlie their position to the "totalitarian belief" that "government has authority just because it's good for citizens." "Notwithstanding the Rights of the People," Toronto *Globe and Mail*, 7 November 1989, p. A8.

31. *Hegel's Philosophy of Right*, trans. T. M. Knox (London: Oxford University Press, 1967), p. 235, addition to para. 37.

suggested.[32] A better appreciation of the dimensions of the required transformation may emerge from the predicaments considered in the next chapter.

32. For a superb vindication of a form of political discourse that dispen-
ses entirely with any appeal to the idea of rights, see Edward Andrew,
"Simone Weil on the Injustice of Rights-Based Doctrines," *The Review of
Politics* 48, no. 1 (Winter 1986): 60–91. More generally, see Andrew's excellent book *Shylock's Rights*.

5

Citizenship

The world is still too young to fix many general
truths in politics.

David Hume

A revolution was needed to bring men back to
common sense.

Jean-Jacques Rousseau

For twenty-nine days in the autumn of 1969, for reasons that are
somewhat obscure, the Strategic Air Command of the United States
went on full alert. Nuclear-armed B-52s "were pulled off their rou-
tine training and surveillance duties and placed in take-off positions
on runways across the United States, fully armed, fueled, ready to
fly attack missions anywhere in the world."[1] No public announce-
ment was made of the orders to initiate the alert. No newspapers
reported the alert. Only a handful of American citizens had any
awareness that something out of the ordinary was occurring. "The
alert amounted to a secret between the White House and [military
and political leaders inside] the Soviet Union."[2] It is difficult to
conceive of anything of more immediate and more urgent interest
to ordinary citizens, both in the United States and throughout the
world, than the possibility of one superpower readying itself for
all-out nuclear war against its rival superpower (and doing so for
no apparent reason!). Yet no civilians anywhere were privy to this
confidence between the White House and the Kremlin. This puz-

---

1. Seymour M. Hersh, *The Price of Power: Kissinger in the Nixon White
House* (New York: Summit Books, 1983), p. 124.
2. Ibid.

98

zling episode may therefore stand as a fateful allegory of the predicament of the contemporary citizen.[3]

LIBERAL CITIZENSHIP

> From an Aristotelian point of view a modern liberal political society can appear only as a collection of citizens of nowhere who have banded together for their common protection.
> Alasdair MacIntyre, *After Virtue*

Even in theory, citizenship seems to be a shrinking status. Let us consider, for instance, the conception of citizenship articulated by one leading contemporary liberal theorist. Bruce Ackerman, in his influential book *Social Justice in the Liberal State*, presents a systematic account of liberal citizenship.[4] Defined negatively, citizenship excludes beings (stones, lions, Martians) with whom it would be impossible to have an argument about social justice. Or put positively, citizenship in the liberal state may encompass any creature with whom we could have a justificatory dialogue about power relations, *including* talking apes or Martians with whom we could communicate about the disposal of scarce resources. Citizenship, as Ackerman formulates it, involves competent participation in a conversation in which moral claims to the appropriation of material resources are either upheld or rebutted.

On Ackerman's account, a liberal citizen is anyone who can utter the magic words: "I am at least as good as you are, therefore I should get at least as much." Ackerman refers to this "thin thread of mutual intelligibility" as the "minimal dialogue" requirement for citizenship.[5] Even a being from a different planet or an ape, if capable of uttering "No" when confronted with human appropriation of resources to which the Martian or ape objects, and if able to accompany this "No" with a set of noises bearing a semantic content that could be interpreted to be "interrogatory, not imperative"

3. The mystery has perhaps now resolved itself. The Soviets admitted, twenty years later, that the Soviet military was involved in combat activity in Egypt commencing in October 1969.

4. Bruce A. Ackerman, *Social Justice in the Liberal State* (New Haven: Yale University Press, 1980), chap. 3.

5. Ibid., p. 75.

(not merely "No. Stop taking that! It's mine!" but "No. Why is it yours? Why not mine?"), would have a putative claim to citizenship.[6] A talking ape, Ackerman notes, would have a stronger claim to citizenship than a human being whose brain was damaged to the extent of precluding participation in an intelligible dialogue about the justifiability of power relations.[7]

Ackerman bases his conception of citizenship on a notion of participation in political dialogue, but it is a dialogue where the topic of conversation is always the same and the parties to the discussion always utter the same monotonous formula. The object of political talk is always the distribution of material resources, and claims in this domain are always put forward and repelled by the same "thin, but fundamental, assertion": "because I'm at least as good as you are."[8] It is no wonder, then, that Ackerman limits the occasions for such exchanges, lest the "civic dialogue" become too wearisome for the participants.[9] This might be less of a problem if the topic of conversation in a liberal polity extended to the substance of the common life shared by these shapeless "citizens."

Citizens within this polity do not debate the substance of civic ties that give life or richness to the community of which they are members. They do not debate whether there are social or collective resources that they might wish to devote to beautifying or ennobling their shared living space. For instance, Ackerman seems to rule out the legitimacy of even the most modest state-funded grants for the arts, let alone more ambitious collective projects.[10] There is

6. Ibid., p. 71.

7. Ibid., p. 80.

8. Ibid., p. 78. This assertion, says Ackerman, should occupy "the entire conversational field."

9. Ibid., p. 96.

10. Ibid., pp. 182–185. Cf. John Rawls, *A Theory of Justice* (Oxford: Oxford University Press, 1971), pp. 331–332: while public funds for the arts and sciences are permissible if those who do not benefit directly are satisfied that they are receiving adequate indirect or compensating benefits, "the principles of justice do not permit subsidizing universities and institutes, or opera and the theatre, on the grounds that these institutions are intrinsically valuable." But Ronald Dworkin parts company with his fellow liberals on this issue in "Foundations of Liberal Equality," in *The Tanner Lectures on Human Values*, vol. 11, ed. Grethe B. Peterson (Salt Lake City: University of Utah Press, 1990), p. 85 n. 44.

no conversation about the kinds of individual or social purposes that might be *worthy* of pursuit, since questions of this sort would violate the whole liberal agenda, premised on the bracketing of any content.[11] Instead, the citizens discuss one thing and one thing only: who gets what for the pursuit of individual life-projects. Where power is used to hog resources, the power holders are compelled by argument to make the supreme community-defining acknowledgment that no one is better or worse than anyone else. As Ackerman puts it, "it is this chain of questions and answers that binds all citizens together to form a liberal state."[12] Needless to say, the citizens of this community would never have occasion to deliberate in common about whether there are, in fact, more important subjects of political conversation than the distribution of material resources for individual purposes.[13] Indeed, citizens are even barred from forming a societywide judgment that the very existence of future citizens constitutes a collective good, since this would put too great a constraint on the judgments of individuals about their own good. Consequently, Ackerman does not even allow a legitimate interest of the state in promoting a stock of future generations of citizens (say, through family allowance benefits) unless this accords with the individual preferences of the existing generation.[14] As always, the very thinness of the civic affiliation is elevated into the defining principle of liberal citizenship.

11. As Ackerman puts it, "a liberal state cannot justify its use of power when this requires us to weigh the intrinsic merit of competing conceptions of the good affirmed by different citizens." *Social Justice in the Liberal State*, p. 115.

12. Ibid., p. 96.

13. The question of a societywide collective good goes by the board in Ackerman's political philosophy: "The liberal rejects the idea that a political community may legitimately further a collective good. . . . For him, the overriding fact is that he finds himself among a large number of individuals, each one of whom affirms his own good" (ibid., p. 227). And "citizens create a *society of individuals* by talking to one another about their social predicament" (p. 100). Political community exists strictly to preside over the fair allotment of life-options for individuals.

14. Ibid., pp. 126, 225–227. If "lifestyle" choices dictate that the present generation exercises its right to "call it quits forever," so be it. This is at a far extremity from Burke's idea of politics as a partnership between the living, the dead, and the yet to be born. As Roger Scruton says, "liberals have great difficulty in seeing how [such a partnership] might be justified, the dead and the unborn being excluded in the nature of things from the

We seem to be very distant indeed from the substantive ideals of citizenship articulated by liberal political philosophers at the end of the nineteenth century.[15] Nor is Ackerman alone among contemporary liberal theorists in emptying the concept of citizenship of virtually all meaningful content. With welfare liberalism, the chief focus is on individual entitlements and the amelioration of inequalities. Since in the just society the state is merely the agent of moral principles that are in principle universal, it is hard to see why a theory of fair distribution would have much to say about the kinds of political attachment that are bracketed behind the veil of ignorance along with other contingencies of personhood. As the grounding affirmation of liberal thought is that of the equal moral worth of all individuals in abstraction from any substantive roles or attributes, perhaps the only coherent liberal idea of citizenship is some notion of world citizenship.[16] Although Rawls nods in the direction of the grander themes of Mill's *Representative Government*,[17] he emphasizes that his own principle of participation (stipulating an equal chance for all to be involved in the constitutional process of government) delineates a more modest vision: "The principle of participation applies to institutions. It does not define an ideal of citizenship; nor does it lay down a duty requiring all to

---

social contract among the living." "In Defence of the Nation," in Scruton, *The Philosopher on Dover Beach* (Manchester: Carcanet, 1990), p. 318; cf. pp. 306, 319.

15. See Andrew Vincent and Raymond Plant, *Philosophy, Politics and Citizenship: The Life and Thought of the British Idealists* (Oxford: Basil Blackwell, 1984), chaps. 1 and 9 (pp. 1–5 and 162–183); and C. B. Macpherson, "Do We Need a Theory of the State?" *Archives européennes de sociologie* 18, no. 2 (1977): 223–244.

16. Joseph Carens undertakes to show that the underlying logic of each of the leading versions of liberalism (Rawlsian, Nozickian, utilitarian) tends in this cosmopolitan direction. "Aliens and Citizens: The Case for Open Borders," *Review of Politics* 49, no. 2 (Spring 1987): 251–273. Cf. Scruton, "In Defense of the Nation," p. 320. The leading liberal theories, whether contractarian, utilitarian, or Nozickian rights theory, all seek what Rawls in section 41 of *A Theory of Justice* refers to as "an Archimedean point." That is, one is called upon to imagine that one did not inhabit any particular society, and then to ask oneself what kinds of rational standards or moral principles one would find compelling from such a contextless perspective. Is it, then, surprising that citizenship, to the extent that it is a topic at all, tends to be a self-dissolving category within such theories?

17. Rawls, *A Theory of Justice*, pp. 233–234.

take an active part in political affairs. . . . In a well-governed state only a small fraction of persons may devote much of their time to politics. There are many other forms of human good."[18] As for libertarian liberalism of the Nozickian variety, the status of citizenship seems to vanish altogether. As Joseph Carens observes: "Citizens, in Nozick's view, are simply consumers purchasing impartial, efficient protection of preexisting natural rights. Nozick uses the terms 'citizen,' 'client' and 'customer' interchangeably."[19] These features of liberal theory also have their counterpart in an attenuation of the language of citizenship at the level of political practice: "It is a symptom of the crisis of citizenship in the 1980s that most political rhetoric, whether of left or right, addresses the electorate not as citizens but as taxpayers or as consumers."[20] It is difficult to imagine how members of a liberal society can hope to be citizens of something, somewhere, when even the ideals of citizenship developed in liberal theory leave them adrift, as "citizens of nowhere."

These theoretical dilemmas are likely to remain irresolvable as long as the liberal injunction on judgments of content remains in place. As we have seen, liberal conversation as Ackerman sets it up is based on the ultimate conversation stopper: "For my judgment in these matters is at least as good as yours is."[21] Upon this non

18. Ibid., pp. 227–228.

19. Carens, "Aliens and Citizens," p. 272 n. 3. Cf. George Armstrong Kelly, *Hegel's Retreat from Eleusis* (Princeton: Princeton University Press, 1978), p. 106.

20. Michael Ignatieff, "The Myth of Citizenship," *Queen's Quarterly* 94, no. 4 (Winter 1987): 981.

21. Ackerman, *Social Justice in the Liberal State*, pp. 176, 182. Ackerman's formulation of liberalism requires us to assume not only that each citizen is as good as every other and, less evidently, that each citizen's judgment about what is worthwhile in life is as good as every other's, but, even more ambitiously, that each citizen, qua participant in the decision-making process, is as good a liberal statesman as every other (pp. 279, 284, 319). This would require us to base our liberal political system on the extraordinary assumption that, on principle, Neville Chamberlain was as good a liberal statesman as Winston Churchill (on the grounds that it would be illiberal to assume otherwise!). Given this mandatory abstraction from judgments of substance, it is not surprising that Ackerman argues that decision by lottery is perfectly consistent with the moral postulates of political liberalism (pp. 285–289, 298, 301). Lottery, in common with majoritarian procedures, offers a method of political decision making "that recog-

sequitur Ackerman builds an entire theory of citizenship. It is striking that a political philosophy that exalts dialogue as the heart of the liberal vision at the same time looks for ways to cut short the discourse so as to avoid what would otherwise be an inevitable fate: the tedious repetition by all citizens, in all contexts, of one and the same mantra.[22] As an alternative to the liberal theory of citizenship, I propose a definition of citizenship that is the exact converse of that offered by Ackerman. Instead of citizenship defined as participation in a dialogue whose basic premise is the impermissibility of weighing the intrinsic merit of competing conceptions of the good, let us have citizenship defined as active participation in a dialogue that indeed weighs the substantive merit of competing conceptions of the good and that aims at transforming social arrangements in the direction of what is judged, in this active public dialogue, as the best possible (individual *and* collective) good.

WHITHER CITIZENSHIP?

> Full Canadian citizenship is worth all the oil in Arabia and all the fish in any sea.
>
> Brian Mulroney, speaking at the
> First Ministers' Conference on
> Aboriginal Rights, 1987

In the sections that follow, I turn from liberal theory to liberal practice. The outlook here is, if anything, even bleaker. Before I offer my appraisal of contemporary realities, let me begin with some preliminary clarifications. It might be thought that a theory of citizenship is merely another name for democratic theory; however, this is not quite the case. What is the difference between democracy and citizenship?[23] Democracy is a mode of social and political orga-

---

nizes each citizen's standing as a statesman whose political judgments are entitled to equal respect" (p. 289). Imagine choosing between the policies of Chamberlain and the policies of Churchill by random selection! Yet if the general moral structure of liberalism is exhausted by the proposition "X is as good as Y and Y is as good as X," then this is indeed perfectly consistent.

22. Ibid., p. 254. Cf. p. 96.

23. The distinction between citizenship and democracy is illustrated by John Burnheim's book *Is Democracy Possible?* (Berkeley; University of California Press, 1985), which offers an argument for radical democratiza-

nization within the political community. Citizenship is a form of attachment to the political community itself; it implies, as well, the capacity to give effect to this attachment through various kinds of competent social, legal, and political praxis. In the ideal case, citizenship is active membership in a political community where the very fact of such membership empowers those included in it to contribute to the shaping of a shared collective destiny. But one can be impelled to forms of democratic activity without being moved by bonds of citizenly commitment; conversely, it is possible to feel a strong sense of citizen identity in the absence of provisions for broad democratic activity. The republican theorist, in contrast to the pure partisan of democracy, is concerned not only with securing the greatest civic participation for the greatest number, but also with elevating the quality of civic participation. So while the republican theorist obviously prefers good citizenship exercised by many to good citizenship exercised by a few, good citizenship exercised by a few may be preferred to ignorant and intolerant citizenship exercised by many. For example, as we see from John Stuart Mill's ideas about a differential franchise, with extra votes for intellectuals,[24] Mill was not always concerned with maximizing democracy; he was, however, always concerned with maximizing good citizenship. However, to the extent that enlarged democratic participation serves to offset feelings of disaffection that would otherwise beset the political community, and helps to strengthen forms of political competence (as it regularly does), citizenship theory includes but is broader than democratic theory, and the inquiry into citizenship subsumes the inquiry into democracy.

Our definition above indicates two dimensions to the theory of citizenship, which we may for convenience label as civic identification and civic competence. Let us start with the question of competence. The most forceful challenge to the standard faith in possibili-

---

tion, conjoined with an argument for radical dissolution of political (i.e., state-focused) citizenship. See, for instance, pp. 117–118: "The illusion that democracy can be assured by so-called democratic control of the state is disastrous. The state cannot be controlled democratically. It must be abolished."

24. J. S. Mill, *On Liberty and Considerations on Representative Government*, ed. R. B. McCallum, (Oxford: Basil Blackwell, 1946), pp. 216–222 (*Representative Government*, chap. 8).

ties of meaningful democratic citizenship has been stated by Schumpeter. "In the realm of public affairs," he writes, "there are sectors that are more within the reach of the citizen's mind than others. This is true, first, of local affairs. Even there we find a reduced power of discerning facts, a reduced preparedness to act upon them, a reduced sense of responsibility." And, he goes on, "when we move still further from the private concerns of the family and the business office into those regions of national and international affairs that lack a direct and unmistakable link with those private concerns," we are, he claims, struck by "the fact that the sense of reality is so completely lost. Normally, the great political questions take their place in the psychic economy of the typical citizen with those leisure-hour interests that have not attained the rank of hobbies, and with the subjects of irresponsible conversation. These things seem so far off; they are not at all like a business proposition; dangers may not materialize at all and if they should they may not prove so very serious; one feels oneself to be moving in a fictitious world." The private citizen musing over national affairs, Schumpeter concludes, "expends less disciplined effort on mastering a political problem than he expends on a game of bridge."[25] The counterchallenge to this stark account can of course be that what Schumpeter treats under the heading of "human nature in politics" in fact reflects contingent, and corrigible, historical conditions, and that Schumpeter's presentation, in common with all universalizing propositions about human nature, hypostatizes a particular set of social relationships and historically shaped social practices. One wishes that this could suffice to dispose of Schumpeter's pessimism about democratic citizenship. But his description, whether universal or not, fits the existing realities so accurately that, with respect to the corrigibility of this condition, the onus of proof surely remains on the shoulders of the partisan of democracy.

The following example exposes the gravity of the problem. According to a survey conducted in 1984, fully 81 percent of Americans polled thought that current U.S. policy is to resort to nuclear

25. Joseph A. Schumpeter, *Capitalism, Socialism and Democracy* (New York: Harper & Row, 1976), pp. 260–261.

weapons "if, and only if, the Soviets attack the United States first with nuclear weapons"; however, it has always been open government policy that nuclear "first use" is a legitimate military response to Soviet conventional attack.[26] In other words, more than four-fifths of the American people found themselves completely in the dark about the stance of their own government on this preeminent, and possibly life-and-death, public issue. In the face of reports like these, it is hard to say whether one feels dismay or relief in learning that, for instance, in the U.S. congressional elections in 1986, only 33.4 percent of potential voters exercised their franchise (a postwar low).[27] How does modern citizenship fare if it depends upon the effectiveness of modern democracy? A clear indication of the depth of the problem is the fact that leading democratic theorists have had resort to the desperate hope that technological gadgets of some kind will furnish salvation of the democratic ideal, as Robert Paul Wolff, Benjamin Barber, and Robert Dahl have variously proposed.[28] Far from achieving the required positive reciprocal relationship between citizenship and democracy spoken of at the beginning of this section, the forms of citizenship presently available do little to bolster democratic practice, just as available modes of democratic activity provide a very inadequate support to a healthy citizenship.

Let us now turn to consider the question of citizen identification. Citizenship is a problem for liberals for the following reason. According to the pure liberal model, the state ideally acts as guarantor of maximal latitude and minimal hindrance in the forming of preferences by individual choosers and consumers. But this pure liberal model surely cannot govern the citizen's relation to the state itself. To be sure, some are immigrants, refugees, or exiles. But most of

26. Cited in McGeorge Bundy et al., "Back from the Brink," *Atlantic Monthly*, August 1986, p. 36.

27. *Congressional Quarterly Weekly Report*, 14 March 1987, p. 485. This figure represents a percentage of the voting-age population.

28. Robert Paul Wolff, *In Defense of Anarchism* (New York: Harper & Row, 1970), pp. 34–37; Benjamin Barber, *Strong Democracy* (Berkeley: University of California Press, 1984), pp. 273–278, 289–290; Robert A. Dahl, *Democracy and Its Critics* (New Haven: Yale University Press, 1989), pp. 338–341; and Dahl, *Controlling Nuclear Weapons: Democracy Versus Guardianship* (Syracuse: Syracuse University Press, 1985), chap. 5.

us find ourselves in the midst of a political community we have not chosen, and the state would be in very serious trouble if we all adopted the stance of radical distanciation required for free consumer choice in respect of the political communities to which we belong. Liberal citizenship taken to the extreme would put everyone in the position of the emigrant who can choose to go anywhere, and whose choice remains in principle subject to supersession by a further choice. We find an instance of this extremity of the liberal mentality in a book by A. John Simmons entitled *Moral Principles and Political Obligations*, the arguments of which issue in a kind of bizarre hyperliberalism:

> We will normally have good reasons for obeying the law, and for supporting some types of governments of which our own may be one. But the reasons we have for obeying the law will be the *same* reasons we have for obeying the law when we are in foreign countries. And if we have reason to support our government it will be the *same* reason we have for supporting any other similar government. Thus . . . we are not *specially* bound to obey *our* laws or to support *our* government, simply because they are ours (or because of what their being ours entails). Insofar as we believe ourselves to be tied in some special way to our country of residence, most of us are mistaken.[29]

On a modest interpretation, it may appear that this tells us no more than that no doctrine of political obligation can oblige us to be led into folly and wickedness simply because we happen to belong to one tribe rather than another ("my country right or wrong"). However, examining this passage more carefully, we can detect far more radical implications. Simmons's purpose is not merely to warn against the excesses of patriotism (citizenship as tribalism); he is saying that even where what is legally and politically required of us is reasonable and just, our reasons for complying will always coincide with those of, say, a foreign tourist subject to the political authority of an alien power. If this is correct, it is hard to see how any sense at all could be made of citizenship as a normative principle. Although Simmons is suspicious of analogies between family and polity, it may help us to appreciate what is

29. A. John Simmons, *Moral Principles and Political Obligations* (Princeton: Princeton University Press, 1979), p. 194.

jarring about the statement quoted above if we consider our reaction to someone who claimed that the fact that our child or our spouse was ours offered no special reason for privileging our moral commitment to their welfare (except that their proximity tended to make them natural recipients of *general* moral reasons for advancing the welfare of other individuals). Like citizenship, devotion to one's family would then appear as an indefensible prejudice. To be consistent, this hyperliberalism should apply the same attitude of detachment to family life as it does to political community. This would spell the end of the family no less than it spells the end of citizenship.

To put the problem in Rousseauean terms: A civic relationship to the state presupposes an underlying attachment to a settled political community. This in turn presupposes an attachment to a set of customs, traditions, historical practices, and established norms that are particularistic and therefore necessarily in some measure exclusive (even if benignly so). If the relationship to the state is not mediated by a sense of commitment to an enduring political community, then citizenship is something hollow (as, for instance, commitment to East Germany as a political unit proved to be hollow as soon as the means of state coercion were removed). Yet the whole of modern existence, of which liberalism tends to function as a theoretical encapsulation,[30] eats away at the sources of these solidaristic attachments; so that we are ultimately driven to the opposing alternatives of spiritless cosmopolitanism and reactionary nationalism: General Motors and Panasonic on the one side, Armenian and Azeri atavism on the other. The citizen is left to choose, as it were, between rule by remote functionaries in Brussels and rule by local zealots.[31]

30. Cf. John Gray, *Liberalism* (Minneapolis: University of Minnesota Press, 1986), p. 82: "Liberalism . . . is the political theory of modernity."

31. This dialectic is given a succinct formulation by Alain Touraine in an interview with *Le Figaro* (9 October 1990, p. 11), in which he refers to "une évolution très générale de la société vers une formidable dissociation du culturel et de l'économique. Plus le domaine économique se mondialise, plus celui de l'identité individuelle se localise" (a very general evolution of the society toward a formidable dissociation of cultural and economic matters. The more the economic domain is globalized, the more the domain of individual identity is localized). In consequence, citizenship is

The globalization of contemporary politics and economics has enormous implications for a theory of democratic citizenship. When we are concerned with the repair of cracked sidewalks or a dilapidated drain system in our local community, we can at least in principle convene an assembly of the whole community to decide on priorities and allocations of resources (even if in fact we choose to delegate responsibility for such issues to administrators or political representatives). But when the issues to be deliberated include what action to take in response to the thinning of the ozone layer, how to regulate relations between the developed and the developing halves of the planet, how to manage nuclear proliferation, and so on, it is not even in principle possible for the five billion citizens of this planet to gather on the hillside of some stupendous Pnyx to deliberate about problems of global scale. (It would, I suppose, be possible in principle to attach plebiscitary voting devices to a billion television sets, but that prospect hardly offers much reassurance in this context.) If the phenomenon of globalism presents troubling difficulties for a theory of citizenship, so does the national question, with its opposing challenge of particularism. It is no doubt true that, as T. H. Green put it, "just as there can be no true friendship except towards this or that individual, so there can be no true public spirit which is not localized in some way."[32] This poses no problem for those who base citizenship on national exclusivity. But it certainly remains a problem for those inclined to see nationalism as the Pandora's box of modern politics (and Mr. Gorbachev is surely not alone among contemporary statesmen in having good reason to see it as such!). Indeed, it is not impossible to imagine that once this Pandora's box of European nationalism is reopened among the newly liberated peoples of the Soviet bloc, one might come to look back upon the preceding forty years of Stalinism as a golden age of interethnic harmony.[33]

---

squeezed out from both ends, namely, globalizing tendencies on the one hand, and localizing tendencies on the other.

32. Thomas Hill Green, *Lectures on the Principles of Political Obligation* (London: Longmans, Green, 1955), p. 175; quoted in Leslie Green, *The Authority of the State* (Oxford: Oxford University Press, 1988), p. 218.

33. It is the fear of tribal citizenship (not an idle fear) that prompts Ralf Dahrendorf's emphatically liberal idea of citizenship as the provision of a set of common entitlements "in order to set people free to be different."

Roger Scruton has offered what he presents as a Hegelian argument that a political identity capable of sustaining itself must be rooted in prepolitical forms of allegiance and membership. However, Scruton departs from Hegel when he insists that "the liberal state must depend . . . upon some other loyalty than loyalty to itself,"[34] for Hegel himself placed a heavier emphasis upon attachment to the *Staat* than upon attachment to the *Volk*. George Armstrong Kelly seems to be more faithful to Hegel in arguing that citizenship must have a primary political focus, and that focus must be the state.[35] As Rousseau correctly anticipated, the core identity of the modern citizen consists in being a payer of taxes—not a condition likely to foster deep bonds of attachment toward the political community (or alternatively, political community is experienced above all else as a community of those sharing in a gargantuan national debt).[36] The characteristic relationship of the citizen

---

See "Blind to the Greater Liberty," London *Times*, 9 November 1990, p. 14. Perhaps what theorists of citizenship need to think about, in order to surmount the quandary of liberal citizenship without losing what is best in liberal politics, is the possibility of a "cold patriotism" centering on political and constitutional traditions, as opposed to the "hot" patriotisms of national, religious, ethnic, and class filiation. Dahrendorf notes that ideas of this kind are the subject of some recent work by Habermas, but he doubts that a philosopher's patriotism can solve the problem: either it will make demands on citizenship that involve too much of a departure from liberalism or it will, for those who long for more, leave the heart unmoved. See Jürgen Habermas, "Historical Consciousness and Post-Traditional Identity," in Habermas, *The New Conservatism*, ed. Shierry Weber Nicholsen (Cambridge, Mass.: MIT Press, 1989), pp. 249–267.

34. Scruton, "In Defence of the Nation," p. 319.

35. George Armstrong Kelly, "Who Needs a Theory of Citizenship?" *Daedalus* 108 (1979): 21–36. See, in particular, Kelly's critical judgment on John Dewey: he "believed intensely in the value of citizenship . . . without much respect for its focus" (p. 34). Those faulted by Kelly for disparaging the state include a range of thinkers of diverse persuasions: "welfare liberals like Rawls, minimalists like Hayek and Nozick, conservatives like Oakeshott, and communitarians like Nisbet" (p. 22). For further elaboration, see chapter 4 of Kelly, *Hegel's Retreat from Eleusis*, especially pp. 100–109. Cf. Vincent and Plant, *Philosophy, Politics and Citizenship*, p. 170.

36. According to Jürgen Habermas, the very genesis of the modern state in the sixteenth and seventeenth centuries was defined by the rising need for capital in the mercantilist era: "The modern state was basically a state based on taxation, the bureaucracy of the treasury the true core of its administration." Citizenship as a relationship to the state is therefore from its inception a relationship to a national entity organized for fiscal pur-

to the locus of political authority resembles the situation of one's being hit for yet another never-to-be-repaid handout by a sponging distant relation. Nietzsche described the state as "the coldest of all cold monsters";[37] this comes unattractively close to how ordinary citizens increasingly experience their relationship to the state. Kelly goes to the heart of the matter when he writes: "If it should be asked, 'Who needs a theory of citizenship?' my answer would be, 'The state,' " and then confesses that, however urgent the need, he has no theory of citizenship to make available, "for it cannot be done under present conditions."[38] It goes without saying that before one can come up with solutions for our dilemmas, one must first become aware of what those dilemmas are. But the latter are not likely to make themselves apparent within a liberal theoretical framework and liberal categories that render thinking about citizenship well-nigh unintelligible.

One writer on citizenship correctly describes the development of citizenship in modern capitalist societies as governed by a steady movement from the particular and ascriptive to the universal and abstract, conceived according to the image of a series of outwardly expanding concentric circles; he then lets himself be carried by the implacable logic of this development to embrace the notion of extending civic privileges to encompass the "citizenship" of infants and fetuses, of insects and bacteria, and even of plants and rocks.[39]

---

poses. Habermas, *The Structural Transformation of the Public Sphere*, trans. Thomas Burger (Cambridge, Mass.: MIT Press, 1989), p. 17. Cf. Max Weber, *General Economic History*, trans. Frank H. Knight (New Brunswick, N.J.: Transaction Books, 1984), p. 337.

37. *Thus Spoke Zarathustra*, first part: "On the New Idol."

38. Kelly, "Who Needs a Theory of Citizenship?" p. 35. It should be noted that Kelly's argument is based on a distinction that he develops, not relevant for my purposes, between "the normative state" and "the empirical state." Kelly appears to want the majesty of the state, but without its familiar day-to-day functions: the empirical state in the twentieth century has exhibited a growing proclivity to be "telocratic" (purpose governed), whereas the normative state is obliged to be "nomocratic" (rule governed). The crux of Kelly's analysis seems to be that "the crisis of citizenship" (p. 30) is mainly to be traced to this discrepancy between what the state ought to be (a dispenser of justice) and what it has largely become (a dispenser of bureaucratic favors).

39. Bryan S. Turner, *Citizenship and Capitalism* (London: Allen & Unwin, 1986), pp. 92–105. For a rebuttal of Turner on this point, see J. M. Barbalet,

While some readers may dismiss this vision of universal citizenship as merely perverse, it helps, I think, to illustrate the incoherence of the underlying assumptions of much modern thinking about citizenship. In fact this infinite extension of the scope of citizenship is the natural outcome of the liberal conception (pursued to its conclusion by some contemporary socialists and social democrats) that the decisive problem of citizenship is the elimination of varieties of exclusion from the rights and privileges of membership in civil society, and that therefore a theory of citizenship can proceed in abstraction from questions of the substance of civic relationships.[40] This can be illustrated by theoretical debates about immigration (the liberal question of citizenship par excellence). In "Aliens and Citizens,"[41] Joseph Carens challenges Michael Walzer's argument that, except in special cases, the admission of outsiders to citizenship should be at the discretion of the existing political community.[42] However, both Carens and Walzer, at least in this context, are in agreement in defining the issue of citizenship in terms of the moral principles governing rightful admission to membership. Yet this reflects the liberal conception focusing on questions of formal membership, of inclusion and exclusion, entry and nonentry, as opposed to the classic theories of citizenship of Aristotle and Rousseau devoted to the substantive functions of political membership. The former concerns how one becomes a citizen (what entry requirements must be met); the latter, what one does as a citi-

---

Citizenship: Rights, Struggle and Class Inequality (Milton Keynes: Open University Press, 1988), p. 18.

40. As George F. Will rightly says, "it is a question how much the density of a society can be thinned before the idea of citizenship becomes too attenuated to hold meaning." *Statecraft as Soulcraft* (New York: Simon & Schuster, 1983), p. 55.

41. Carens, "Aliens and Citizens," pp. 264–270.

42. Michael Walzer, *Spheres of Justice* (New York: Basic Books, 1983), pp. 31–63. As Carens rightly argues in an unpublished essay entitled "Migration, Morality, and the Nation State," the theoretical warrant for closure cannot be, as it is for Walzer in chapter 2 of *Spheres of Justice*, simply that that is what is willed by the community that excludes would-be citizens; rather, it must rest upon the substance of what is worth preserving in the way of life that is under threat from outsiders. Though Walzer's conclusions in this context are moderately illiberal, his unwillingness to base them on judgments of substance is eminently liberal.

zen.[43] According to the liberal conception, once one has secured formal entry into the political community, one may be a citizen in good standing and yet do absolutely nothing after having attained to membership: not vote, not participate in jury service, not read newspapers or keep oneself informed politically. Even conformity to the laws does not count toward citizenship, since breaking the laws does not deprive one of citizenship in this formal sense. It is just this sort of nonactive membership that would be intolerable from the point of view of an Aristotelian or Rousseauean (or even Millian) account.[44] The most that a liberal theory of citizenship can envisage is a more extensive civic membership, whereas what is needed is theoretical reflection, in the tradition of the classic theories, on possibilities of a more intensive civic experience. The paradox of liberal citizenship is that while it limits the question of citizenship to formal considerations of inclusion and exclusion (*who* is a citizen), it offers the barest resources, theoretical or practical, for answering this very question. Therefore, finding such an answer to the question set by the problem of liberal citizenship itself requires that we shift to another way of setting the problem of citizenship (*what* is a citizen).[45]

Canadian Prime Minister Mulroney, in the quotation that heads this section, feels called upon to affirm the pricelessness of citizenship in his polity precisely because those with whom he must negotiate the terms of continued federation insist upon putting a price tag on this citizenship (dollars for oil in the case of Albertans; dollars

43. For an illuminating presentation of the Aristotle-Rousseau tradition of what Richard Flathman calls "high citizenship," and a critical probing of that tradition as well as of the opposing "low citizenship" tradition of Hobbes and Oakeshott, see "Citizenship and Authority: A Chastened View of Citizenship," in Richard E. Flathman, *Toward a Liberalism* (Ithaca, N.Y.: Cornell University Press, 1989), pp. 65–108.

44. The Australians at least try to incorporate a minimum condition of more active citizenship with mandatory voting requirements. To be sure, an exceptional democracy like Israel goes much further with a very heavy dose of compulsory military service; and military service is included as a component of citizenship to a lesser extent in the case of certain other liberal democracies.

45. For a similar distinction between the "who" and the "what" of citizenship, see Morris Janowitz, *The Reconstruction of Patriotism* (Chicago: University of Chicago Press, 1983), p. 4.

for fish in the case of Newfoundlanders). Actually, one wonders how many of Mulroney's fellow citizens would share his conviction that the status of being a citizen has a worth that is beyond price and beyond calculation. A recent opinion poll in Mulroney's home province of Quebec is very interesting from the point of view of a theory of citizenship. A mere 38 percent of Quebeckers (French and English) define their political identity primarily in terms of Canada; given a chance to reaffirm or repudiate their citizenship in another referendum, a bare majority of 51 percent would choose to remain full members of the Canadian political community. (Both of these figures would obviously be substantially lower if only francophone Quebeckers had been polled.) Yet "a strong majority would refuse to pay more taxes to get an independent state."[46] Contemporary citizenship, it seems, judging at least by those surveyed in this poll, is like membership in a club for which one has little or no enthusiasm; but equally, one has no wish to exchange it for membership in an alternative club if the latter involves paying a new set of membership fees.

MODERN QUANDARIES

> On the whole, our present situation more or less resembles that of a party of absolutely ignorant travellers who find themselves in a motor-car launched at full speed and driverless across broken country.
>
> Simone Weil,
> *Oppression and Liberty*

The theme of citizenship has been at the heart of the tradition of Western political thought. Many of the classic texts of theory in the West have been in effect treatises on citizenship: book 3 of Aristotle's *Politics*, Rousseau's *Social Contract*, Hegel's *Philosophy of Right*, and the writings of Tocqueville and John Stuart Mill. I think it is fair to say that the late twentieth century has yet to produce a work approaching these masterpieces of the tradition, and that a global theory of citizenship remains one of the leading desiderata of con-

---

46. "For Quebeckers, the Ties That Bind Seem to Be Mainly Economic," Toronto *Globe and Mail*, 14 April 1990, p. D2. Details of the poll, conducted by Sorécom, can be found in *L'Actualité*, 1 May 1990, pp. 7–13.

temporary social theory.[47] However, before we allow ourselves to indulge hopes for a full-blown treatise on citizenship in the manner of the traditional classics, we should, more modestly, at least attempt to survey the problems and perplexities in the character of modern social and political life that impede the writing of such a treatise.

If the modern experience of citizenship is largely incoherent, liberal theory, as we glimpsed in the preceding two sections, tends to reflect this incoherence rather than help to resolve it. Needless to say, this is not an incapacity unique to liberals. As Sheldon Wolin points out: "The democratic citizen does not appear in any substantial form in the writings of Barry Commoner, the titular leader of the Citizens' Party, or Michael Harrington, the theoretician of Democratic Socialists of America. Most Marxists are interested in the 'masses' or the workers, but they dismiss citizenship as a bourgeois conceit, formal and empty."[48] At the opposite end of the political spectrum, in Canada a pressure group calling itself the National Citizens' Coalition actually devotes its energies to mobilizing opinion against what are thought to be excessive public responsibilities of the state, and thus effectively campaigning against citizenship on behalf of "individual liberty." In the nineteenth century, social critics like Tocqueville and Mill argued powerfully for the central human worth of political citizenship, and they spelled out the social and cultural requisites of such an experience of citizenship.[49] The complexities and traumas of life in the twentieth century have not rendered less urgent this case for citizenship. Yet our understand-

---

47. That this theoretical desideratum has a political salience as well is expressed in the following lament uttered by a British journalist in 1988: "Something is rotten in the state of Britain, and all the parties know it. . . . The buzz-word emerging as the salve for this disease is something called citizenship. . . . Somewhere out there is an immense unsatisfied demand for it to mean something." Hugo Young, quoted in Derek Heater, *Citizenship: The Civic Ideal in World History, Politics and Education* (London: Longman, 1990), p. 293.

48. Sheldon S. Wolin, "What Revolutionary Action Means Today," *Democracy* 2, no. 4 (Fall 1982): 18.

49. The Mill referred to here is the Mill of *Considerations on Representative Government* and the reviewer of Tocqueville's *Democracy in America*. Of the Mill of *On Liberty* and *Utilitarianism*, a rather different judgment might be made.

ing of what citizenship is, and our sense of its place within our life, is today terribly unfocused. Few if any social critics speak to our current discontents with the power or authority of a Tocqueville or Mill. Citizenship rings hollow within the context of our established political vocabulary, failing to draw forth resonances of an older idiom of politics.

There was no "problem of citizenship" when Aristotle formulated his famous definition of citizenship in book 3, chapter 1, of the *Politics*.[50] The citizen is "a man who shares in the administration of justice and in the holding of office," or one who "enjoys the right of sharing in deliberative or judicial office," that is, one who performs the "function of deliberating and judging." Here Aristotle merely articulates in a theoretically satisfying way the reality of the polis as it would have been unreflectively conceived by anyone who exercised the responsibilities or fulfilled the duties of citizenship.[51] Today, however, it is otherwise. Citizenship *is* a problem to be pondered rather than a reality to be described. Indeed, where amidst our multiple identities as clients of the state, as constituents of various pressure groups, or merely as privatized consumers can we locate anything that we may characterize as pertaining specifically to the status of citizen?[52] To be sure, we can cite the case of jury duty, or even the periodic ritual of voting.[53] But is there really

50. The phrase "the problem of citizenship" comes from Michael Walzer's essay of that title in *Obligations: Essays on Disobedience, War, and Citizenship* (New York: Simon & Schuster, 1970).

51. This is not to deny that Aristotle might at the same time have known, by the time he wrote the *Politics*, that the understanding of citizenship of which he was the spokesman had already had its day. As M. I. Finley notes, "Aristotle and the classical *polis* died at about the same time. When his contemporary Diogenes said, 'I am a cosmopolites [citizen of the universe],' he was proclaiming that citizenship had become a meaningless concept." *The Ancient Greeks* (New York: Viking Press, 1970), p. 113.

52. Cf. Barber, *Strong Democracy*, p. 221: "The very term *constituent* has been transmogrified from a noble word signifying constitutional author into a term for voter and thence into an almost derisive synonym for *client*—for the individual whom representatives must please and pacify in order to retain their offices."

53. For a good statement of the liberal case that voting is not to be so easily dismissed as constitutive of modern citizenship, see Judith Shklar, "American Citizenship: The Quest for Inclusion," in *Tanner Lectures*, vol. 11, ed. Peterson, pp. 387–413.

anything less episodic in our experience of political life that can give substance to modern citizenship? Is it even meaningful for us to invoke this classical notion in a time of highly attenuated public involvement, where the imperatives of private consumption overwhelm the satisfactions of collective responsibility, and where the complexities of modern life tend to defeat the possibility of a privileged political identity that stands out from the fragmented plurality of social roles?

If citizenship is associated with a stable sense of principles of coherence within a society and a firm sense of one's place within the structures of social order that confer such coherence, it does not require high theoretical acumen to detect a crisis of citizenship in Western societies. We all feel ourselves to be more and more at the mercy of large and impersonal bureaucracies, subject to technological forces beyond our comprehension, driven hither and thither by global economic conditions that appear increasingly inscrutable. Unemployment and inflation, like two imperious bullies, take their turns in tormenting us. At the same time, modern societies are today prone to a variety of social dislocations: a serious and pervasive crisis of the family; a profound realignment of gender roles; major convulsions in the distribution of work and leisure; a substantial intellectual challenge to and political assault upon the modern welfare state; a devaluation of standards of general cultural and intellectual life that begins to resemble a plunge into the abyss; and a detachment from political involvements and institutions bearing political authority. It would be reassuring, but a false reassurance, if we could at least pin the blame for all of this on one large villain, such as capitalism or the permissive society. The bottom line, from the point of view of citizenship, is that these conditions make it hard to sustain any real sense of efficacy or to continue to draw a sense of worth from political membership. Traditionally, political philosophy has sought to discipline and focus our reflection in such moments of confusion and uncertainty. What resources can our traditions of political reflection make available amid our present perplexities?

Going back to Aristotle's classic statement in the *Ethics* and *Politics*, political membership has been considered to be, not a partial role or discrete set of activities, but the most encompassing and comprehensive status within human life. Politics was taken to be what Aristotle termed the architectonic science: that which organized all less inclusive activities into a meaningful whole.[54] It followed that the status of citizen did not constitute one role among others, but rather was that privileged identity that served to integrate and make sense of a person's other roles in society and that thereby defined what it was to be fully human.[55] This classical sense of politics, which is easily assumed to be impossible in a modern setting, was briefly reborn in the public spirit of student demonstrators in Tienanmen Square, firing the moral imagination of spectators in the West. Relative to this ancient conception, it is not easy to imagine what day-to-day citizenship could mean in a context where the civic functions of deliberating and judging are largely the monopoly of politicians and bureaucrats. We are left not with the definition of a concept but merely with the statement of a puzzle.

John Dunn characterizes the dilemma of citizenship quite sharply in his observation of "the increasingly alienated vision of the nature of human societies and politics which has developed over the last two and a half centuries": "If the entire field of political and social relations surrounding an individual agent is taken as given, and his or her potential contribution to politics is then assessed in purely instrumental terms, virtually all political action will appear as necessarily futile; and the balance between comparatively certain cost and highly uncertain gain will become prohibitively discouraging to political agency."[56] As the sense of efficacy shrinks, so too do the bonds of civic allegiance to the political community. In the early nineteenth century it was still possible for Hegel to conceptualize the state as a substantive moral community, express-

54. The fact that we today deny that politics is an architectonic science, and deny that the idea of an architectonic science makes sense, does not prove that we don't have one, as I try to argue in the last section of this chapter. The architectonic science of our society is economics as a science of production bereft of a telos. In Aristotelian terms, this is as if the architect were subject to the sovereign authority of the bricklayer; as if the latter, convinced that bricklaying is an end in itself, obliged the former to design a set of plans for bricks to be laid upon bricks right up to the heavens.

55. On citizenship as a role among other roles, see Barber, *Strong Democracy*, pp. 220–221, 228–229.

56. John Dunn, *Rethinking Modern Political Theory* (Cambridge: Cambridge University Press, 1985), p. 38.

ing and enveloping the cultural and historical identity of its members—as a locus for collective self-consciousness. For us today, near the end of a century characterized in significant measure by experiences of moral and political estrangement in the citizen's relation to bureaucracy and the state, it is difficult to credit or recapture this grand vision of the moral authority of the state. Perhaps more compelling for us are the insights of Rousseau in the eighteenth century concerning the overpowering obstacles to the experience of a genuine *Sittlichkeit* in the modern state.

The barriers to effective citizenship are many. One basic problem may be formulated as follows. Much of what most profoundly affects the destinies of human beings today far surpasses the competence of individual states, however gigantic: global degradation of the environment, the planetary scale of economic activity, the power of multinational corporations, issues of hemispheric redistribution between the affluent and the starving halves of the Earth, and so on. States as we know them are scarcely equal to such challenges, let alone political communities closer in scale to the ancient polis. Conversely, demands for democratization and popular participation would necessarily mandate the shifting of responsibilities for political deliberation and decision to the level of local assemblies or even neighborhood councils. One suspects that the kind of deliberative bodies that would make possible a sense of meaningful participation could tackle issues of only a trivial nature, while those capable of dealing with the truly fateful issues of our time would inescapably be located at a level utterly remote from the common citizen. Present political realities seem to require the realization of something like the ancient Stoic image of a *cosmopolis*, a universal polis, for a citizenship that would be neither intangible nor pointless. (Nicely symbolic of our predicament is the question of a political response to the AIDS menace: our plagues today all seem to be global plagues.) The impossibility of this Stoic vision hardly needs utterance.[57]

Another major stumbling block is that the typical political debates of today are so technically specialized (budgets, weapons sys-

---

57. Cf. Michael Walzer, "The Moral Standing of States: A Response to Four Critics," *Philosophy & Public Affairs* 9, no. 3 (Spring 1980): 227–228.

tems, coordination of economic and technological growth, management of energy demands without uncontrollable deterioration of the environment, centralized command of the total resources of the society, etc.) that it is difficult to imagine how the ordinary nonexpert citizen could hope to contribute at all.[58] Perhaps the centuries-old ideal of meaningful citizenship, dating back to the polis, is now simply outdated.[59] The local concerns and forms of competence, relations of community and sentiments of membership, of the popular citizenry are largely, and increasingly, an irrelevancy to the reality of the modern state; the state itself is not yet an irrelevancy, but much in the historical evolution of the present-day world is tending in this direction.[60] These challenges to the idea of citizenship in a modern republic are merely the most obvious ones.

Where do we look for solutions? One possibility would be to trace the quandaries of contemporary citizenship back to the term itself. The Latin-derived words *citizen* and *citizenship*—like the Greek-derived words *politics* and *political*—refer back inextricably to *local* realities: the city, the polis.[61] Obviously, these original connotations have been all but effaced, and perhaps therein lies the root of our dilemma. Thus some theorists have proposed a return to the *city* as the only meaningful locus of citizenship.[62] But as I

58. For a helpful account of these problems as they have figured in the writings of Robert Dahl, see H. D. Forbes, "Dahl, Democracy, and Technology," in *Democratic Theory and Technological Society*, ed. R. B. Day, R. Beiner, and J. Masciulli (Armonk, N.Y.: M. E. Sharpe, 1988), pp. 227–247. See also my commentary in the introduction to the same volume, pp. ix–xii.

59. Such is the view of, for example, Henry Kariel in "Beginning at the End of Democratic Theory," in *Democratic Theory and Practice*, ed. Graeme Duncan (Cambridge: Cambridge University Press, 1983), pp. 251–262; and also John Dunn in chapter 1 of *Western Political Theory in the Face of the Future* (Cambridge: Cambridge University Press, 1979), pp. 1–27.

60. For a very measured response to such anxieties about the looming obsolescence of the existing nation-state, and hence of national citizenship, see Dahl, *Democracy and Its Critics*, pp. 318–321.

61. For discussion, see Nancy L. Schwartz, "Communitarian Citizenship: Marx and Weber on the City," *Polity* 17, no. 3 (Spring 1985): 530–548, especially pp. 531–532. As Schwartz notes on p. 531 n. 2, *city* and *citizen* share the same etymological root.

62. See, for example, Robert A. Dahl, "The City in the Future of Democracy," *American Political Science Review* 61, no. 4 (December 1967): 953–970.

have noted above, it seems fanciful to think that town-hall democracy will prove equal to our political needs in a world where the most pressing political crises have to do with war and peace, depletion of global resources, the imperial power of megacorporations, and so on. Another version of the same line of thought proposes that we seek out forms of quasi citizenship within civil society that will offer alternatives to state-oriented citizenship. The pluralist route to a theory of citizenship plays down the importance of a direct relationship to the state and highlights the relationship to substate forms of community. At the end of his book *The Twilight of Authority*, Robert Nisbet offers a nice encapsulation of "the view that citizenship must be rooted in the groups and communities within which human beings actually live":[63]

> Every voting study has shown us that the impulse to participate in politics, to the degree that it exists at all, is closely dependent *not* upon primarily political values and objectives but upon economic, social, and cultural ones. If there is to be a citizenship in the useful and creative sense of that word, it must have its footings in the groups, associations, and localities in which we actually spend our lives—not in the abstract and now bankrupt idea of *patrie*, as conceived by the Jacobins and their descendents.[64]

Nisbet distinguishes two main traditions of thought about citizenship in the West: one, which he associates with Plato, Hobbes, and Rousseau, that extinguishes all loyalties other than that to the state in the interests of the state; the other, identified with Hegel, Tocqueville, Burckhardt, Kropotkin, and above all Burke, situates

63. Robert Nisbet, *The Twilight of Authority* (London: Heinemann, 1976), pp. 286–287. As George Kateb notes, in recent decades the Left has engendered its own versions of Nisbet's vision of pluralist citizenship. "Comments," in *Participation in Politics*, NOMOS 16, ed. J. Roland Pennock and J. W. Chapman (New York: Lieber-Atheron, 1975), pp. 89–97. Commenting on the student movement of the sixties, Kateb writes: "The aim is to rehabilitate the idea of citizenship and to extend the practice of citizenship into as many areas of life as possible; from the original locus of citizenship, i.e., public affairs, to private institutions and associations and activities of almost every sort" (p. 91). Needless to say, the Left anarchist tradition has always gone in this direction (as Nisbet's invocation of Kropotkin attests).

64. Nisbet, *Twilight of Authority*, pp. 285–286. This theme of local versus national citizenship is pursued also in Nisbet's "Citizenship: Two Traditions," *Social Research* 41, no. 4 (Winter 1974): 612–637.

citizenship in the plural loyalties of ethnicity, localism, regionalism, religion, and kinship. However, the Hegelian-Tocquevillean solution of intermediary citizenship breaks down (as it does, arguably, in the prevailing political order) if the intermediate associations, instead of conducting us toward forms of political loyalty at a higher level, function merely to channel demands made on the state by self-seeking social groups. This is what we know today as interest-group politics. Rather than furnishing an education in citizenship, it offers an education in anticitizenship. Rather than serving to alleviate the problem of cultivating allegiance to the state under modern conditions (as it does on the Burke-Hegel-Tocqueville model), it serves to exacerbate that very problem. All individuals know what they want from the state, all have their wish-lists, all are taught and encouraged by the groups and associations to which they belong to dwell on these insistent demands; but no one knows why they might wish to belong to a larger political community, of which state authority is the most visible incarnation. In the words of George Armstrong Kelly, "there is a darker side to pluralist citizenship."[65]

The intuition that I am trying to explore in this chapter is that participation in political community is a real human good. But if such participation is to be meaningful, it must be upheld by a source of enduring commitment. What is to sustain this commitment? Liberalism, in principle, finds it theoretically impossible to locate a substantive basis for this commitment. Modernity *has* offered, in the last two centuries, an answer to this puzzle about citizenship, but I must confess that this answer—nationalism—makes me feel extremely uncomfortable. It is the strength of liberalism that it articulates what is unattractive about this modern answer to the puzzle of citizenship. It is even more embarassing to confess that I have no alternative answer to suggest. My contribution, I hope, is to clarify that the puzzle is indeed a puzzle, whereas the liberal will tend to assume that there is really nothing much to worry about here.

Other quandaries are yet to be addressed. Many would hold that the ideal of equal citizenship will necessarily remain hollow until it

---

65. Kelly, "Who Needs a Theory of Citizenship?" p. 33.

can be set upon the foundation of fully egalitarian gender relation-ships—in the household and in the sphere of work as much as in the political arena. I do not deny the power of this challenge to the civic status quo, but it raises a host of questions that still await examination: Does equal citizenship presuppose a transcendence of gender? Does the very distinction between *citoyen* and *citoyenne* undermine the republican ideal? *Can* citizenship be genderless? These questions will appear irrelevant to some feminists who, in order to enlarge the participation of women in the civic arena, will put more rather than less emphasis on gender differences. How-ever, to the extent that feminism begins to take on the features of yet another of modern society's group egoisms (a kind of gender nationalism), it raises in another guise the same kinds of quandaries of pluralism dealt with elsewhere in this section. Other theorists of citizenship will contend that the chief obstruction to effective citizenship lies in the deep cleavages of class in liberal societies, and that a redemption of the ideal of citizenship can consist only in a transcendence of class division.[66] This is, no doubt, a promising and indeed urgent path of political aspiration. For instance, the spectacle of class-segregated pubs in England ("lounge bars" and "public bars"—a form of class apartheid) is, no less than racially segregated facilities in other benighted parts of the world, a noto-rious affront to the very idea of common citizenship. But what would a class-transcendent social membership actually look like? Were it possible, would we want a universal middle class? Un-speakable! A universal working class? Even worse. A universal aris-tocracy? Self-evidently impossible. (I think that universal aristoc-racy is what socialism means for many socialists, and that it is what communism probably meant for Marx.) But what would it mean to conceive a classless society, where the members were associated with no class in particular? I know of no form of political reflection, Marxist or non-Marxist, that begins to address this perplexing di-lemma.

66. The classic theorist of citizenship and class is of course T. H. Mar-shall. Marshall's legacy for contemporary theories of citizenship is reexam-ined in Turner, *Citizenship and Capitalism*, and Barbalet, *Citizenship*. See also David Held, "Citizenship and Autonomy," in Held, *Political Theory and the Modern State* (Stanford: Stanford University Press, 1989), pp. 189–213.

In sum, I cannot pretend to have the answers to these and other quandaries of modern citizenship. But one needn't see, in all of this, grounds for despair—not, at least, if one takes one's bearings by the great tradition of theory from Plato to Rousseau to Marx to Nietzsche, whose leading strength consists more in the critical location of ills than in the supplying of nostrums. Ultimately, whether these quandaries turn out to be impassable or not may depend much more upon the practical imagination of actual political agents than upon the contrivances of theorists. I shall return to this question in the epilogue.

SPIRITUAL IMPASSE

> I do not have to tell you, my dear Mill, that the greatest malady that threatens a people organized as we are is the gradual softening of mores, the abasement of the mind, the mediocrity of tastes; that is where the great dangers of the future lie.
>
> Alexis de Tocqueville,
> letter to John Stuart Mill, 1841

> A serious threat is hovering over European culture. . . . The threat emanates from an onslaught of "mass culture" from across the Atlantic. We understand pretty well the concern of West European intellectuals. Indeed one can only wonder that a deep, profoundly intelligent and inherently humane European culture is retreating to the background before the primitive revelry of violence and pornography and the flood of cheap feelings and low thoughts.
>
> Mikhail Gorbachev,
> *Perestroika*, 1987

In the previous section we scanned a number of deep quandaries at the social and political level, in the face of which the creation of a less enervated citizenship looms as an immense puzzle. However, it may be that these quandaries are as nothing compared with the phenomenon of cultural and spiritual torpor that blocks richer possibilities of political membership in liberal societies. According to a recent poll, 39 percent of the Canadian public believes in horoscopes.[67] What hope is there for an educated citizenry if four out

---

67. *Toronto Star*, 27 June 1987, p. A4.

of ten members of an advanced, Western liberal democracy believe in astrology?

It is impossible to reflect on citizenship with any seriousness without attending to the cultural dimension. This raises, inescapably, questions of political and cultural education, modes of socialization, as well as forms of economic practice that shape, and are shaped by, a dominant social and political culture. We have to be socialized to citizenship. Either we inhabit a culture that stimulates political energies and enlivens political imagination or we inhabit one that stifles and dulls the cultural resources that nourish citizenship. In order to participate in civic life one must be fitted for it, and this in turn presupposes a certain level of public culture. The contemporary "citizen" is unfitted for citizenship, not merely because of deficiencies in the political system, but because the nature of modern modes of consumption thoroughly privatizes individuals and renders them incapable of experiencing anything genuinely public.

Political citizenship depends on a shared culture and a sense of rootedness.[68] The point of this emphasis on a common culture is surely not to intellectualize politics. As Christopher Lasch remarks in reply to the charge that his criticism of mass culture aims at a universal intelligentsia: "I can't imagine a less attractive prospect than a society made up of intellectuals."[69] The political problem with mass culture is not that it renders people uncultured or philistine, but that it privatizes and deracinates them, that is, undermines the cultural conditions of citizenship.[70] Henry Fairlie, in a wonderful essay entitled "The Decline of Oratory," marvels at the enthusiasm with which long political speeches could be relished by large popular audiences in the small towns of mid-nineteenth-century America (his example is the Lincoln-Douglas debates of 1858), as

68. An argument along these lines is spelled out in Wilson Carey McWilliams, "Democracy and the Citizen: Community, Dignity, and the Crisis of Contemporary Politics in America," in *How Democratic Is the Constitution?* ed. Robert A. Goldwin and William A. Schambra (Washington: American Enterprise Institute, 1980), pp. 79–101.

69. Christopher Lasch, "Popular Culture and the Illusion of Choice," *Democracy* 2, no. 2 (April 1982): 88.

70. See Christopher Lasch, "Mass Culture Reconsidered," *Democracy* 1, no. 4 (October 1981): 7–22.

compared with the boredom induced by contemporary speechmaking.[71] Walt Whitman's dictum, "To have great poets there must be great audiences, too," applies no less to politics, and it takes a special kind of audience to elicit "the flame of great oratory."[72] Part of Fairlie's diagnosis of this decline is "that there are almost no common allusions that a politician can make":

> As recently as a few decades ago, a politician could refer to Job or even to Balaam's ass and be confident that his audience would understand the reference. It made a great difference when even in semi-literate families everyone heard the Old Testament read every Sunday, and when in the homes of the humblest there were likely to be copies of the Bible and of Shakespeare. The constituents of the great English radical, John Bright, were cotton spinners and weavers in the mill town of Rochdale. When they asked why he had refused office, he answered with the story of the Shunammite woman who, when Elisha said, "Shall I do aught for thee with the king?" replied, "I dwell among my own people." Cotton workers who left school at the age of 8 did not need the allusion explained to them.[73]

However urgent the need for citizenship, all the ingenuity of political scientists like Barber and Dahl,[74] with their designs for the fabrication of new modes of democracy, will be to no avail; for citizenship, dependent on the ethical and spiritual resources of a political community, cannot be manufactured. Exposed by the history of the modern West to the triple solvent of Protestantism, capitalism, and the liberal ethos, it is not to be wondered at that our cultural resources for the cultivation of citizenship are slender.

Just as we can (and must) be socialized to the exercise of citizenship, so we can (and in our circumstances inevitably are) socialized to its nonexercise. The ethos of a liberal civilization in this regard is captured well by Robert Dahl when he writes, commenting on industrial democracy but with application to democratic citizenship

71. Henry Fairlie, "The Decline of Oratory," *New Republic*, 28 May 1984, pp. 15–19.

72. Ibid., p. 18. The line from Whitman is quoted from Todd Gitlin, "New Video Technology: Pluralism or Banality," *Democracy* 1, no. 4 (October 1981): 60.

73. Fairlie, "Decline of Oratory," p. 17. The story of the Shunammite woman is in 2 Kings 4: 13.

74. See note 28 above.

generally, that "affluent American workers, like affluent workers in many other advanced countries and the middle class everywhere, tend to be consumption-oriented, privatistic, and family-centered. This orientation has little place for a passionate aspiration toward effective citizenship in the enterprise (or perhaps even in the state!)"[75] It has been a staple of the republican tradition, from Aristotle to Machiavelli to Rousseau, that a life of free self-government presupposes a certain political economy—in particular, modes of ascetic discipline and self-restraint. The assumption was that there must be a "political economy of freedom," to use a phrase of Oakeshott's that he employed in a sense antithetical to the one intended here.[76] But the economic practices of contemporary societies seem to rule out the very possibility of restraint of wants and desires in the interest of political liberty. If, as the classic theorists all assumed, endless desire-fulfillment is incompatible with the sober demands of citizenship, then it would appear that for us, infinite consumption is in and citizenship is out.

What I would call the pure liberal doctrine of citizenship has received a provocative recent statement in a *Time* essay by Charles Krauthammer:

> [The current] triumph of apolitical bourgeois democracy has been a source of dismay to some. They pine for the heroic age when great ideologies clashed and the life of nations turned on a vote in Congress. On the contrary. I couldn't be happier that the political century is over, and that all that's left is to shuffle cards on the cruise ship. . . . A few weeks ago, a producer from U.S. public television came to ask my advice about planning coverage for the 1992 elections. Toward the end, she raised a special problem: how to get young adults interested in political coverage. I offered the opinion

75. Robert Dahl, "Power to the Workers?" *New York Review of Books*, 19 November 1970, p. 22.

76. Michael Oakeshott, *Rationalism in Politics and Other Essays* (London: Methuen, 1962), pp. 37–58. For an example of analysis of the political economy of freedom in *my* sense (or what one might also call "moral economy"), see Emile Durkheim, *Professional Ethics and Civic Morals*, trans. Cornelia Brookfield (London: Routledge & Kegan Paul, 1957), pp. 1–41, 71–72. Oakeshott's idea is that a free society is one that minimizes the regulation of economic life; Durkheim's idea is that regulation of economic relationships can be a good thing if it helps to build up agencies of moral solidarity within the society.

that 19-year-olds who sit in front of a television watching politics could use professional help. At that age they should be playing ball and looking for a date. They'll have time enough at my age to worry about the mortgage and choosing a candidate on the basis of his views on monetary policy. To say that, of course, is to violate current League of Women Voters standards of good citizenship. Let others struggle valiantly to raise the political awareness of all citizens. Let them rage against the tides of indifference. They will fail, and when they do, relax. Remember that indifference to politics leaves all the more room for the things that really count: science, art, religion, family, play.[77]

Relative to this statement on behalf of "apolitical bourgeois democracy," John Stuart Mill would certainly have to be counted as an intrepid civic republican! Now obviously, few self-professed liberals would express themselves as bluntly as Krauthammer does here, nor would many of them actually share his disparaging view of political participation; but the more important point is that the pure liberal doctrine of citizenship (or anticitizenship) aptly expresses the realities of a liberal society.

What exactly is wrong with the pure liberal theory? Isn't it true that "there are many other forms of human good" besides politics?[78] Isn't it true that we have a lot else to worry about (and a lot else to get satisfaction from) than budgets and defense policies and welfare reform? In any case, why should the relationship to the political sphere be anything other than an instrumental one? I am not confident that I can answer these objections adequately, but the beginning of an answer can be sought by reflecting on the unprecedented responsibilities borne by politics in our day. The stakes are of an entirely novel scale. In the words of John Dunn:

> At a time when the leaders of the most powerful nations on earth may at any moment find themselves with at best a few minutes in which to decide whether or not to unleash thermonuclear war, it is hardly open to rational dispute that human beings have a more urgent and a more baffling need to grasp what prudence really is than they have ever had before. Nor is it readily disputable that the political project of reconstructing the states and societies to which we

77. Charles Krauthammer, "In Praise of Low Voter Turnout," *Time*, 21 May 1990, p. 82.
78. Rawls, *Theory of Justice*, p. 228.

belong to embody such prudence is apocalyptically more complex and formidable than it must have looked to a would-be Legislator in the Greece of the fourth century B.C. or in eighteenth-century Geneva.[79]

Citizens in ancient states never had to fear that poor political calculations could obliterate the species, or could contaminate the environment irreversibly for all succeeding generations, or could make the planet uninhabitable for billions of human beings. Today, these things are necessarily in the balance, and they utterly transform the toll of noncitizenship. So it is not just a case of saying that it would be great for us to be Aristotelian citizens again (or for the first time). It is rather that the alternative to at least minimal citizenship, which is still far beyond what the majority of us can exercise, is that we are effectively excluded from deliberations that will decide not only our own fate but that of our descendants, and perhaps the fate of the species as a whole. Can we really accept that we will be denied a voice in the determination of issues of this magnitude? It is the "apocalyptic potential"[80] of contemporary politics that renders citizenship that is more than formal membership not a privilege but a moral necessity.

As I sought to consider in earlier chapters, what a liberal public culture makes available is a phony individualism and a phony pluralism, and what ultimately prevails is neither the individualism nor the pluralism but merely the phoniness.[81] The outstanding liberals of the nineteenth century were not debarred from raising the kinds of questions I have been broaching, but present-day liberal philosophers seem to have been mysteriously relieved of the anxieties of their forebears. Herein lies, in important measure, the inadequacy of contemporary liberal theory; it offers modes of criticism of

79. Dunn, *Rethinking Modern Political Theory*, p. 11.

80. This is the theme of Hans Jonas's important book *The Imperative of Responsibility: In Search of an Ethics for the Technological Age* (Chicago: University of Chicago Press, 1984). For commentary, see my essay "Ethics and Technology: Hans Jonas' Theory of Responsibility," in *Democratic Theory and Technological Society*, ed. Day, Beiner, and Masciulli, pp. 336–354.

81. For a discussion of how easily it can come to pass that the language of autonomy serves merely to legitimize a culture in which everything is reduced to the lowest common denominator, see Alain Finkelkraut, *La Défaite de la pensée* (Paris: Gallimard, 1987), pp. 149–179.

liberal practice, to be sure, but leaves unjudged, and in principle beyond judgment, much of what most demands criticism. A just society that offered even the most perfect realization of the egalitarian ideals articulated by Rawls and Ackerman could well leave intact some of the most debilitating and demoralizing features of life in a modern society. Social equality by itself can refer to a mode of existence that is either high or low, the equality of Marx's race of aristocrats or the equality of Nietzsche's race of "last men," depending on the conditions of life in which individuals participate equally. This is why the redressing of inequalities cannot on its own lead us to the vision of a way of life that is substantively enriching (which necessarily implies attention to the substance of that way of life, not merely to the fair distribution of its spiritful or spiritless benefits).[82] As Wilson Carey McWilliams writes, "indignity, not inequality, is our real complaint. A great many Americans would forgo material gains if they felt they were listened to or even that their listening mattered." But the problem, as McWilliams sees it, is that "in the mass state, indignity is inherent."[83] This is in no sense a disparagement of egalitarian aspirations. To the contrary, it is an indispensable condition for the effectuation of more promising possibilities of citizenship that Western societies become a great deal more egalitarian than they are presently (as I try to explore in the next chapter). But then equality as such is not the ultimate goal, it is the conduit to a further destination.

Liberalism counsels us to abstain as far as possible from moral judgments (which the liberal identifies with moralistic judgments)

82. This negativism of contemporary liberal theory is a trait shared with certain contemporary versions of neo-Marxism—for example, the later work of Habermas, which has come increasingly to approximate to liberal formalism. A theory focusing on the lifting of constraints upon dialogue and the leveling of asymmetries of power needs to say more about why the postemancipatory society embodies a positive good. Having emancipated ourselves from the countless inequalities that still remain, what precisely will we have emancipated ourselves *for*? This is, of course, a problem that goes back to Marx himself, with his rhapsodizing of contentless freedom; it is, one might say, the mark of Marx's own philosophical liberalism. Cf. Serge-Christophe Kolm, *Le Libéralisme moderne* (Paris: Presses Universitaires de France, 1984), p. 92.

83. McWilliams, "Democracy and the Citizen," p. 100. Cf. p. 99: "Those social critics who suggest that capitalism and private wealth are the root

concerning the chosen ways of life of individuals within society. Yet the very concern to articulate an ideal of citizenship already violates this proscription. Imagine the following alternative to the model citizen: someone hooked on cocaine, committed above all to the satisfying of his or her physical urges (even if this involved no criminal behavior, apart from the purchase of the drug), apathetic as regards public affairs in one's own society and beyond, and indifferent to the plight of other human beings, including those immediately affected by this "lifestyle." From a civic republican perspective, it would be impossible to avoid judging this a defective way to exist. Even if the only one in any way affected by this behavior is the individual himself or herself (though this is virtually unimaginable and probably incoherent), the judgment would have to be the same. The liberal would necessarily see this as an encroachment upon the moral space of the individual agent. Or rather, one is allowed to make *private* judgments about the satisfactoriness of such ways of life, but these can admit neither of theoretical sanction nor public enforcement. Beyond the reactions of personal morality (how we respond to such behavior as private individuals), this is a matter for individuals to work out for themselves. It is their own affair. To this, the republican must answer: If this constitutes moral encroachment upon the prerogatives of the individual, then both at the level of theory and at the level of politics, moral encroachment is the only course of sanity.[84] It would be insane, theoretically and politically, to regard choice of "lifestyles" as a private affair, not a public affair; for if it is not a matter of public concern whether members of a society are good citizens or bad citizens, what *is* of legitimately public concern? If the political community cannot permissibly concern itself with this, what can it concern itself with?

---

of all the ills of American democracy are guilty of making our problems appear less severe than they are."

84. It is the prospect of entailments like these that motivates Richard Flathman's critique of civic republicanism, in "Citizenship and Authority." Flathman's argument is that a more ambitious exercise of citizenship would go hand in hand with a strengthening of political authority, and that this invigorated fusion of citizenship and authority would have deleterious consequences for liberal individuality. One way in which he characterizes this fear is that civil disobedience would be "a logical and a psychological impossibility" in a regime of energetic citizenship (p. 104 n. 44).

One can also picture from other angles, ways in which the minimalist moral vision of liberalism runs afoul of a more demanding ideal of citizenship. Consider the political problem of pornography. The standard liberal response is to say that while one may not approve personally of these practices, female models who make themselves available for such purposes are exercising legitimate rights and prerogatives as "owners of their own bodies" that ought not to be subject to state interference (such as the municipal antipornography ordinances in Minneapolis). One typical way in which the liberal will criticize such state action is by appeal to John Stuart Mill's classic distinction between self-regarding and other-regarding acts. But this distinction assumes that one can differentiate neatly between actions that impinge on others, which can be politically and juridically regulated, and actions that impinge only on oneself, for which state regulation is strictly illegitimate. But do the choices of adult female models to exhibit themselves in pornographic publications affect only themselves? Is it not the case that all women must contend with the consequences arising from the propagation by such publications of demeaning and degrading images of the status of women? If this is so, there may be good grounds, overlooked by the libertarian liberal, for submitting the question of pornography (or even ordinary television advertising, in many cases) to public and not just private deliberation. One might restate this challenge to liberalism in the language of citizenship by saying that women who exercise these career options injure the prospects of common citizenship for the entire class of their fellow women. (Reasoning of this sort no doubt prompted legislators of the state of New York recently to ban the sport of dwarf tossing practiced in certain taverns in that state. That the dwarfs being tossed were consenting adults was not considered decisive; what was decisive was that they were allowing themselves to be degraded, and thereby helping to degrade the status of equal citizenship of fellow dwarfs.) So we see how, by framing problems of political theory in terms of an egalitarian conception of citizenship, often-debated issues within liberal society may be reformulated in nonliberal categories.

Throughout the last two hundred years of our intellectual tradition, grave fears have been expressed of the unavoidable advent of universal mediocrity, leveling, and homogenizing banality in

modern democratic societies—from the last-ditch efforts of Burke
in the eighteenth century to uphold the waning symbols of regal
grandeur in Europe, to the anguished aristocratic pathos of nineteenth-century liberals like Tocqueville and J. S. Mill, to the more
radical cries of warning of Nietzsche, Weber, and Heidegger. It
would require childish naivety to imagine that these concerns do
not pose an immense challenge to any reflection on the possibilities
of an invigorated experience of politics within liberal societies.[85] It
suffices to consider the range of periodicals available in the average
North American corner store, and to ask oneself what percentage
of these contain any significant political or socially critical content
(or what percentage of the general North American periodical read-
ership is presently capable of being moved by such content). The
results of this thought experiment are not encouraging. What one
will encounter are "flesh magazines, tennis and golf magazines,
skiing and surfing magazines, model railroad magazines, needle-
craft magazines, camera magazines, stereo magazines, fitness mag-
azines, car magazines, field and stream magazines, hairdo maga-
zines, romance magazines, horoscope magazines, gun magazines,
stamp and coin magazines, music magazines, upscale city magazines, and celebrity magazines."[86] No one who pursues this reflection can be in very much doubt about what constitutes the liberal
way of life.[87] What scale of moral revolution would be required for

85. For a highly relevant survey of mass culture—relevant, that is, to
its bearing upon possibilities of competent citizenship—see Habermas,
Structural Transformation, section 18.

86. Gitlin, "New Video Technology," pp. 68–69. Gitlin juxtaposes the
fringe of opinion magazines that "address their readers much of the time
as citizens" (*The Nation, The New Republic, Harper's, The Atlantic, Mother
Jones, The New Yorker, National Review, The American Spectator*) to this dominant magazine culture: "depoliticized, indeed anti-political, valuing private goods over public needs. In this culture, the common good is always
being parcelled out into separate pursuits of private happiness." For a
survey of the most widely read periodicals in the United States, see *The
World Almanac and Book of Facts 1990* (New York: Pharos Books, 1989), pp.
363–364. By way of contrast, see the report on Soviet newspaper culture
in Lawrence Martin, "Press Is a Prime Example of Life in the Slow Lane,"
Toronto *Globe and Mail*, 2 March 1987, p. A7.

87. The U.S. Information Agency has recently arranged to have unsold
copies of glossy American magazines shipped every month to Eastern
Europe. A leading publisher involved in the venture observed, with a
theoretical perspicuity that eludes some of the notable political philoso-

the ordinary liberal citizen to be attracted to the kind of cultural and political publications currently being devoured by the newly liberated citizens of Eastern Europe?

We seem to end up in an uncomfortable impasse. According to our argument, it is only by locating some more substantial possibility of political membership that we can hope to avoid a fate described by Nietzsche as "going to pot on egoistic pettiness and squalor, ossification and self-seeking,"[88] or in Burke's words, the fate of being "disconnected into the dust and powder of individuality," becoming "little better than the flies of a summer."[89] On the other hand, a more real relationship to the political world already requires a transcendence of the ungrounded or deracinated character of modern culture. Thus the inescapable vicious circle: a deeper engagement with politics only when freed from our barbaric social culture; a less barbaric culture only when political membership is deepened and enhanced. The exit from this vicious circle is barely imaginable. I doubt that the impasse admits of a theoretical resolution; yet one can conceive it being surmounted by new experiences, new constellations of social solidarity, new modes of life arising with a spontaneity that confounds all the expectations of social scientists. To predict the sources of such spontaneous regenerations of solidarity is certainly not the responsibility of theory. The theorist can, however, say what Rousseau said: that "the inference from what has existed to what is possible is a sound one."[90] So on that basis, we may be assured either that past instances of invigorated citizenship in liberal societies—such as the civil rights movement of the 1960s, itself rooted in the powerful ethos of the black churches—may be resuscitated, or that we may find parallels in our own experience in the West of the possibilities of an enriched practice of citizenship that have been disclosed in the last decade in the dockyards of Gdansk, on Tiananmen Square and Wenceslas

---

phers of our day: "Magazines like *House Beautiful* and *Road and Track* are a reflection of the American way of life and we want to expose that way of life." Quoted in the *Toronto Star*, 5 February 1990, p. A16.

88. Friedrich Nietzsche, *Vom Nützen und Nachteil der Historie*, section 9.

89. Edmund Burke, *Reflections on the Revolution in France*, ed. Conor Cruise O'Brien (Harmondsworth: Penguin, 1969), pp. 194, 193.

90. Jean-Jacques Rousseau, *Du contrat social*, book 3, chap. 12.

Square, and in the streets of Manila and Leipzig. In either case, the specific shape of these possibilities is unforeseeable and therefore beyond the purview of the limited powers of theory.

During 1989 the peoples of Eastern Europe offered a school of citizenship for the West. Prior to the end of the 1980s it would have been hard to imagine just how prescient Hannah Arendt could turn out to be when she wrote a quarter of a century ago: "Whatever the outcome of our present predicaments may be, if we don't perish altogether, it seems more than likely that revolution, in distinction to war, will stay with us into the foreseeable future. Even if we should succeed in changing the physiognomy of this century to the point where it would no longer be a century of wars, it most certainly will remain a century of revolutions."[91] (The bicentennial of the French Revolution was celebrated throughout Eastern Europe, with Polish, Hungarian, Czech, Bulgarian, East German, and Romanian reenactments of the events of 1789.[92]) Of course, in reading the above passage by a leading critic of liberalism anticipating a renewal of the revolutionary tradition in modern politics, in a book meant to challenge what she saw as an impoverished experience of citizenship in American liberalism, we confront a deep irony: that all of the revolutions or attempted revolutions of the late 1980s, in China, Hungary, Poland, East Germany, and Czechoslovakia, were liberal revolutions, revolutions on behalf of bourgeois freedoms. On the other hand, I think it would be perfectly consistent with Arendt's point of view to suggest that the instruction offered by the stunning success of these revolutionary movements has less to do with the moral and political adequacy of prevailing bourgeois liberalism than with the yet to be realized possibilities of enriched citizenship in the liberal societies of the West. In other words, the citizens of China, East Germany, and Czechoslovakia may have more to teach us about political freedom than we have to teach them.

91. Hannah Arendt, *On Revolution* (New York: Viking Press, 1965), p. 8.
92. Following the inauguration of a non-Communist government in Czechoslovakia, Václav Havel told his followers: "Historians will have to analyze this period . . . this peaceful revolution . . . and tell us what happened." One might presume to say that in *On Revolution*, Arendt "explained" these revolutions several decades before they actually happened.

In the Soviet Union, as glasnost gained political momentum, officials announced that it was necessary to suspend live broadcasts of sessions of the Supreme Soviet because so many people watched them that there was a drop in productivity—not something that would pose a threat in any Western democracy! Liberal citizenship, even if its worth is somewhat less than all the oil in Arabia and all the fish in any sea, certainly counts for something. But whether its worth is sufficient to rescue us from the atomizing, deracinating, and "massifying" tendencies of modernity is a question that one trembles to ask.

THE LIBERAL REGIME

> A social contract [must allow for the fact] that society as a whole has no ends or ordering of ends in the sense that associations and individuals do.
>
> John Rawls, article in *American Philosophical Quarterly*, 1977

Leo Strauss has, at least among his followers, popularized "regime" as a translation for the Greek term *politeia*.[93] This retranslation is still rather misleading, since current English usage tends to associate *regime* with a particular government or governing elite (e.g., the Brezhnev regime),[94] but it has at least highlighted the unacceptable narrowness of the usual translation, "constitution." Whatever one may think of other aspects of Strauss's reading of classical texts, I think this introduction of the term *regime* to convey an ancient meaning can help us to draw invaluable lessons from classical philosophy for the understanding of all human societies, including our own liberal society.

---

93. See, for example, Leo Strauss, *Natural Right and History* (Chicago: University of Chicago Press, 1953), pp. 136–138, 193; *What is Political Philosophy?* (Chicago: University of Chicago Press, 1988), pp. 33–34; *The City and Man* (Chicago: University of Chicago Press, 1977), pp. 45–46. Cf. Nathan Tarcov and Thomas L. Pangle, "Epilogue: Leo Strauss and the History of Political Philosophy," in *History of Political Philosophy*, ed. Leo Strauss and Joseph Cropsey, 3d ed. (Chicago: University of Chicago Press, 1987), pp. 925–927, 931–933. Also Claude Lefort, *Democracy and Political Theory*, trans. David Macey (Cambridge: Polity Press, 1988), pp. 2–3.

94. Thus G. A. Kelly takes *regime* to have a narrower, not a broader, signification than *state*. "Who Needs a Theory of Citizenship?" p. 34.

Part of what is entailed by the Platonic-Aristotelian conception of regime (and what Strauss took it to mean) is that all action, in particular all political action, asserts certain claims to truth whose authority either can or cannot be vindicated. All rule by statesmen is meant to be authoritative for everyone within the society. We all live within the horizon of norms and moral expectations imposed by leaders of our society whose example is, again, authoritative. The presumption is that these norms are true, that the way of life we take to be exemplary within our society is a true exemplar—whether, as in ancient Greek society, the exemplary life of the warrior or orator or, as in our society, the exemplary life of the lawyer or software inventor or ambitious entrepreneur. Political arguments in any society, including our own, commonly boil down to who these exemplary types should be. Again, this invariably contains an implicit claim to truth, a claim that this or that exemplar is authoritative for the whole society—that we should all model ourselves upon, or judge ourselves by the standard of, the successful warrior or orator or corporate lawyer or entrepreneur. Every society exists and orders itself as a society by its commitment to one or several of these exemplary types being true. We all live according to the dictate of a set of putative truths, the grounding of which, for Plato at least, requires turning political practice into philosophical practice and turning kings into philosopher-kings.

It hardly needs remarking that this whole idea of authoritative standards of social life is virtually untranslatable into our own modern categories of moral and political life. *We* would say that these people have these values, and those people have those values, and that it would be a mistake (a violation of liberal principles) for either these values or those values to be considered authoritative for the whole society. Within the grip of these liberal categories, it is pretty much impossible to get the talk of moral knowledge off the ground at all. The very notion of knowing virtue, of grasping cognitively a moral reality, is quite bewildering to modern ears. To be sure, we can make sense of the idea of knowledge as the basis for a claim to rule—in the sense of technical knowledge, technical expertise. (This is something like what Francis Bacon in the seventeenth century had in mind when he proclaimed "Knowledge is power.") So we can certainly make sense of the rule of knowers, in the sense of technical experts. But moral knowledge? Our very term *values* implies that these things cannot be known; they depend on individual choices and preferences. They are, by definition, not objects of cognition but objects of volition; not rational, to be apprehended by the knowing intellect, but volitional, products of one's will. Yet there is something to be said for Plato and Aristotle's way of talking about moral and political experience. Let us consider the notion, assumed by all members of a modern society, that no values are authoritative (or no values ought to be) in a liberal society that is faithful to itself. Aren't liberal principles themselves intended to be universally authoritative, and if so, not reducible to mere "values"? Aren't they thought to be true in some basic sense? This was brought out very forcefully in the uproar surrounding the Salman Rushdie affair. To say that Khomeini's death threat against the author of *The Satanic Verses* offends our "liberal values" sounds pathetically weak. Moreover, if someone responds that "Islamic values" are no less legitimate for Muslims than "Western values" are for us, how are we to answer, if not by forsaking the language of values? In fact, even the liberal has to claim ultimately to know a moral reality that is either valid because it is knowable, or nothing—of no political consequence. Politics is itself the realm of competing claims about what is authoritatively true—true not for me or you as individuals, but true for all of us.

And the same goes for the allocation of priorities in a society, or the ranking of practices, or the appointment of roles, as mentioned earlier. For instance, one might consider that Hannah Arendt's arresting presentation in *The Human Condition* of modern society as, quintessentially, a society of laborers or a society of jobholders is an account of the modern regime, of the norm-enforcing ethos of modernity. By a jobholder's society Arendt meant a society in which it is dictated that "whatever we do, we are supposed to do for the sake of 'making a living' "; a society governed by the "trend to level down all serious activities to the status of making a living."[95] As she puts it: "Even presidents, kings, and prime ministers think of their offices in terms of a job necessary for the life of society."[96] Again, it is certainly wrong to conceive liberal society, as it

---

95. Hannah Arendt, *The Human Condition* (Chicago: University of Chicago Press, 1958), pp. 126–127.

96. Ibid., p. 5. What Arendt offers here is simply a book-length elaboration of Rousseau's suggestion, in book 3, chapter 15, of *The Social Contract*,

is often conceived, as merely offering a neutral grid within which individuals can pursue their self-defined activities. Every society is shaped as the society that it is by an implicit ranking of activities, or by the definition of a certain range of activities as paradigmatically worthy of pursuit—or by the canonization of certain activities as supremely human, relative to other activities that are correspondingly stigmatized. This is as true of liberal society as it is of every other society. According to Arendt, what defines a modern society, whether liberal or socialist, is that it tends increasingly to conceive itself as a society of laborers, where the primary energies of human activity are drawn to the collective goal of maximizing the productivity of the society as a whole, maximizing the possibilities of production and consumption. Far from it being obvious that this should be the overriding task of a society, Arendt argues that it is unique to the modern age that this defining goal has the centrality it now has. "The modern age," she writes, "was as intent on excluding political man, that is, man who acts and speaks, from its public realm as antiquity was on excluding *homo faber*."[97] A given society may accord paradigmatic status to the activity of being a warrior, or being a citizen, or being a worshipper of the civic deity; the life of the society may be governed according to the moral reign of poets or priests. Ours, Arendt claims, gives such status specifically to the vocation of being a jobholder, of contributing to the net productivity of the social whole.

The liberal regime is a regime of producers and consumers, not of citizens. (More strictly, it is increasingly a regime of servicers and consumers of services; for production, it seems, looms less and less large in economically advanced liberal societies.) If one takes this thought seriously, it will certainly tend to puncture the liberal presumption that a liberal political order can and should remain impartial toward the conflicting ends and aspirations of different

---

that the moderns have avoided the ancient institution of slavery by the expedient of universal slavery. Cf. Marx: "The bourgeoisie has stripped of its halo every occupation hitherto honored and looked up to with reverent awe. It has converted the physician, the lawyer, the priest, the poet, the man of science, into its paid wage laborers." Karl Marx and Friedrich Engels, *Basic Writings on Politics and Philosophy*, ed. Lewis S. Feuer (Garden City, N.Y.: Anchor Books, 1959), p. 10.

97. Arendt, *Human Condition*, p. 159.

individuals and groups within society. The Platonic-Aristotelian view is that any neutrality of this sort is impossible. If Plato and Aristotle are right that any political community must embody some ranking of ends, then the liberal notion of a society without an ethos and a state without a regime must be severely confusing as far as the understanding of liberal society is concerned. My judgment is that Plato and Aristotle *are* right about this, and that therefore liberal theorists indeed breed confusion. In fact we would be better off with the ancient theoretical framework of parts and wholes, assumed by the liberal theorist to be long ago dead and buried.

What defines liberalism is its desire *not* to be a regime, an organized social and political ordering of ends. It fails to fulfill this desire because it cannot do so. Once it is admitted that the liberal regime *is* a regime, we can set about addressing the more interesting theoretical question of whether it ought to be a regime of laborers, of consumers, or of citizens, and why.[98]

98. One might also read the account of liberalism given by Alasdair MacIntyre in *Whose Justice? Which Rationality?* (Notre Dame, Ind.: University of Notre Dame Press, 1988), pp. 335–347, as an effort to characterize the liberal regime. On p. 336, MacIntyre offers his own statement of the thesis of this section and of this book: "Liberal individualism does indeed have its own broad conception of the good, which it is engaged in imposing politically, legally, socially, and culturally whenever it has the power to do so, [and] in so doing its toleration of rival conceptions of the good in the public arena is severely limited."

6

Socialism?

One may care less for the efficiency of the capitalist process
in producing economic and cultural values than for the kind
of human beings that it turns out and then leaves to their
own devices, free to make a mess of their lives.

Joseph A. Schumpeter

If, as has been suggested thus far, the matter with liberalism is
that it has no matter, no substance, what of the leading ideological
alternative to liberalism on the level of contemporary social-political
realities—namely socialism? How does socialist theory, if not socialist practice, fare in relation to the critical standards by which I
have sought to judge liberal theory? Put otherwise, is socialism, or
can it be convincingly conceived as, a genuinely postliberal social-
political philosophy?[1] The problem that we confront here, however, is that, from our theoretical perspective, arguments on behalf
of socialism are still largely framed within categories that are of a
piece with the terms of liberal discourse that I have attempted to
criticize in preceding chapters. To address this problem, I will try
sketching the lines of a possible alternative way of formulating the
case for socialism, one that I will label, for reasons that I hope
will clarify themselves in what follows, the *political* argument for
socialism. Whether socialist practice can surmount the quandaries
of liberal capitalism may, after all, depend decisively on the character of the defining terms by which one fashions or refashions notions of socialism.

1. John Gray has recently described himself as committed to "postliberal theorizing," but the kind of theory that he appeals to in this context,
that of Hobbes, seems to me to be preliberal rather than postliberal. See
his *Liberalisms: Essays in Political Philosophy* (London: Routledge, 1989), pp.
234–236.

SOCIALISM AND CITIZENSHIP

The standard case for socialism turns on an argument about distributive justice, an argument concerning social and economic rights or entitlements, and it has the concept of equality as its defining term. In what follows I shall merely put this argument to one side, neither discounting its validity nor acknowledging its force; in other words, I suspend judgment about the force of the standard argument. I wish to sidestep these issues, for I believe it is possible to construct an alternative case for socialism that revolves around citizenship rather than social justice, around political enfranchisement rather than economic entitlements, and that substitutes the concept of solidarity for that of social equality as its pivotal term. It is an argument of which intimations may be drawn from Rousseau, J. S. Mill, and perhaps even Marx.[2] As I say, I want neither to repudiate nor to endorse the conventional argument, but merely to suggest other terms in which the question of socialism might be debated.

The question I want to ask is whether it is possible to elaborate a justification of socialism that does not depend upon principles of distributive justice. Michael Walzer, in the context of an argument for a more developed system of communal provision in the United States, notes: "One might also argue that American citizens should work to build a stronger and more intensely experienced political community. But this argument, though it would have distributive consequences, is not, properly speaking, an argument about distributive justice."[3] It is important to pose this question on account

2. Since the reference to Marx may elicit some surprise, let me mention one supporting text. In the *Grundrisse*, trans. Martin Nicolaus (New York: Vintage, 1973), pp. 487–488, Marx observes that for the ancients "the question is always which mode of property creates the best citizens," and that in this respect antiquity is loftier than modernity. This quotation is taken from James T. Knauer, "Rethinking Arendt's *Vita Activa*: Toward a Theory of Democratic Praxis," *Praxis International* 5, no. 2 (July 1985): 185–194. Knauer, on pp. 192–193, attempts to draw from the work of Hannah Arendt the outlines of a theory of social justice conceived as instrumental to political equality, i.e., political justice, a theory that agrees very well with the one I attempt to sketch in this chapter.

3. Michael Walzer, *Spheres of Justice: A Defense of Pluralism and Equality* (New York: Basic Books, 1983), p. 85. Walzer himself offers a definition of

of the prominence lately accorded to theories of distributive justice within contemporary political philosophy.[4] The disproportionate attention devoted to questions of fair distribution and social justice make it necessary to consider the other argument that Walzer notes but does not pursue.

The problem with basing the argument for socialism strictly on the claims of social justice is that this way of proceeding runs the risk of getting enmeshed in the language of rights and entitlements that defines (and in my opinion disfigures) liberalism as a political philosophy and is thus liable to distract from what Marx considered the key question about socialism, namely the quality of social relations between human beings. Let me refer here to a familiar case. Rawls's theory offers an extreme instance of what one may call socialism through the back door, that is, a possible justification of socialist measures by means of a theory of distributive justice that gives only the most minimal account of shared ends and does it on the basis of a thoroughly instrumentalist conception of rationality. I propose the opposite theoretical strategy, eliminating the intermediate problem of fairness of distribution and going straight to questions of shared ends and the basis of social solidarity (which is, at best, a derivative issue for Rawls).

Justice is of course a central and ineliminable term of political discourse. However, social justice does not exhaust our political concerns. It is questionable whether it is, as Rawls claims, the "first virtue" of social institutions, and it is certainly not the only virtue. Citizenship is also one of the essential needs that we have as politi-

---

socialism focused on the invigoration of participatory politics in "Civility and Civic Virtue in Contemporary America," *Social Research* 41, no. 4 (Winter 1974): 609, 611.

4. As John Dunn well observes, one of the outstanding weaknesses of modern political understanding "is the absurd overemphasis in political philosophy, ever since the constitution of political economy and the formation in reaction to it of socialist theories, upon distributive justice. In any political society which permits the open discussion of political choices, justice in the distribution of material goods is an inevitable focus of dispute. But the degree to which modern philosophers, whether Marxist or liberal, concentrate their imaginative energies upon this problem reflects a quite ludicrous level of misjudgment." *Rethinking Modern Political Theory* (Cambridge: Cambridge University Press, 1985), p. 186.

cal beings. When one argues for a given set of institutions, it is not immediately obvious how one should weight these different claims. Perhaps it is unnecessary, since both require the same set of institutions (namely, socialism under some description). But it does not seem to me guaranteed in advance how the argument for distributive justice will be decided, and we would therefore be well advised to question whether considerations of social justice should have ultimate supremacy, in case our need for justice and our need for citizenship should, perchance, conflict.

Suppose I could establish an irrefutable claim to various socioeconomic goods, based, say, on desert. Let us say that I can prove that I deserve a certain share of the social benefits and advantages available for social distribution. Suppose further that the cost of my obtaining what I actually deserve is that political activity and civic collaboration with others in my society is thereby impaired (because, for instance, the material conditions for replete political membership for those others are thereby denied, or because feelings of mutuality and fellow-feeling are damaged by the resultant inequalities). It seems quite reasonable to me, in such circumstances, to regard this as too high a cost for getting what I in fact deserve, in fulfillment of the principles of distributive justice. A public-minded citizen would wish to forgo his or her rightful entitlements in this case. Now I do not want actually to affirm the initial supposition. Rather, my point is that it is quite intelligible to assert the priority of politics over economics, which in this context means that as citizens we are prepared to subordinate questions of social and economic distribution to questions of political membership. Now of course it is possible that struggles over equalizing distribution may themselves actually forge bonds of political community and solidarity (we know that this often happens), and I certainly do not wish to exclude such possibilities. But I see no necessary relation between the two issues, and it seems to me important to establish an independent argument for egalitarian political commitments that does not rest upon the contingencies of economic distribution and the entitlement claims to which they give rise. In any case, one might want to establish the relative priority of economic parity and political democracy in defining one's idea of socialism. Does one seek social equality for its own sake, or in relation to a further end, namely that it makes us better citizens and promotes a shared experience of political community?

My contention, then, is that arguments about distributive justice do not exhaust the arguments for socialism, and that even if the former arguments were somehow definitively settled one way or the other, arguments that adduced other considerations could proceed nonetheless. This point is reflected to some extent in certain varieties of socialist rhetoric, such as Bennite socialism in Britain, where the decisive arguments are often framed in terms of participatory democracy and, in particular, of radical democratization of the party system. (This, of course, does not deny the social-economic dimension of these arguments, related as they are to a struggle against a particular class system.) But even supposing that the two sets of concerns, socioeconomic and civic-political, could easily converge, the question remains whether we wish to conduct the argument for a socialist society within the language of economic rights or that of political goods, and this choice between one rhetoric or the other at the same time involves a choice of substance between rival conceptions of socialism.

Up to now, I have been presenting arguments to suggest why it would be unwise to limit the case for socialism to a derivation from social and economic entitlements, and why it would be sensible to introduce other considerations. It remains to indicate what would be the shape of an alternative argument. In barest outline, the claim would be that socialist arrangements would heighten political identity and enhance civic consciousness, and thereby reverse or at least mitigate the trend toward depoliticization and "civil privatism" documented by Habermas among others. Socialism, in short, would make us better citizens. This, of course, is an empirical claim, dependent on counterfactual projections about how a genuinely socialist transformation would affect the quality of political life. In the absence of solid empirical grounding for this claim, I shall content myself for now with some more casual observations that tend to support my case. My intention is more to intimate the lines upon which such an argument could be developed than actually to fill in its content in any detail.[5]

5. Similar lines of reflection are pursued in Philip Green's instructive book *Retrieving Democracy: In Search of Civic Equality* (Totowa, N.J.: Rowman

There is one rather simple way to demonstrate that the advancement of socialism must go hand in hand with a much more active sense of citizenship. The societies with which we are here concerned are nonsocialist and appear to be little inclined to socialism. These societies are at the same time massively depoliticized. By socialism, of course, I do not mean merely the election of socialist parties committed to greater government spending. I mean a large-scale transformation of attitudes, institutions, and relationships in society with a view to the achievement of shared purposes and social justice through the public disposal of collective resources ("common ownership of the means of production" is the standard formulation). Such a transformation would be unthinkable without a general shift of consciousness throughout the society. This shift of consciousness, in turn, would presuppose a thorough politicization of the whole population. A major turn toward socialist ideals and the corresponding political objectives would not come about unless people in very large numbers took an extremely active interest in politics and seriously concerned themselves with problems of political change. In short, they would have to exercise citizenship in the fullest way. In the West, intimations of such a politicization have been witnessed, for example, in the black voter registration drive associated with the presidential campaigns of Rev. Jesse Jackson, and in certain aspects of the nuclear disarmament movement.

No doubt one could employ the same reasoning to argue that in systems of state socialism the natural means of politicizing people is through the mobilization of discontent and protest against the prevailing (that is, state-socialist) mode of social organization. In fact this is precisely what we have seen at the end of the 1980s throughout Eastern Europe, with results that, from the point of view of the concerns of this chapter, have been very impressive. Therefore it seems hard to deny that the same argument that supports socialism in capitalist societies works in the opposite direction

---

& Allanheld, 1985). In *A Preface to Economic Democracy* (Berkeley: University of California Press, 1985), pp. 94–110, Robert Dahl considers an argument of the same form on behalf of workplace democracy. He examines arguments for and against the view "that democracy within firms would improve the quality of democracy in the government of the state by transforming us into better citizens and by facilitating greater political equality among us" (p. 94).

in the case of socialist (but, at least until recently, equally depoliticized) societies in the Eastern bloc. Perhaps the thesis here comes
to no more than the self-evident observation that political change
of any sort presupposes that the people who will undertake it have
been politicized to the appropriate degree. But I think more is entailed; the societies in need of political change (whether West or
East) are not simply unjust, oppressive, or prone to corruption
but are also, and above all, depoliticized. When a community is
mobilized to rectify injustices, whether economic or political, it is
at the same time educated to citizenship. The most powerful example of this in our time has been the Solidarity movement in Poland.

This argument concerns the gains to citizenship that would ac-
crue from working or struggling toward socialism, or participating
in socialist movements, rather than from fully formed socialist institutions themselves. It would be easy to indulge in speculations
about the flowering of political activity and civic involvement under
socialism, but it is difficult to see any empirical grounds for assuming that the entrenchment of social equality would automatically
lead to a full and active political life. It might simply lead to equal
participation in consumerist indolence. Whether civic activity blos-
somed in a postcapitalist society would depend not on the achievement of social equality per se, but rather on how one defined and
conceived socialism, whether within socioeconomic categories or
in broader terms (and, needless to say, a radical democratization
of active citizenship *would* be central to the version of socialism
that I am advocating). If socialism is defined in terms of shared
civic responsibility rather than economic justice, then the achievement of a socialist order will, by definition, usher in a new republicanism.

There is, however, one important respect in which egalitarian
social conditions certainly do foster citizenship and civic solidarity.
If there exist substantial disparities of wealth and opportunity, the
common exercise of citizenship will be blocked by social divisions
and feelings of relative deprivation. (In this connection, it should
not be too difficult to speculate on the likely political implications
of the significant erosion of the middle class, and the consequent
polarization of rich and poor, that has been unfolding in North
America over the last decade.) This is a theme familiar in republican
political thought—for instance, in Aristotle, Machiavelli, and Rous-

seau.[6] And if inequalities impair the forms of mutuality required for the joint exercise of citizenship, it is reasonable to expect that the converse would hold as well, namely, that social equality would encourage forms of shared experience and common sentiment, which would in turn likely issue in richer political relationships.[7] It was this hope that prompted Aristotle and Rousseau, among others, to insist upon the easing of class divisions in a well-constituted society. It must be said again, though, that social equality would be no more than a necessary condition of good citizenship, not a sufficient condition. A socialism which resulted in a universal bourgeoisie—Sweden?—would remain subject to Rousseau's polemical opposition between *bourgeois* and *citoyen*.[8]

The argument that I am putting forward is neither classical liberal nor classical socialist. To show this, let us abstract two positions that lie at opposite poles. One line of argument would be that political and legal rights are all-important and that all attention should

6. Cf. Robert A. Dahl, *Democracy and Its Critics* (New Haven: Yale University Press, 1989), p. 333; and Dahl, *Preface to Economic Democracy*, pp. 10, 68–70, 110. See also Cass R. Sunstein, "Beyond the Republican Revival," *Yale Law Journal* 97, no. 8 (July 1988): 1552–1553.

7. Cf. John Dunn, *The Politics of Socialism: An Essay in Political Theory* (Cambridge: Cambridge University Press, 1984), p. 53: "The redistribution of all substantial aggregations of private wealth in a society like Britain (or even the United States) would make a relatively trivial once and for all contribution to the material welfare of the great majority. But to live in a society which contrived to preserve all the other merits of these countries, but which no longer set off the distress of their less fortunate members by the gross luxury of a tiny parasitic class would at least make it easier to see the society itself as a single community and membership within it as a human bond with some genuine moral significance."

8. Jean-Jacques Rousseau, *On the Social Contract*, ed. R. D. Masters (New York: St. Martin's Press, 1978), p. 54n and pp. 137–138 n. 32. It is an odd fact that both ends of this French dichotomy can be translated by the same German word: *Bürger*. (The German *bürgerlich* at the same time annuls the English distinction between civil and civic.) This seems to indicate that the relation between *bourgeois* and *citoyen* contains aspects of convergence as well as of tension. Perhaps the explanation for it has to do with T. H. Marshall's suggestion that the rise of modern citizenship coincides with the bourgeois triumph over feudalism. "Citizenship and Social Class," in Marshall, *Class, Citizenship, and Social Development* (Garden City, N.Y.: Anchor Books, 1965), pp. 92–93. Cf. Ralf Dahrendorf, "Citizenship and Beyond: The Social Dynamics of an Idea," *Social Research* 41, no. 4 (Winter 1974): 675–676.

be directed at these rather than at social and economic disparities. The converse argument would be that legal-political freedoms are merely formal and that everything really hangs on whether the formal rights are given substance at the level of social and economic arrangements. Against the former position, it would be reasonable to argue that, say, blacks in South Africa will never get a meaningful voice in the conduct of their own affairs unless they attain sufficient social and economic leverage to force the whites to accord them a share in political power. This view is supported by the example of blacks in the United States, where their political power has grown in proportion to their social and economic gains, namely, the consolidation of a black middle class. But one could go on to argue (this is the second perspective) that political representation would be superfluous once social and economic equality had been firmly established, since the latter is, in any case, the real object of and rationale for the former. This line of reasoning, in my view, would be quite wrong. In fact, one of the main arguments for expanding social and economic entitlements is, precisely, in order to provide for the disenfranchised a meaningful enfranchisement. Again, it is not a question of the sense of solidarity being in the service of the passion for equality, but rather of social equality working to elicit greater political solidarity.

Thus far, the impression may have been conveyed that the struggle for equality belongs strictly within the sphere of social and economic competition. However, it would be wrong to assume that the concept of equality applies exclusively to the realm of social status and economic distribution. The concept of citizenship implies a conception of equality as well, and equality must prevail within the limits circumscribed by a given definition of citizenship. If we are regarded as citizens with respect to any legal and political rights or responsibilities, we must also be treated as equals within that same domain. Partial citizenship is an incoherent notion; the idea of unequal citizenship amounts to a contradiction in terms. If we are defined as citizens in any respect, we enjoy (or should enjoy) equality within the terms specified by that definition of citizenship. Therefore civic equality is synonymous with citizenship.[9]

9. As Michael Walzer points out, according to the usage of the French Revolution, the title *Citoyen* connoted a universal status in a way that the title *Monsieur*, at the time, did not. Walzer, "Citizenship," in *Political*

If the concept of equality can be given a political rendering distinct from its usual social-economic meaning, so too can the concept of justice. This calls for a further clarification of the relationship between the theory here sketched and standard theories of justice. Although my version of the socialist argument certainly has implications for the formulation of principles of distributive justice, it should be fairly clear from what I have already said that it is not centrally a theory *about* justice (or at least social justice). When we shift from equality for equality's sake to equality for citizenship's sake, the primary concern is no longer with what is just (for individual citizens) but with what is good (for the community as a whole); or rather, social justice is sought to the extent that it promotes political citizenship. A theory of social justice seeks to explain why the society should establish more or less distributive equality in terms of entitlement—what is due to individual members. Strictly speaking, my theory offers no such account. It seeks to argue for equality in terms of something else, something that transcends or supplements the claims and entitlements of individuals, namely political well-being. But citizenship, too, yields an account of justice, though not social justice. The claim to participate in general deliberation is also a claim to justice, to political justice; this is the sense that the term *justice* has in Aristotle's political philosophy. Justice, after all, is not exclusively a social concept; it also evokes a political meaning. When we refer to injustice in South Africa, for instance, we certainly do not refer only to social disadvantages; even if the levels of income among the races suddenly became equal, the nature of the political system would continue to violate our sense of political justice. Following Michael Walzer one might even include the latter dimension of justice under the heading of "distributive justice," for claims to participate in a political system necessarily call for principles of distribution for arbitrating among such claims. According to Walzer, citizenship, like social justice, is a distributive question.[10]

Innovation and Conceptual Change, ed. T. Ball, J. Farr, and R. L. Hanson (Cambridge: Cambridge University Press, 1989), p. 211. On "the equality implicit in the concept of citizenship," cf. Marshall, *Class, Citizenship, and Social Development*, pp. 92–93.

10. Walzer, *Spheres of Justice*, chap. 12.

The point of my argument has been to show that one can have other than egalitarian reasons for embracing socialism and that one can support socialist goals without being already committed to social equality per se. (I am assuming that arguments about distributive justice are inherently murky and that the case for full-bodied political citizenship is more straightforward; though here too, undoubtedly, the desirability of the end will be severely contested.) To reformulate the problem along these lines carries the advantage that it shifts the focus to the distinctively political benefits of socialism and away from the theoretically confusing issue of economic costs.[11] In discussions of the relative merits of socialism and liberal capitalism, it is generally assumed that the relative inefficiency of socialist economies exhibits the political inferiority of socialism. It is hardly ever considered that it may in fact constitute a political *advantage* of socialism that such economies operate less efficiently and thus offer fewer goods to be distributed. If indeed economic disadvantages yield political advantages, the reason is—as political philosophers from Plato onward have always recognized—that too much affluence breeds poor citizens. This kind of reflection is integral to Rousseau's way of thinking, with its resolute subordination of the economic to the political. The same thought finds expression within more recent political thought in the work of Hannah Arendt (which likewise subordinates economics to politics): "Economic growth may one day turn out to be a curse rather than a good, and under no conditions can it either lead into freedom or constitute a proof for its existence."[12] It is fairly astonishing to what a small degree factors such as low crime rates, as well as low rates of unemployment, are considered suitable measures of political achievement in the evaluation of existing socialist societies. It strikes me that one need not be a partisan of the Soviet system to accept as a legitimate standard of political comparison the odds of being murdered on the streets of Moscow as opposed to the streets of Wash-

11. For a consideration of certain political advantages of "actually existing" socialist regimes—a treatment informed by the political thinking of Plato—see Hans Jonas, *The Imperative of Responsibility: In Search of an Ethics for the Technological Age* (Chicago: University of Chicago Press, 1984), pp. 145–151.

12. Hannah Arendt, *On Revolution* (New York: Viking Press, 1965), pp. 219–20.

ington. On the converse side, it is scarcely less stunning that pervasive drug taking, rampant sexual exploitation, the addiction to consumerist "lifestyles," and the ubiquity of the credit card in Western societies are not commonly taken as key indicators of political debility relative to other societies.[13] Or to pick another topical example, we could ask ourselves: Have we carried our identification of political freedom with consumer freedom so far that it is unthinkable to see the infinite availability of pornographic publications in West Berlin relative to East Berlin hitherto as at least one political advantage to be reckoned on the side of the latter?[14] Again, what seems to loom largest is the criterion of economic productivity; the truly political consideration—the question of what promotes good citizenship—appears less important.[15]

Some arguments for socialism regard politics as the means and economic equality as the end. Here this perspective is reversed: economic equality is the means and greater exercise of political citizenship is the end. At the outset I referred to my endeavor as the political argument for socialism in order to distinguish it from the social-economic argument. Of course, the latter is also a political argument, at least in the content of the commitment it elicits, if not in the quality of the grounds upon which it is based. Perhaps the

13. In a speech on 26 July 1986, Fidel Castro declared, not without justification, that widespread drug use in the United States served to demonstrate the inability of Americans to practice virtue. In my view Castro was quite right to point to narcotics abuse as among the appropriate terms of comparison by which to measure the moral and political qualities of socialist versus nonsocialist societies.

14. According to Alexander Solzhenitsyn, the invasion of Western-style "freedom" commenced even before the barriers between East and West were lifted. He writes: "The iron curtain did an excellent job of defending our country against everything good in the West . . . but the curtain didn't quite go all the way down, and allowed the liquid dung of a debauched and decadent 'pop mass culture' to ooze underneath." Quoted in Michael Scammell, "A Great Man Eclipsed," *Times Literary Supplement*, 16–22 November 1990, p. 1234.

15. It is striking that even the authors of the much-publicized manifesto of the "Movement for Socialist Renewal" (drafted in November 1985) restrict their critical analysis of the relative strength of East and West chiefly to economic comparisons, agreeing entirely with Lenin's view that the decisive test of the success or failure of socialism would be whether it could outstrip the productivity of labor in capitalist economies. (In retrospect, it is clear that this document was an early statement of "Gorbachevism.")

contrast would be brought out more sharply by dubbing mine the "civic" argument for socialism. This theoretical strategy may be summed up in the notion that socialism should be pursued not on account of equality for its own sake, but because it makes us better citizens or promotes citizenship generally, or rather, that greater equality is justified insofar as it makes better citizens and encourages citizenship. My conclusion is that even those who are not persuaded that egalitarianism for its own sake is justified might nonetheless have good grounds for embracing socialism if they could be shown the truth of the civic argument.

RECONCEIVING SOCIALISM

We may well be disconcerted to find on reflection that we have considered as the most appropriate argument on behalf of socialism one that in significant measure abstracts from the actual content of socialist politics. This forces us to confront much more directly a problem we have so far avoided, and which is at the heart of the current crisis of socialism that all thoughtful socialists have acknowledged—namely, that it is anything but clear on what bases we are, today, to attach a clear and compelling content to the socialist idea. My argument up to this point would seem to imply that a definite sense of what we all understand by socialism already exists. Yet it would not be surprising if the altered terms of my case for socialism at the same time produced important modifications in the very conception of socialism. For the sake of simplicity in the preceding argument I have presupposed a more or less traditional definition of socialism in terms of ownership of means of production, or public disposal of collective resources. However, the specific circumstances of our contemporary situation (not excluding widespread public skepticism about the efficacy of state ownership) may well force us to consider a *re*definition of what socialism means, or of what core commitments constitute grounds for identifying oneself as a socialist.[16] In order to face up to this problem as

16. For a thoughtful attempt to redirect socialist thought away from its preoccupation with the question of ownership, see Robert A. Dahl, *After the Revolution?* (New Haven: Yale University Press, 1970), pp. 115–140. An invaluable guide to the sorts of rethinking that are required is Alec Nove, *The Economics of Feasible Socialism* (London: George Allen & Unwin, 1983).

directly as possible, let me submit for consideration what we can call the three principles of moral economy in a postliberal state. For each of these principles, some remarks are offered that are in keeping with the political argument presented thus far. As should be already apparent, the intention has not been to establish a compelling case for socialism, but merely to offer suggestions for how to conduct the political debate, an argument whose real point is to highlight problems in the ways the debate is usually conducted.[17]

Full Employment

Even Western societies in the developed world have had sufficient experience of mass unemployment to measure how profoundly it demoralizes those who suffer it directly as well as the society as a whole. In the light of both the social realities of our century and the specific contours of our argument, it would thus be reasonable to say that the first precept of a redefined socialism ought to be an overriding commitment to the goal of full employment, backed up by the agency of state planning. To be sure, it would appear that the redefinition of socialism centering upon this particular goal leads to certain paradoxes. In China, by 1976 the policies of the Cultural Revolution had produced very high unemployment in the cities. An important motivation behind the move toward private enterprise by the Deng Xiaoping regime was to eliminate this unemployment. But given these facts, it seems odd to say that the development of a mixed economy in China since 1976 represents a betrayal of socialist aspirations. (The opposite conclusion must be drawn in say Hungary, where, even before the upheavals of 1989, socialist economists were being tempted by their experiments with market socialism to experiment as well with Western-style unemployment, in order to spur efficiency and competitiveness.) In theory, of course, unemployment can be overcome without state planning, but those who put their faith in the market are not likely to view unemployment as necessarily an evil, nor full employment as nec-

---

17. For a tough-minded and grimly realistic challenge to conventional renderings of the socialist idea, see Dunn's *Politics of Socialism*. It should be added that Dunn would not view with any greater equanimity the kind of alternative conception formulated here. Ibid., pp. 56–57.

essarily a good. The British experience, in particular, shows how unemployment serves the market by disciplining workers to conform themselves to market imperatives.

The reason for regarding full employment as the foremost political priority for state action is that no one subject to chronic unemployment can consider himself or herself, or be considered by the society, as a citizen in any meaningful sense.[18] Thus this formulation of the present-day meaning of socialism (focused upon productive employment within the society, and not, say, nationalization of industries or public intervention in the economy per se) remains consistent with the preceding argument, that socialism should be defined and justified not in terms of amelioration of the social condition, but in terms of expanded citizenship. To put it in the form of a principle applicable to the policies of social democratic government: Public intervention in the workings of the economy is politically desirable, *whether or not it is economically more efficient,*[19] when it tends to draw more members of the society into a stable sense of being full citizens, or gives those already citizens a deepened or enlarged sense of political membership. The same principle can be applied to the urgent problem of housing in capitalist societies. How could a society that permits, as North American society permits, countless people to remain homeless, flatter itself that it offers an experience of common citizenship for its inhabitants?[20] Without

18. Cf. Dunn, *Politics of Socialism*, p. 54: "The prospect of a capitalist economy permanently unable to supply a large proportion of the society's adult members with gainful employment is not a pretty one. What sense can such victims be expected to make of their membership in a society which remains complacently or maliciously capitalist in its values?"

19. Socialists have always made the sanguine assumption that the supersession of capitalism would be accompanied by a higher standard of living (having your cake and eating it). But this assumption has turned out to be eminently falsifiable. If the socialist ideal delineates an intrinsically worthwhile form of life, it is not unthinkable that the ideal might be embraced at the price of (heresy!) a *lower* standard of living.

20. See Mary Ellen Hombs and Mitch Snyder, *Homelessness in America* (Washington: Community for Creative Non-Violence, 1986), p. xvi, for a hair-raising estimate of the numbers of these subcitizens: 1 percent of the population. In November 1988 the General Accounting Office of the U.S. Government let it be known that it considered credible the possibility that the homeless might actually exceed 1 percent. *The World Almanac and Book of Facts, 1990* (New York: Pharos Books, 1989), p. 37.

certain minimal conditions of membership, such as adequate shelter and a reasonable prospect of reasonable employment, the promise of citizenship shows itself to be the merest pretense.

Any argument on behalf of socialist transformation presupposes an answer to the question "What is socialism?" or "How ought socialism to be conceived in the given historical context?" By proposing that the goal of full employment be made central to the definition of socialism, I have sought to supply an answer to this question: socialism today must signify a determination to put people to work, by any available means, utilizing the full powers and resources of the state, and to see to it that no one is deprived of the dignity of employment. The argument for this interpretation of socialism can be made on civic grounds. Without work one possesses no stable location in the world, no proper locus for one's dignity as a member of the society; and without the latter there can be no citizenship. (Such assumptions about the relationship between employment and citizenship have prompted the recent development of workfare programs in the United States.[21]) If being a citizen is a basic good within a good society, then full employment, as the condition of full citizenship, has priority over other social purposes.[22] Today socialism must be defined, in the first

21. See Lawrence M. Mead, *Beyond Entitlement: The Social Obligations of Citizenship* (New York: Free Press, 1986). Mead's argument is that welfare policies that tie entitlements to obligations to the society (that is, work in return for welfare benefits) would do more to enhance equality, not simply in the sense of economic equality but in the deeper sense of shared citizenship, than policies that confer entitlements with no corresponding duties or obligations. The concerns that inform Mead's book also run through Morris Janowitz, *The Reconstruction of Patriotism* (Chicago: University of Chicago Press, 1983). For critical scrutiny of the prescriptions offered by Mead and Janowitz, see Robert K. Fullinwider, "Citizenship and Welfare," in *Democracy and the Welfare State*, ed. Amy Gutmann (Princeton: Princeton University Press, 1988), pp. 270–278. On the possible political advantages of workfare, cf. Benjamin Barber, *Strong Democracy* (Berkeley: University of California Press, 1984), pp. 210–211.

22. The principle of full employment is, to be sure, very noble sounding. Put into practice, especially when conjoined to the notion that employment is not simply a right (i.e., an option) but a social obligation, it acquires perhaps a harsher ring. However, it may be argued that the presence of an enduring underclass in American society is a problem of such desperate urgency that, analogous to the forcing to be free of Rousseau's citizens, the members of this underclass can permissibly be forced to be more equal

instance, not in terms of nationalization or social equality as such, but rather in terms of a publicly organized resistance against the evil of unemployment; and this, as I have presented it, is an aspect of what I have called the civic argument for socialism.[23]

DECENT EMPLOYMENT

But what if—horrors!—capitalism turns out to offer the only prospect of meaningful full employment; what if it turns out to be not only the more efficient producer of goods but also the more efficient producer of jobs?[24] The critic of capitalism will of course reply that not just *any* jobs will do; that the kinds of jobs generated by contemporary capitalist societies are no better than, perhaps in fact worse than, unemployment. Yet this reply is not entirely satisfactory. On the basis of what historical experience of capitalist and socialist economies can we hope for any guarantee that every job will be decent and satisfying? Marx's vision of a society in which all forms of labor are individually and socially rewarding, because those that are not are rendered technologically redundant, appears to be not an inch closer to realization today, after a century of unmatched economic growth and technological progress. If such a thing were

---

partners in the social and economic life of the whole society. The Soviets are evidently less compromising than Westerners on the relation between work and citizenship, though admittedly this is expressed fairly unpleasantly in the Stalinist constitution of 1936: "It shall be the duty and honor of every able-bodied citizen of the USSR to work, according to the principle 'he who does not work, does not eat.' " Quoted in Mead, *Beyond Entitlement*, p. 214. The source of this Stalinist principle is, remarkably enough, St. Paul. 2 Thess. 3:10. These observations may well remove some of the moralistic luster of socialist rhetoric about full employment. In any case, it seems pretty clear that what full employment really means in, say, Soviet society is precisely workfare—that is, compulsory menial labor at the minimum wage.

23. It is not only socialists, to be sure, who recognize the threat to citizenship posed by unemployment. For discussion by a leading liberal of the relationship between work and citizenship, see Judith Shklar, "American Citizenship: The Quest for Inclusion," in *The Tanner Lectures on Human Values*, vol. 11, ed. Grethe B. Peterson (Salt Lake City: University of Utah Press, 1990), pp. 413–439, especially pp. 433–439.

24. For some information concerning episodes of unemployment in socialist societies, see Michael Ellman, *Socialist Planning*, 2d ed. (Cambridge: Cambridge University Press, 1989), pp. 179–187.

possible, why has not a single government, left or right, simply abolished drudgery?[25] Even a socialist might begin to suspect that drudgery is not, within the range of finite expectations, abolishable.[26]

On the other hand, nothing dictates that one cannot continue to include the demand for full *and rewarding* employment as a reasonable object of socialist aspiration. After all, my purpose here is to clarify the nature of coherent socialist ideals; and an ideal, by definition, defines the direction in which hopes transcend realities.

The Plato Principle

The basic moral intuition underlying the commitment to some version of socialism is of course that it is offensive that certain members of society earn incomes that are grossly out of relation to their real contribution to the welfare of society (because of arbitrary aspects of the social system of one sort or another). When one reflects on the wealth accumulated by a Mick Jagger, or Jane Fonda, or Wayne Gretzky, this intuition seems eminently sound. And the arbitrariness of the social criteria that establish these gross disparities appears all the more outrageous when one considers how, humiliated by seeing the obscene forms of consumption around them, those who are most severely deprived are effectively excluded from the possibility of sharing in a real political community with those who are most privileged. It hardly requires a full-blown theory of distributive justice to see that gross inequalities are bound to spawn widespread perceptions of injustice that cannot help but do violence to

25. Michael Ellman's conclusion seems pretty much on the mark: "The CMEA [Comecon] countries do not differ fundamentally from the capitalist countries with respect to the rationality of the economic system, the labour process, the division of labour, and the social ownership of the means of production. In both groups of countries, most of the population is forced to engage in dreary labour in an inefficient, stratified, unequal society in which the means of production are not in social ownership." Ibid., p. 325.

26. On some relevant problems, see Fred Hirsch, *Social Limits to Growth* (Cambridge: Harvard University Press, 1976), pp. 41–51, especially p. 42. Hirsch argues that better equipping people for more attractive jobs does not actually increase the supply of such jobs, but merely intensifies the competition in a zero-sum game.(In Hirsch's terminology, sought-after kinds of employment are positional goods.)

sentiments of shared citizenship. While material incentives may be necessary for the efficient working of a modern economy, it is difficult to see why these incentives must be of the scale of the existing ratios between the wealth of the highest-paid earners and that of the lowest-paid earners. (Do the Soviet Union and Hungary really require Soviet and Hungarian multimillionaires in order to reform their economies?) One can certainly seek to alter the magnitude of the disparity without entirely eliminating private incentives. But it remains open to the political philosopher to endorse greater equality either on grounds of the unfairness of existing arrangements or on grounds of the consequences for possibilities of solidarity and a greater sense of commonality (insofar as a distribution of material resources that is manifestly inegalitarian tends to undermine the perception of shared citizenship).[27]

In Plato's *Laws*, we have an ancient precedent of a political philosophy that mandates publicly enforced equality not for the sake of equity in the social relations between individuals, but for the sake of social order and the health of the polity. In book 5 (744d–745a), Plato introduces the principle that in order to avert the possibility of civil strife between rich and poor, which would be otherwise unavoidable, all citizens of the society must be guaranteed a basic minimum of property, and no one ought to be allowed to accumulate total property exceeding five times the original allotment. If someone does accumulate more—"by finding something or being given something, or by money-making, or some other such stroke of luck—let him dedicate the surplus to the city."[28]

---

27. For some helpful reflections on the extremity of inequality in contemporary American capitalism and its adverse implications for democratic citizenship, see Dahl, *After the Revolution?* pp. 105–115, and Dahl, *Dilemmas of Pluralist Democracy* (New Haven: Yale University Press, 1982), pp. 170–186.

28. Plato, *The Laws*, ed. Thomas L. Pangle (Chicago: University of Chicago Press, 1988), p. 132. Cf. Plato, *Republic*, 421d–422a, 552a–b. The same line of thought is to be found throughout the writings of Rousseau, and it forms the philosophical ground of his own egalitarian politics. For one among many relevant texts, see Rousseau, "Political Economy," in *Social Contract*, ed. Masters, pp. 230–232. What I have called the Plato principle also finds expression in the following passage from book 2, chapter 11, of the *Social Contract*: "Do you want to give stability to the State? Bring the extremes as close together as possible: tolerate neither opulent people nor

Applied to modern conditions, the Plato principle would yield the result that if a streetsweeper earned $25,000 a year, a corporate lawyer could not earn more than $125,000.[29] While not perfectly egalitarian, the universal application of this five-to-one ratio would certainly have a revolutionary impact on capitalist societies as they now exist. Contemporary welfare states of course operate on a principle something like this, but with results that are less egalitarian. No one can question the feasibility of this proposal since (unlike certain other socialist projects), given the legislative will, it can be implemented instantaneously; at most, one can claim that putting it into practice would diminish economic efficiency. Yet, as I have suggested above, this possibility of lower economic prospects should not necessarily count against it as a political proposal.

Karl Marx was certainly right to criticize socialists for making fair distribution the be-all and end-all of a good society.[30] The question of just distribution ought to be strictly subordinate to the question of the richness or emptiness of the shared mode of life of a society. However, the width of disparities in wealth and income bears not a small relevance to the quality of social relations, as Marx could

---

beggars. These two conditions, naturally inseparable, are equally fatal to the common good" (ed. Masters, p. 75n).

29. In *A Preface to Economic Democracy*, p. 105, Robert Dahl refers to wage and salary differentials in the United States of ten to one, twenty to one, and even one hundred to one, among individuals employed within the same firm. For elaboration by a noted economist of a proposal very similar to the one I have drawn from *The Laws*, see Lester C. Thurow, *The Zero-Sum Society* (New York: Basic Books, 1980), pp. 200ff. Plato's proposal is actually considerably more radical than the one advanced here, for Plato proposed the equalization of total property holdings, rather than merely that of income. As J. M. Barbalet demonstrates convincingly in *Citizenship* (Milton Keynes: Open University Press, 1988), pp. 52–54, the reduction of income differentials may leave untouched substantial inequalities of wealth, with adverse consequences for the ideal of equal citizenship. (Cf. Thurow, *Zero-Sum Society*, pp. 168–177.) In order to ensure that equalization of incomes was not rendered nugatory by advantages associated with established property, my version of the Plato principle would have to be supplemented by a severe inheritance tax and a severe capital gains tax, as well as devices to equalize access to credit between those with capital and those without it.

30. Karl Marx, "Critique of the Gotha Programme," in Karl Marx and Frederick Engels, *Selected Works* (New York: International Publishers, 1968), pp. 321–325.

scarcely have denied. The same considerations apply to the problem of citizenship. Of course, it may be that equalization of material resources barely begins to go to the heart of what is required for sentiments of social and political solidarity within a political community. And there may be a whole multitude of possibilities for promoting such civic solidarity and bridging class boundaries that have little or nothing to do with income equalization.[31] On the other hand, it is difficult to see how one could truly speak about membership in a common political community when, to use Rousseau's phrase, citizens are increasingly divided into beggars who are forced to sell themselves and rich people who have the wherewithal to buy them.[32]

Liberal and socialist critiques of capitalism are typically founded on conceptions of distributive justice. However, as the very reference to Plato reminds us, there are other bases for a critical stance toward an economic system as inexorably dynamic and morally destabilizing as capitalism.[33] Regardless of one's idea of justice, another salient aspect of capitalism, noted with anxiety by conservatives as well as socialists, is its corrosive effect upon the moral order of a society and its tendency, at least in the long run, to undermine the sentiments of common purpose that are vital for a stable sense of citizenship.[34] (I say in the long run because, as

31. A persuasive argument along these lines is sketched by Mickey Kaus (drawing upon some of Michael Walzer's ideas about equal citizenship) in "For a New Equality," *New Republic*, 7 May 1990, pp. 18–27. The same analysis, applied to the policies of the post–World War II Labour government in Britain, can be found in Marshall, "Citizenship and Social Class," pp. 101, 113–114, 132; p. 113: "Equality of status is more important than equality of income."

32. Rousseau, *Social Contract*, bk. 2, chap. 12.

33. For discussion of one possible source of critical reflection on capitalism that is neither liberal nor socialist in inspiration, see my "Hannah Arendt on Capitalism and Socialism," *Government & Opposition* 25, no. 3 (Summer 1990): 359–370.

34. Irving Kristol accuses left-wing radicals of succumbing to "highly apocalyptic notions of the present." But Kristol's own assessment of the present is not much less apocalyptic: "The inner spiritual chaos of the times, so powerfully created by the dynamics of capitalism itself, is such as to make nihilism an easy temptation." *Capitalism Today*, ed. Daniel Bell and Irving Kristol (New York: Basic Books, 1971), pp. 11, 13. In a similar vein, see also Daniel Bell, *The Cultural Contradictions of Capitalism* (New York: Basic Books, 1976). The same ambivalence toward capitalism, and the

Charles Taylor has argued, there is no problem of meaning in a capitalist civilization while it is in the process of building itself up. It is only later, when capitalism is "in the saddle," that the problem of sustaining the meaning of it all arises.[35]) This too entails a certain egalitarian commitment—a civic egalitarianism, that is, an egalitarianism of shared purpose.

Because socialism and liberal capitalism have presented themselves as the two principal ideological alternatives subsequent to

---

gloomy pathos that accompanies it, is already to be found in Schumpeter's celebration of capitalism's achievements and dismay over its self-annulling tendencies. (This attitude is captured well in the title of Kristol's book *Two Cheers for Capitalism* [New York: Basic Books, 1978]; the choice of title is explained in the book's preface.) Like the neoconservatives, Schumpeter scorns radicals for failing to appreciate the extent to which the greatest feats of the modern world are owing to mentalities fostered by capitalism, but at the same time adopts a critical perspective that suggests, no less than that of the radical, that capitalism is morally problematical to a profound degree. See Joseph A. Schumpeter, *Capitalism, Socialism and Democracy* (New York: Harper & Row, 1976), p. 129: The radical's "adverse verdict about capitalist civilization rests on nothing except stupidity, ignorance or irresponsibility. . . . But a completely adverse verdict may also be arrived at on a higher plane." Reading Schumpeter and his successors, one is tempted to ask whether capitalism is more unloved by its enemies than by the enemies of its enemies. Similar lines of thought on the moral conditions of capitalism's capacity to sustain itself are pursued in Kristol, "A Reply," *The Public Interest* no. 22 (Winter 1971): 104–105; Kristol, "Capitalism, Socialism, and Nihilism," *The Public Interest* no. 31 (Spring 1973): 3–16; and (from a point of view that seems more receptive to socialist possibilities) Hirsch, *Social Limits to Growth.* For a helpful scan of these issues, see Raymond Plant, "Hirsch, Hayek, and Habermas: Dilemmas of Distribution," in *Dilemmas of Liberal Democracies,* ed. A. Ellis and K. Kumar (London: Tavistock, 1983), pp. 45–64.

35. Charles Taylor, "Interpretation and the Sciences of Man," *Review of Metaphysics* 25, no. 1 (September 1971): 42–43. Max Weber, in a key formulation, stated: "Capitalism at the time of its development needed labourers who were available for economic exploitation for conscience's sake. To-day it is in the saddle, and hence able to force people to labour without transcendental sanctions." But if transcendental sanctions are dispensable, by virtue of what can capitalism be expected to remain in the saddle indefinitely? Can it not at some point fall out of the saddle? Weber refers in the same passage to "the impersonality of present-day labour . . . its joyless lack of meaning," without considering the problems that this might pose for the self-maintenance of the work ethic in the absence of a larger horizon of meaning. Max Weber, *The Protestant Ethic and the Spirit of Capitalism,* trans. Talcott Parsons (London: George Allen & Unwin, 1948), p. 282 n. 108.

the defeat of fascism, it is easy to exaggerate the contrasts between capitalism and socialism, and to understate the similarities. Yet one would have to be thoughtless indeed to go on assuming that socialism can be counted on to resolve the predicaments examined in our critical probing of liberalism. Historically, and with increasing apparentness as we near the close of this century, socialist politics has been caught within the very same predicaments. Like liberalism, it is an ideology focused chiefly on building economic productivity and expanding opportunities for freedom in exploiting nature, not on building character or enriching the experience of citizenship.[36] Even the committed socialist would have to be rather foolish to feel any complacency about the superiority of socialism to liberalism in respect of the problems raised in these chapters. As Alasdair MacIntyre quite correctly observes: "That a systematically lower standard of living ought to be preferred to a systematically higher standard of living is a thought incompatible with either the economics or the politics of peculiarly modern societies. . . . A community which was guided by Aristotelian norms would not only have to view acquisitiveness as a vice but would have to set strict limits to growth."[37]

The reorientation of political thinking implied in MacIntyre's challenge lies outside the horizon of traditional socialism just as much as it lies outside the horizon of liberalism. Still, socialism may hold certain advantages that ought not to be overlooked. Daniel Bell cites an incisive remark by Schumpeter to the effect that "stationary feudalism was an historical entity, stationary socialism an historical

36. For more detailed consideration of some of the affinities between socialism and capitalism, see "Hannah Arendt on Capitalism and Socialism." Cf. Václav Havel in the title essay of *The Power of the Powerless*, ed. John Keane (London: Hutchinson, 1985), pp. 26–27, 38–39, 45, 68, 89–92; and Havel, *Disturbing the Peace*, trans. Paul Wilson (New York: Vintage Books, 1991), pp. 10, 13–16, 168. Also Alasdair MacIntyre, *After Virtue* (Notre Dame, Ind.: University of Notre Dame Press, 1981), p. 33.

37. Alasdair MacIntyre, *Whose Justice? Which Rationality?* (Notre Dame, Ind.: University of Notre Dame Press, 1988), p. 112. Cf. T. H. Marshall, "Value-Problems of Welfare-Capitalism," in *The Right to Welfare and Other Essays* (London: Heinemann Educational Books, 1981), pp. 120–121: "Materialism, profit-seeking, quantity-worship and growth-mania are not characteristics of capitalism alone, but permeate the whole of modern technological mass society."

possibility, but stationary capitalism an historical contradiction in terms."[38] What this implies for our argument is that because socialism contains at least the theoretical possibility of a stationary economy, it retains advantages over capitalism, owing to the mounting social and environmental problems spawned by limitless growth, that are yet to be fully appreciated in modern societies.

There is one last advantage to a socialist outlook that may bear mention. For anyone who has looked to socialism as the solution to history's riddles, a glance at most of the regimes that have called themselves socialist in our epoch should suffice to dispel one's imaginings. But it is not yet fully clear that the antidote to political hubris exists in the liberal West. It may well be that the Western liberal democracies, led by the United States, have won the Cold War, as some have recently claimed.[39] On the other hand, it might just as well be true that the gradual rapprochement between the two leading superpowers owes as much to the anxiety of the American nation concerning its fitness to maintain its position in the world as to the anxiety of the Soviet Union concerning *its* position in the world. At any rate, it is hard to see how shifting global destinies, with all their uncertainty, could warrant self-satisfaction on either side. Nor should it be assumed that the events of 1989 mark the end of socialism. Indeed, it is conceivable that the anti-Communist revolutions currently under way in Eastern Europe will have the effect of redeeming the socialist ideal no less than the regimes they have displaced served to discredit that ideal. In particular, socialism may come to be newly appreciated by the politically emancipated themselves as they begin to experience the unemployment, high housing costs, and other forms of unpleasantness associated with a free market.[40] Let us hope that the nearing of the end of the second millennium brings a mood of political reflectiveness

---

38. Bell, *Cultural Contradictions of Capitalism*, p. 240.

39. See, notably, Francis Fukuyama, "The End of History?" *The National Interest* no. 16 (Summer 1989): 3–18. For the most part, Fukuyama's argument is suffused with obnoxious gloating, though it is punctuated by moments of liberal self-doubt.

40. The situation of those in what was formerly East Germany (a wholesale collapse of industry, and staggering rates of unemployment) bears a particular pathos, given the cruel disparity between their expectations when they joined the West and their present plight.

and reserve commensurate with the awesome responsibilities exercised by centers of political power today.

Let us now sum up the preceding discussion. The experienced economic inadequacies of command economies and state-run enterprises in mixed economies have left nondogmatic socialists in a state of some anxiety in regard to whether adjustments in socialist doctrine can be made that absorb these lessons of socialist experience and yet leave the socialist ideal with some meaningful content, so that it remains something more than an empty radicalism or an egalitarian rhetoric uttered in order to assuage middle-class guilt. I have proposed three specific principles or guidelines of socialist practice, none of which has anything to do with public ownership:

1. Every employable member of the society is to be guaranteed a job at the behest of public authority. A Western society that consents to, or promotes,[41] the unemployment of 10 percent of its working population should come to be seen in the same light, and be subject to the same degree of moral censure, as a society that arbitrarily disenfranchises a tenth of its adult citizenry. The contemporary salience of this principle is related to the fact that as political regimes in Eastern Europe move in the direction of a free market system, they will almost certainly have to accept significant levels of unemployment. Capitalist societies, while they may not necessarily welcome unemployment, have shown themselves willing to tolerate it as a price of economic efficiency; and previously communist social orders may consent to pay the same price.[42] It would not be a negligible contribution to socialist

41. While it might seem unlikely that any modern government would actually promote unemployment (as opposed to simply accepting it as the price of inflation-fighting measures in an unemployment-inflation trade-off), it is arguable that this was precisely the weapon deliberately used in the early years of Margaret Thatcher's government to discipline the trade union movement.

42. Consider, for example, unemployment figures for post-Communist Poland: January 1990, 55,000; February 1990, 186,000; March 1990, 266,000; June 1990, 511,000; September 1990, 926,000; October 1990, in excess of one million; end of 1990, likely to exceed 1.3 million. *The Economist Intelligence Unit Country Report: Poland* no. 4, (1990), pp. 14–15. While market reforms in the Soviet Union may spur unemployment there as well, Mikhail Gorbachev has put on record that guaranteed employment must be a defining socialist commitment: Gorbachev, *Perestroika* (New York: Harper & Row, 1987), pp. 86, 100.

theory to clarify the nature of this price, namely debased citizenship for those who are displaced to the margins.

2. Public authority is obliged to do everything in its power to render it more likely that the kinds of jobs actually available to
members of the society do not destroy the soul.

3. The ratio of the highest to the lowest income in the society shall
not exceed, say, five to one. This ratio shall be implemented
by a publicly enforced, non-loophole-ridden, redistributive tax
system. In a just social order it should be impossible for anyone
to say what Leona Helmsley reportedly said to her maid: "We
don't pay taxes. Only little people pay taxes."

The purpose of these policies is not to maximize social equality for
its own sake, but to support and enhance a sense of citizenship and
common involvement in the doings of the society one inhabits.
Thus my argument remains, as it was intended to be, a civic argument for socialism.[43]

It may be asked: Why call this a brand of socialism if it has
nothing to do with public ownership or socialized ownership of
some kind? Indeed, in the United States, where there has been less
of a socialist tradition than in other liberal democracies, many a
theorist committed to these three ideals would probably not iden-
tify himself or herself as a socialist. But I think it may be conceded
that the greater the public intervention in the workings of the market, the more valid the socialist label; and by any standard, the three
proposals discussed involve a large degree of deliberate political
intervention in the economy. Also, with these proposals I am assuming the retention of what the best welfare states already provide. Therefore, for instance, the United States, lacking a system
of socialized medicine, would be required to provide one. I should
hasten to add that nothing here rules out socialized ownership.
Naturally, any socialist will be sympathetic to workers' coopera-
tives, public agencies to meet basic needs, and so on. My point,
rather, is that even if various experiments in noncapitalist owner-

43. One should not overlook internal connections between the three
principles. Thurow draws out one such connection in arguing that the
most effective means of narrowing differentials in income is by committing
the state to the provision of universal employment. *Zero-Sum Society*, pp.
203–206.

ship prove unworkable in the face of imperatives of global competition, there would still be ideals to which chastened socialists could and should remain faithful. Is it possible that in a socialist society according to the civic model, citizenship would be sufficiently robust, feelings of solidarity sufficiently pronounced, and the commitment to care for disadvantaged members of one's society sufficiently strong that the whole society would become like one very large kibbutz? Not very likely; but to the extent that these socialist ideals were realized, the super-kibbutz analogy would have some force in this respect at least: that the regulation, by the collective decision making of the society as a whole, of tolerable margins of relative income, security of employment, and thus life prospects generally, would be in some way analogous to the collective regulation within the kibbutz of the relative income, job security, and life prospects of its members; and to this extent the residual fact of private ownership would be of less relevance. Even if there is no general socialization of property, there would be, one might say, a socialization of the perils of living in a modern society.

Of course, liberals will protest that theirs is an egalitarian philosophy too. But the question to be raised is whether a neutralist metatheory permits them to give a sufficient account of their own egalitarianism. Are we offering merely a beefed-up welfare state? Perhaps; or let us say, a beefed-up welfare state plus a greater sense of political involvement, by all citizens, in its fate. For as we have seen all too clearly from the politics of the 1980s, one of the major political problems of the welfare state is that even where it continues to receive grudging support from taxpayers, it is vulnerable to attack so long as socially egalitarian policies of the state are seen by citizens as an imposition by an alien power. Perhaps the repudiation by socialists of the principle of state neutrality can help them to do a better job than liberals of upholding egalitarianism in the eyes of the political community that will decide its future.

For the state to take charge of restructuring the economy to ensure full employment (if necessary, through employment *by* the state), to maximize humanly rewarding employment, and to equalize the distribution of wealth and income, are large and ambitious public purposes. But the larger the undertakings of the state, the greater the demands placed upon citizenship. We can glimpse here intimations of a vicious circle. For the state to undertake responsibilities of this dimension would require a resolution of the dilemmas of citizenship treated in the previous chapter; the state would have to act as the agent of a shared purpose embraced by the whole political community, supported by a general and generous civic identification felt by members of that political community.[44] So measures at the level of public policy intended to strengthen and expand the experience of citizenship would themselves require the support of an already consolidated commitment to the state as the locus of citizenship and the agent of shared purposes: a classic chicken-and-egg problem.

We have examined a variety of strategies by which one might develop a brief for socialism, with the purpose of expanding the assumed range of theoretical options. (In any case, the *last* argument by which to persuade anyone in the last decade of the twentieth century of the desirability of socialism is that of Karl Marx—namely, its vastly superior potential for economic efficiency.) One would hope that the proposed principles are sufficiently straightforward and mutually reinforcing to provide a clear and coherent direction; unfortunately, things are not as simple as one would wish. Some of the problems have already been touched on: What if the guarantee of a full-employment economy requires a level of economic activity so dynamic that it jeopardizes other concerns that tend to engage socialists, such as environmental problems? What if a stationary or no-growth economy (desired for the sake of establishing a saner form of social existence) entails that the goal of full employment could only be secured at the price of forgoing the goal of decent employment? What if the only way to guarantee full employment in an economic environment shaped by a highly competitive global economy is precisely by propagating soul-destroying, tedious work (e.g., by placing everyone in front of a computer terminal from nine to five)? What if, as I mentioned earlier, the principle of full employment in practice means forced drudgery at low wages? All of these pose real political challenges. However, the question of what sort of public policy would guaran-

44. The notion of citizenship bears a similar burden in David Miller, *Market, State and Community: Theoretical Foundations of Market Socialism* (Oxford: Clarendon Press, 1989), part 3, especially chap. 9. Miller, unfortunately, is still attracted to the liberal neutralist metatheory criticized above.

tee both employment for all *and* kinds of employment that would not wreck the higher human capacities of those employed is not one that we can reasonably expect a political philosophy to answer.[45] To say in a little more detail why this is not the rightful task of theory is the purpose of the concluding chapter.

45. Admittedly, socialism may present itself as a less than satisfying theory if it enumerates what all of us cherish—work, security, happiness, a sense of efficacy and empowerment, a decent life—while offering little definite guidance (certainly far less than it could once have confidently offered) on how to secure these good things.

7

Epilogue: The Limits of Theory

> When it comes to the communal self-reassurance of the
> modern democratic societies, most of the work gets done
> not by deep thinkers (e.g. people attracted by Plato and
> Kant) but by superficial dreamers—people like Edward Bel-
> lamy, Henry George, H. G. Wells, Michael Harrington,
> Martin Luther King. These are the people who dangle car-
> rots before democratic societies by suggesting concrete
> ways in which things might get better—become more dem-
> ocratic, fairer, more open, more egalitarian, more decent.
> They supply local hope, not universal knowledge.
>
> Richard Rorty, article in the
> *London Review of Books*, 1987

From the point of view that sees theory as demanding hard, sober,
realistic answers to pressing social problems, the reflections offered
in this book are bound to appear unsatisfactory. Let us close, then,
with one more statement of why the problem may lie not with the
inadequacy of our theoretical efforts in previous chapters (though
these may be regarded as feeble on other grounds), but rather with
the inappropriateness of the critic's demands.

I admit freely that the critical probing of contemporary liberalism
in this work has been conducted on the assumption that theory as
such is a pure indulgence whose end is simply the enhancement
of our understanding, not the supply of nostrums for an improved
practice. For many, this limited conception of theory will appear as
an inexcusable extravagance, on grounds that it fails to take seriously the central problem that has exercised political philosophers
from Francis Bacon onwards, namely, the problem of theory and
practice. This reproach can be answered by reflecting on the fact
that since the seventeenth century, thinkers ranging from Bacon to
Marx have advanced a succession of theories that, if applied, were
supposed to lead to practical salvation. The experience of modernity, if nothing else, has taught us what to expect of such promises.

Modern theorists on the whole accept as a matter of course John Stuart Mill's dictum that "the test of real and vigorous thinking, the thinking which ascertains truth instead of dreaming dreams, is successful application to practice."[1] Of the great modern thinkers, Rousseau alone had a more sensible view of the relation of theory to practice. In *Emile* he declares that he has no reason to apologize for the fact that his philosophy amounts to "dreaming dreams"; at least he gives his dreams as dreams, which others are not careful to do.[2]

Ever since Marx, in the eleventh thesis on Feuerbach, castigated philosophers on the grounds that they had hitherto merely interpreted the world whereas the need was to change it, many theorists, Marxist and non-Marxist, have presumed that they must strive for a unity of theory and practice, that is, that they must, by means of their theoretical activity, help to change the world. Yet those who make this presumption generally do not recognize fully what it entails. This unhappy notion of theory translated into practice would be unmasked if it were obliged to confront the strict Marxian premises that uphold the doctrine of theory-practice unity. In its classic Lukácsian version, the Marxist argument is that a unity of theory and practice comes into reality only through the vehicle of a specific social class. I accept this Lukácsian argument, but, contrary to Lukács, I deny that such a social class exists or is remotely conceivable in our present circumstances.[3] As Lukács correctly perceived, if one is to speak of theory-practice unity at all, the decisive question is that of the social class that is to supply mediation or transmission of theory. To illustrate: Ronald Dworkin's political philosophy satisfies this condition, for it is disseminated by the class of professional lawyers and jurists trained in the liberal academy. The later writings of Herbert Marcuse exhibit the virtue of trying to specify the constituents of a new proletariat; the only problem is that the candidates nominated for this role (e.g.,

1. John Stuart Mill, *Utilitarianism, On Liberty, Considerations on Representative Government*, ed. H. B. Acton (London: Dent, 1972), pp. 211–212.

2. Jean-Jacques Rousseau, *Emile*, trans. Allan Bloom (New York: Basic Books, 1979), p. 112n.

3. My argument is spelled out in "On the Disunity of Theory and Practice," *Praxis International* 7, no. 1 (April 1987): 25–34.

middle-class university students) were not very credible bearers of a not very credible social theory. Before presuming to utter the slogan "theory and practice," we should remind ourselves that we are speaking of political change in mass societies, and that the only possible relation of theory to practice in this context is one of mass ideological conversion. If this is the price to be paid for a unity of theory and practice, would it not be preferable for political practice to remain resolutely untheoretical?

Modernity has given us sufficient experience of the consequences of applications of theory to practice. Invariably, what results is a technocratic vision of politics that stifles the natural resources of ordinary prudence. It is time that theorists adopted a more modest conception of their calling. Theories alone cannot tell us how to reorder the world. At best, they can alert us to some of the dangers of a bad unity of theory and practice, in the form of technocratic understandings of politics. Theory can teach us to limit the intrusions of theory itself into the practical sphere. This function is, to be sure, a negative one, but at least it has the positive effect of helping to roll back the technocratic pretensions to a successful application of theory to practice.

Among contemporary Aristotelians, Gadamer offers the surest guide to Aristotle's essential insight that it is ethos that is decisive in constituting sound judgments, not theoretical considerations of any kind. Whether a society possesses the ethos sufficient to support sound practical judgment owes very little to the influence or guidance of philosophers. Instead, the truth tends to lie in the opposite direction: any influence that philosophers exercise will depend on the ethos that already exists (which explains why poets and intellectuals can be taken seriously in, say, eastern Europe in a way that is nearly inconceivable in the West). On the other hand, it is helpful to remember that we theorize in the context of a society that is to a large degree intoxicated with theory (as it has been since the Enlightenment), where the society expects much of theorists and theorists expect much too much of themselves. So in this context, to deflate the exaggerated promises of theorists may itself be a salutary practical effect of theory.

It is not part of this argument to suggest that theory (mine or anyone else's) is devoid of normative implications; this would be absurd. However, the general normative prescriptions contained in theory cannot instruct us in what we should do here and now. It is not for theorists to answer Lenin's famous question, "What is to be done?" This is entailed by my understanding of the strict division between theory and prudence. Prudence is not a product of theory, nor can it be deduced from theory. It is not that theory is bereft of norms, but merely that these general norms do not extend to telling us how we should go about changing the world (Marx's definition of praxis). If what one means by the unity of theory and practice is that one should not be a hypocrite in the practical choices one makes—that one should not preach socialism and practice capitalism—then obviously no objections are possible. But I would assume that something more is implied by the modern concept of theory and practice. It is when we ascend to questions of large-scale social change that theoretical principles leave us largely at a loss as to how we should proceed.[4]

Here we are likely to encounter the notion that good political practice presupposes an attempted democratization of theory. This implies that everyone can and should become a theorist, which strikes me as far-fetched. John Dunn's characterization of ordinary citizens as "amateur social theorists" is quite misleading in this respect.[5] The books that the contemporary theorist reads—Marx,

---

4. A dramatic case of this problem of application is John Rawls's influential work *A Theory of Justice*, which offers an elaborate account of principles of distribution, yet offers no determinate guidance whatsoever on the substantive distribution yielded by his theory; in principle, it could be appealed to no less sincerely by Mrs. Thatcher and Mr. Bush for an ideological justification of their politics than it could by Marxists and social democrats. On this point, cf. Jürgen Habermas, *Autonomy and Solidarity*, ed. Peter Dews (London: Verso, 1986), p. 207.

5. John Dunn, "Social Theory, Social Understanding, and Political Action," in *Rethinking Modern Political Theory* (Cambridge: Cambridge University Press, 1985), pp. 119–138. Dunn's image of the "amateur social theorist" is misleading, among other reasons because it seems to suggest that ordinary citizens do clumsily or incompetently what real professionals do with more success—whereas Dunn himself makes clear that the latter perspective is far from his own view of things; see ibid., pp. 129, 136–138, 214–215 n. 9. Although Dunn often in his writings seems to suggest that it is primarily the job of thinkers and intellectuals to come up with better solutions for our dilemmas, in at least one place he settles for a more realistic view: "Political theory in general cannot tell human beings what to do. What it can tell them is what not to forget." Dunn, *The Politics of Socialism* (Cambridge: Cambridge University Press, 1984), p. 88.

Weber, Habermas, Rawls, Foucault—are difficult books. It is a challenge to get one's students (or even one's colleagues) to penetrate these texts, let alone the layperson. The suggestion that we attempt to democratize theory does not seem to me a serious one. My argument, though, is that the "aristocratic" nature of theory does not in any way undermine democracy within the sphere of praxis, since theory is not a necessary condition of responsible citizenship. Ordinary prudence unguided by theory is in principle sufficient. My argument, therefore, is a defense of democratic praxis, not at all a critique of it. My critique is, rather, directed at theory, or rather, at the uncalled-for pretensions of theory.

For the sake of convenience, and to avoid needless squabbles over what we are to understand by the term *theory*, let us suppose that it refers to the sorts of research and controversy that fill the pages of the leading philosophical journals. Theory in this sense is certainly of concern to myself, as well as my students and my colleagues, but it would be implausible to imagine that it has any direct or even remote bearing upon the struggles that unfold within the practical sphere. Citizens have enough to occupy themselves with and educate themselves about without also being obliged to acquaint themselves with such recondite texts as those of Adorno, Lyotard, Nozick, Althusser, or Wittgenstein. We should be sufficiently satisfied if ordinary men and women see fit to exercise a more vigorous citizenship, without taxing them with the added burden of being theorists as well.

To this it may be objected that whereas the simplicity and immediacy of ancient political life may have permitted an experience of praxis innocent of theory, the overwhelming complexity and scale of modern society requires a theoretical command of the relevant political issues. The question I wish to raise is: Even assuming that this is so, how will the correct theory of society be mediated to a general public? After all, we live in a mass society, where intellectual movements of every kind are absorbed and reshaped according to the laws of mass consumption and where ideas all too easily become perverted in the guise of mass ideologies. From this I deduce a conclusion exactly opposite to the one stated in the objection: While it may be true that we need correct theory much more urgently than did the citizens of an ancient polis, Aristotle could address more or less directly the gentlemen of his society in a way that would be simply inconceivable in today's mass society.

Let me now expand on the crucial question of the relation between theory and prudence, as I see it. Agreement on first principles may be compatible with a great variation in orienting oneself to practical decisions and judgments of particulars; theoretical judgment underdetermines prudential judgment. Two theorists might be able to achieve a substantial degree of consensus at the level of theory (say, with respect to the most desirable possibilities of democratic participation, or the ideal conditions of social and economic citizenship), yet it is not at all clear that this would put the two theorists in a position to agree on judgments and decisions in the sphere of what Aristotle called "ultimate particulars." It is just the latter that are the object in political deliberation. Theory seems to be of little help in apprehending such "ultimate particulars" and deciding how to comport oneself toward them in practice. Suppose I have arrived at the theoretical conclusion that a given political philosophy represents the most adequate understanding of our situation, or is superior to all known alternatives. Does this philosophy equip one to decide which concrete policy, here and now, is most likely to realize one's theoretical ideals? In choosing strategies? In ranking priorities? It should be obvious that this involves the confrontation with a great number of particulars. It is in the very nature of a particular that it cannot be adequately anticipated by theory. To put the point in a way that accords with insights by philosophers ranging from Kant to Wittgenstein: even if we had an adequate rule, we would require a further rule to *apply* this first rule, then a rule beyond that to apply this next rule, and so on ad infinitum.[6] Eventually we must run out of rules, and we will then

---

6. For some statements of the problem, see Hannah Arendt, *The Life of the Mind*, vol. 1, *Thinking* (New York: Harcourt Brace Jovanovich, 1978), p. 69; Hans Jonas, *The Phenomenon of Life* (Chicago: University of Chicago Press, 1982), p. 199; Hans-Georg Gadamer, *Reason in the Age of Science*, trans. F. G. Lawrence (Cambridge, Mass.: MIT Press, 1981), p. 121; Alasdair MacIntyre, "Does Applied Ethics Rest on a Mistake?" *The Monist* 67, no. 4 (October 1984): 503–504, 507; Charles Taylor, "Justice after Virtue," in *Kritische Methode und Zukunft der Anthropologie*, ed. Michael Benedikt and Rudolf Burger (Vienna: Wilhelm Braumuller, 1985), p. 35. Kant's doctrine of reflective judgment, which is the modern formulation of this insight, is anticipated by Montesquieu in his "Essay on Taste": "Le goût naturel n'est

have to confront the particular without benefit of a rule for the sub-sumption of particulars. But encounter with particulars independent of rules of subsumption is precisely what defines prudence.

Belief in the omnicompetence of theory to direct political judg-ment generally presupposes a deductive model whereby theory determines ultimate principles, from which are deduced maxims for action. Much of contemporary moral theory, whether deonto-logical or consequentialist, is premised upon such a model.[7] If the-ory can be used to locate the correct principles, it is assumed, then one will possess the key to right conduct. The problem with this picture of things is that it offers a wholly false account of the relation between theory and prudence (as Aristotle understood so well).[8] In contrast to this false model, what is implied in the notion of prudential judgment, as I understand it, admits of no deduction from rules or principles. Rather, the task of judgment at its most acute is situated (sometimes tragically) at the intersection of con-flicting and nearly incommensurable moral and political claims: for instance, the claims of the local and particular versus those of the general and universal, the perspective of the involved participant versus that of the detached outsider—or, in Burke's terms, the claims of "kindred" versus those of "kind."[9] No recourse to bind-

---

pas une connaissance de théorie; c'est une application prompte et exquise des règles mêmes que l'on ne connaît pas." (Natural taste is not a matter of theoretical cognition; it is a swift and exquisite application of the very rules that are incapable of being cognized.) Montesquieu, *Oeuvres com-plètes*, ed. Daniel Oster (Paris: Editions du Seuil, 1964), p. 845.

7. For an extreme articulation of these underlying assumptions, see Robert Nozick, *Anarchy, State, and Utopia* (Oxford: Basil Blackwell, 1974), pp. 277–279. Nozick suggests that a set of moral principles should account for moral intuitions in the same way that a scientific explanation accounts for natural phenomena.

8. For an argument drawn from the work of Gadamer to the effect that theoretical considerations necessarily underdetermine practical choices, and that the demand by various philosophers that theory should "ground" ethical and political practice is ultimately hollow, see my essay "Do We Need a Philosophical Ethics?" *The Philosophical Forum* 20, no. 3 (Spring 1984): 230–243. Similar thoughts are developed by Bernard Williams in *Ethics and the Limits of Philosophy* (Cambridge: Harvard University Press, 1985). Where Williams and I differ, however, is that he sees Aristotelianism as one among a variety of foundationalist moral philosophies, whereas I have tried to present it as an *alternative* to foundationalist ethical theory.

9. Edmund Burke, "Letter to a Member of the National Assembly," in

ing principles can release one from this tension-ridden seat of judgment. (For instance, should the Israeli government offer military assistance to the Ethiopian regime in its fight against Eritrean rebels in order to help secure the release of starving Falashas in Ethiopia? As Max Weber articulated most powerfully, political life is full of devil's pacts of this sort.) To attempt to reduce this sometimes tragic responsibility of practical judgment to a deductive entailment from ultimate principles misses the genuine concreteness of the judging situation as well as the consequent pathos of the moral-political agent.

To illustrate further: One may be of the opinion, for good reason, that nationalism is a basically atavistic and potentially lethal tendency of modern politics. Nonetheless, one can hold that a particular upsurge of it, say Lithuanian or Estonian nationalism in the context of contemporary social and political developments in the Soviet Union, can help crucially to further the process of cultural regeneration and political liberation in a given society at a specific historical moment. (On the other hand, as Burke correctly noted, the same act that at one moment of political time would have constituted a sound and constructive reform may at another moment offer an incitement to political disaster.[10]) In principle, there are never rules according to which such judgments can be applied. Nor is it the case that such judgments are marginal ones, serving merely to qualify judgments that are otherwise rule-governed or potentially deducible from a rule-bound theory. Rather, they are of the very essence of political life, so that judgments of, say, the goodness or badness of nationalism are necessarily mediated by considerations of concrete specificity that are in principle outside the competence of rule-governed, abstract theoretical intelligence. This helps explain the force of Aristotle's reference to ultimate particulars, which again brings home to us the necessary shortfall in the relationship between theory and prudence.

Not only is theory not a deductive basis for prudence; it cannot even provide for prudence in a more general way. Rather, to use

---

The Works of Edmund Burke, vol. 4 (London: Oxford University Press, 1934), p. 300.

10. Ibid., pp. 313–315; e.g., p. 314: "The medicine of today becomes the poison of tomorrow."

Aristotelian language, prudence is a product of ethos. And, to borrow a remark by Gadamer, even Aristotle could not restore ethos to an ethically drained polis. It would be sheer folly for us to assert comparable claims on behalf of our own efforts as theorists today. Whatever one may regard as the possible accomplishments of theory, the legislation of a new ethos by a philosophical tour de force cannot be one of them. (This was Rousseau's grim insight: that intellectuals or men and women of theory can do much to undo the ethos of a sound political community, but they can do little to restore it once it is lost.[11]) Gadamer's Aristotelian insight may be expressed as follows: Good theory is no substitute for good socialization, and even the best theory is utterly helpless in the face of bad socialization.[12] To say it once more: We do not need theories of prudence, we need prudence itself.[13]

I cannot accept that practice is really a clouded or un-self-conscious form of theory (a kind of latent, therefore still opaque, theory), and that one necessarily improves practice by making it more conscious with theory, as if pretheoretical practice were in itself somehow deficient. This is the technicist understanding of practice exposed by Oakeshott, Polanyi, Gadamer, and other philosophers. One does not ride a bicycle by having a theory of what it is to ride a bicycle. Neither does one organize a boycott, deliver a speech, canvass contributions to a cause, engage in debate, and so on, by having a theory of how to do so. Such practical activities do not stand in need of theoretical consciousness; far from being necessarily improved thereby, they might just as easily be thrown off track, much as one who tries to ride a bicycle by formulating a theory about it will probably fall off the bicycle.[14] Furthermore, one can

11. For a similar line of thought, cf. Martin Heidegger, "Why Do I Stay in the Provinces?" in *Heidegger: The Man and the Thinker*, ed. T. Sheehan (Chicago: Precedent, 1981), p. 29.

12. See "Gadamer on Strauss: An Interview," *Interpretation* 12, no. 1 (January 1984): 10. Cf. Habermas, *Autonomy and Solidarity*, pp. 207–208.

13. It seems to me that this is a mistake that John Dunn commits in his critique of modern liberalism—as if the shortage of prudence in contemporary politics were a merely theoretical deficiency, to be remedied by better theory. See, especially, *Rethinking Modern Political Theory*, pp. 167–170.

14. Cf. Williams, *Ethics and the Limits of Philosophy*, p. 167: "It is a platitude that a practical skill can, in an individual case, be destroyed by reflection on how one practices it."

engage in adequate and successful practice in conjunction with an inadequate or even false theory of one's practice; for instance, one can make true and important scientific discoveries while entertaining a false philosophy of science, or one can uncover true and important hermeneutic interpretations while adhering to a false hermeneutical theory, that is, a false understanding of the nature of hermeneutic activity.[15] Just as someone with training in linguistics might be awful at learning languages whereas someone without such training might pick up languages effortlessly, so someone with acute theoretical intelligence might be rather obtuse when it comes to judging particulars in the immediate context.

One does not learn to sculpt by studying theories of sculpture. One does not learn to write novels by studying literary theory. More basically, one does not learn to use language, or to form relationships, or to assume practical responsibilities, by mastering theories of various kinds. Why, then, should it be assumed that the way to learn to act (and in particular, to act in concert) politically is by training oneself in theories of politics? It seems surprising that one so often finds theorists inspired by *Marx* averse to a truth that conservatives going back to Burke have understood profoundly: that practice is primary. The fact is that this truth gets forgotten only in the kind of technicized society where *everything* is thought to involve intellectual mastery, that is to say, a society that pathologically misunderstands itself.

The presumption of intellectuals that they can shape practice by theory is certainly not, of course, confined to the Left. Norman Podhoretz claimed, with regard to the neoconservative intellectuals, that the election of Ronald Reagan in 1980 "could be, and was, seen as a mark of their spreading influence"—to which Conor Cruise O'Brien replied:

> Could it be? And was it? And by whom? Clearly it could be and was, by Mr. Podhoretz and some of his pals, afflicted by galloping

---

15. See Hans-Georg Gadamer, *Truth and Method* (New York: Seabury Press, 1975), pp. xvii–xviii; "Correspondence Concerning *Wahrheit und Methode*," *The Independent Journal of Philosophy* 2 (1978): 10. Gadamer's view of theory and practice is challenged by Alasdair MacIntyre in his review of *Truth and Method*, "Contexts of Interpretation," *Boston University Journal* 24, no. 1 (1976): 41–46, especially p. 46; but I find this challenge unpersuasive.

swelled heads. But did anyone else see it that way? Possibly some besotted left-wing intellectual, disposed to magnify the importance of his intellectual opponents, may have suggested something of the kind; though I don't happen to know of any such case. But could anyone outside the charmed circle of a few intellectual coteries and countercoteries ever have dreamed of such a thing? How could a couple of magazines, and a couple of dozen individuals of whom most Americans, and most other people, have never heard, possibly have exercised a determining influence over an American national election? Of course you can imagine—if you are a neoconservative—the esoteric influence of *Commentary*, etc., as spreading out at secondhand, through the media, and so filtering down to the plebs who, when they pressed those levers, were indirectly under the spell of Mr. Podhoretz and his friends without ever having heard of them. But it all seems a mite fanciful to me. Far from thinking of that election as a mark of the "spreading influence" of neoconservative intellectuals, I think that the only intellectual who clearly exercised a significant influence in bringing about the defeat of Jimmy Carter and the election of Ronald Reagan was that eminent paleoconservative scholar, Imam Khomeini.[16]

What applies to the presumed influence of the intellectual Right applies, mutatis mutandis, to the matching conceits of the intellectual Left. Idealist delusions are certainly not the exclusive property of either end of the political spectrum.[17] Yet suppose it *were* possible for theorists meaningfully to prevail upon the key political deliberations within our society. Would we be better off? Should the prospect delight us? I have my doubts. As the example of Max Weber's contribution to the constitution of the Weimar Republic testifies, the most towering theoretical mind of an age can, like any other mortal, commit decisive practical misjudgments in assessing particular circumstances. Why should persons of great theoretical intelligence, or even intellectuals in general, be exemplars of practical reason? Certainly, the writings of Rousseau and Kant should suffice to make us question the connection between theoretical and practical reason. As Conor Cruise O'Brien writes, in criticism of the Pla-

16. Conor Cruise O'Brien, "Trop de Zèle," *New York Review of Books*, 9 October 1986, p. 12.

17. For an example of "the exaggerated importance which the Left attaches to intelligentsia politics," see Maurice Cowling, "The Sources of the New Right," *Encounter*, November 1989, p. 8.

tonism of Simone Weil: "Does the love of good depend on the light of intelligence? It hardly seems so; we can all think of rather stupid people who are kind and honest, and of quite intelligent people who are mean and treacherous."[18] Here I must confess my sympathy for Gadamer's expression of "profound skepticism regarding the role of 'intellectuals' and especially of philosophy in humanity's household of life."[19]

In this context, consider the following statement of metatheoretical principle by Habermas:

> According to my conception, the philosopher ought to explain the moral point of view, and—as far as possible—justify the claim to universality of this explanation, showing why it does not merely reflect the moral intuitions of the average, male, middle-class member of a modern Western society. Anything further than that is a matter for moral discourse between participants. Insofar as the philosopher would like to justify specific principles of a normative theory of morality and politics, he should consider this as a proposal for the discourse between citizens. In other words: the moral philosopher must leave the substantive questions which go beyond a fundamental critique of value-scepticism and value-relativism to the participants in moral discourse, or tailor the cognitive claims of normative theory from the outset to the role of a participant.[20]

Now I do not consider this minimalist position to be an adequate statement of the theoretical mandate of the philosopher, for it would rule out most of the substantive questions of the great tradition of Western political philosophy. But I think it is a politically salutary declaration of the limits of theory: the philosophers are put

---

18. Conor Cruise O'Brien, "Patriotism and *The Need for Roots,"* in *Simone Weil: Interpretations of a Life,* ed. G. A. White (Amherst: University of Massachusetts Press, 1981), pp. 98–99. I have examined this question in more detail in "Hannah Arendt and Leo Strauss: The Uncommenced Dialogue," *Political Theory* 18, no. 2 (May 1990): 238–254.

19. Gadamer, *Reason in the Age of Science,* p. 58.

20. Habermas, *Autonomy and Solidarity,* pp. 160–161; cf. pp. 170–171. Habermas's circumscription of the role of theory is not quite as modest as it sounds, since he immediately goes on to distinguish between "normative theory" and "social theory." While this distinction between moral theory and social theory is rather mysterious to me, it seems that Habermas has in mind that in some respects the place previously occupied by moral and political philosophy will be reoccupied by sociology.

in their place relative to the possibility of general deliberation among citizens. This seems entirely justified, even if one rejects, as I do, Habermas's overly parsimonious account here of the proper dimensions of theory.

It is true that classical theory was intended to bear a relation to the good life, as Habermas expressed eloquently in his inaugural lecture on knowledge and human interest.[21] Nonetheless, I think one can have good practice without good theory, as Aristotle surely recognized, though maybe Plato did not.[22] Nor is one compelled to say that the richest and most interesting theories are a guide to good practice. It is undeniable that few, if any, writings on the Left can match the work of, say, Michael Oakeshott for depth or breadth of theoretical insight; yet one does not necessarily want to apply his philosophy to contemporary practice. Oakeshott himself insists that this cannot be the philosopher's intention. Conversely, one might detect serious deficiencies in Ronald Dworkin's philosophical defense of liberalism, and yet entirely welcome the political authority he would exercise if, say, he were appointed to the U.S. Supreme Court by a future Democratic administration. It seems to me not contradictory that one might, as a theorist, prefer Oakeshott to Dworkin and yet, as a citizen, prefer Dworkin to Oakeshott. Or, to choose our examples from the nineteenth century: *As a theorist*, Nietzsche offers a far richer and deeper source of theoretical reflection than John Stuart Mill, but as a guide to practice, it would be perilous not to favor Mill over Nietzsche. For me, these examples merely illustrate the possible ways in which theoretical and practical interests could cut in different directions. This shows that something can be good theory and yet bad politics, or bad theory and good politics; which in turn shows that theory is not a set of guidelines for practice, just as practice is not theory realized.

Let us explore an example of how the interests of good theory and good practice cut in opposing directions. Hegel spoke for a fine

21. Jürgen Habermas, *Knowledge and Human Interests*, trans. J. J. Shapiro (Boston: Beacon Press, 1971), pp. 301–317.

22. On Aristotle's grounds for affirming the autonomy of phronesis, see the translator's introduction to Aristotle, *The Politics*, trans. Carnes Lord (Chicago: University of Chicago Press, 1984), pp. 18–19; and p. 246 nn. 49–50.

liberal tradition (expressed also in the writings of Kant, Tocqueville, and John Stuart Mill, among others) when he wrote in a famous epigram: "The early morning reading of the newspaper is a kind of realist morning prayer. One's attitude to the world is oriented toward God, or toward a sense of what the world is. The former bestows the same assurance as the latter, that one knows where one stands."[23] Nietzsche spoke for the antithetical illiberal tradition (represented also by Heidegger) when he wrote, in direct reply to Hegel, that newspapers in place of daily prayers were a principal mark of the nihilistic flux and self-annulling character of modern societies.[24] As paraphrased by Leo Strauss: "Not every day the same thing, the same reminder of man's absolute duty and exalted destiny, but every day something new with no reminder of duty and exalted destiny."[25] So should we side with the liberal defenders of the modern press or with its antiliberal detractors? Should philosophers read the newspapers or shouldn't they? Again, it seems reasonable to distinguish sharply between the interests of theory and the interests of practice. Without question, Nietzsche and Heidegger pursue a profound reflection on essential features of modern civilization, including, in Heidegger's words, the securing of "the everydayness of our dawning age," provision of "the ever-useful objectivities of the day," and "the portrayal of all and everything in terms of universal history."[26] Unless one were a dogmatic

23. Karl Rosenkranz, *Georg Wilhelm Friedrich Hegels Leben* (Darmstadt: Wissenschaftliche Buchgesellschaft, 1963), p. 543. For another translation of the epigram, see Hegel, "Aphorisms from the Wastebook," *Independent Journal of Philosophy* 3, (1979): 2. Cf. "The Dialectics of Rationalization: An Interview with Jürgen Habermas," *Telos* no. 49 (Fall 1981): 21.

24. Friedrich Nietzsche, *The Will to Power*, ed. Walter Kaufmann (New York: Vintage, 1968), § 67.

25. Leo Strauss, *The Rebirth of Classical Political Rationalism*, ed. Thomas L. Pangle (Chicago: University of Chicago Press, 1989), p. 31.

26. Martin Heidegger, *Nietzsche*, vol. 4, *Nihilism*, trans. F. A. Capuzzi, ed. D. F. Krell (San Francisco: Harper & Row, 1982), p. 241; Heidegger, *What Is Called Thinking?* trans. F. D. Wieck and J. Glenn Gray (New York: Harper & Row, 1968), p. 66. For representative expressions of Nietzsche's views, see *Basic Writings of Nietzsche*, ed. Walter Kaufmann (New York: Modern Library, 1968), pp. 193, 321, 403; *The Portable Nietzsche*, ed. Walter Kaufmann (New York: Viking Press, 1968), pp. 162, 288; Nietzsche, *The Will to Power*, § 132 (p. 80), § 888 (p. 474); *Complete Works of Friedrich Nietzsche*, vol. 3, *On the Future of Our Educational Institutions* (New York: Russell & Russell, 1964), pp. 40–41, 47–49, 51, 54, 58, 60, 66–67, 70, 84, 134–135;

liberal determined to repel *Kulturpessimismus* at all costs, one would surely not want to close off these luxuriant sources of critical insight. On the other hand, Kant and Mill, with their bland liberalism, make available the practical truth that newspapers are an indispensable condition of responsible citizenship. The press, Mill says, is the modern equivalent "of the Pnyx and the Forum"; more than that, journalists are, he suggests, modernity's answer to biblical prophets.[27] Liberal banalities such as the notion of the importance of a free and active press depend upon a political perspective that may be theoretically less penetrating but without a doubt practically more sound. Yet I do not wish it to be inferred from my argument that Nietzsche and Heidegger are diminished as philosophers because they neglected their duty, as citizens, to read their daily newspapers. Philosophers are not meant to instruct us in how to act, but rather to hold before us shining examples of how to think, that is, how to raise questions and to reflect critically on our assumptions. Plato was wrong to suggest that a class educated in philosophy would furnish the best rulers. If one is looking for inspiring examples of political leadership, one might be better ad-

---

Nietzsche, *Schopenhauer as Educator*, trans. J. W. Hillersheim and M. R. Simpson (South Bend, Ind: Gateway, 1965), p. 89; and Nietzsche, *Gesammelte Werke*, vol. 16 (Munich: Musarion Verlag, 1925), p. 384. For representative expressions of Heidegger's views, see Heidegger, *An Introduction to Metaphysics*, trans. Ralph Manheim (Garden City, N.Y.: Doubleday-Anchor, 1961), p. 103; Heidegger, "The Pathway," *Listening* 8, nos. 1/2/3 (1973): 37; and Heidegger, "Messkirch's Seventh Centennial," *Listening* 8, nos. 1/2/3 (1973): 43, 45, 47. Cf. the unsympathetic stance toward the press of Nietzsche's mentor, Jacob Burckhardt, in *Judgments on History and Historians*, trans. Harry Zohn (London: George Allen and Unwin, 1959), p. 207; and Burckhardt, *Reflections on History*, trans. M. D. Hottinger (London: George Allen and Unwin, 1943), pp. 23–24, 26, 115–116, 160, 165, 170.

27. Mill, *Utilitarianism, On Liberty, Considerations on Representative Government*, pp. 179–180, 201. Relevant texts in Kant are *Kant's Political Writings*, trans. H. B. Nisbet, ed. Hans Reiss (Cambridge: Cambridge University Press, 1970), pp. 55–56, 85. Relevant texts in Mill are *Utilitarianism, On Liberty, Considerations on Representative Government*, pp. 313, 348. Another key text in this liberal tradition is Alexis de Tocqueville, *Democracy in America*, vol. 2, bk. 2, chap. 6. Tocqueville's argument is that the associative function of the newspaper, drawing far-flung individuals into communities of judgment and action, is necessary in order to counter the individualizing tendencies of a large democratic society. See also *Democracy in America*, vol. 1, chap. 11.

vised to seek out an electrician like Lech Walesa or a preacher like Jesse Jackson, rather than persons of great theoretical ability.

It might be thought by many that the greatness of a writer like Marx lies in his capacity precisely for "successful application" of theory to practice (to repeat the phrase of Mill cited at the beginning of this chapter). I would say, to the contrary, that the genius of Marx and Engels lies in their capacity for immersing themselves in particularity. In my opinion, the measure of Marx's greatness lies as much in his political journalism as in his theorizing. One need only compare the unconvincing abstractions of the *1844 Manuscripts* with the wonderful concreteness of the *Eighteenth Brumaire.* Marx's capacity to illuminate the sphere of praxis has less to do with, say, his theoretical appropriation of Hegel than with his ability to digest a huge volume of information culled from newspapers and other sources. As the editors of one collection of writings point out: "The American periodical press was a most important source of information for Marx and Engels. Their friends regularly sent to London newspapers and journals of the most varied tendencies. It is clear from their letters that Marx and Engels were receiving up to thirty newspapers and journals from the USA."[28] Thus Marx represents a way of thinking situated at the opposite extreme to that of Nietzsche; whereas Nietzsche associates the newspaper with all that is wrong with modern politics, Marx is at his best when poring over detailed press reports of the latest advances and setbacks of the working class in any number of political battlegrounds throughout the world. This is in fact the special advantage of reading newspapers. Its educative function consists in the immersion in particularity, contingency, and factuality that it supplies, as well as the attention to detail that is indispensable to political judgment. As

28. Karl Marx and Friedrich Engels, *On the United States* (Moscow: Progress Publishers, 1979), p. 16. In his graveside speech eulogizing Marx, Engels specifically referred to Marx's journalistic work for a variety of periodicals as among his highest achievements; see *The Marx-Engels Reader*, ed. Robert C. Tucker, 2d. ed. (New York: W. W. Norton, 1978), p. 682. For a review (largely critical) of Marx's journalistic contributions to the *New York Daily Tribune*, see the editor's introduction to Karl Marx, *Surveys from Exile*, ed. David Fernbach (New York: Vintage, 1974), pp. 18–33. For evaluations by Engels of the contemporary press, see *On the United States*, p. 322, and *The Marx-Engels Reader*, p. 557.

the newspaper writer or editor must address himself or herself to what actually occurs on a day-to-day basis, the reader is schooled in the happening of the unforeseen and in the never-ending analysis of what is ceaselessly shifting. To be forced to confront particulars is itself to be initiated into politics, where no amount of theoretical training can substitute for the simple knack of telling an able statesman from a clever charlatan, or telling a sound policy from a pack of lies. As Marx himself says: "I was compelled to make myself familiar with practical details," as opposed to "the actual science of political economy."[29]

The lesson I seek to draw from this question of the philosophers' pronouncements concerning the newspaper is not that we should judge the worth of a philosophy according to the soundness of its practical judgments, merely that we should be wary of the assumption that theoretical insights offer any guarantee of reliability in the practical sphere. As we have seen, Aristotle, for one, had a keen appreciation of this, formulated systematically in book 6 of the *Nicomachean Ethics*.[30] Philosophers typically do not tell one how to vote; nor should they. Hegel's political stance was so elliptical that the argument still goes on between Right Hegelians and Left Hegelians. And today there are probably more Left Nietzscheans than Right Nietzscheans! Yet in neither case does this indeterminacy in the least interfere with the power of these philosophies to illuminate the world for us at the level of theoretical insight. If one wants to raise fundamental questions about the nature of political life, one should immerse oneself in Plato, Machiavelli, Rousseau, and Nietzsche. If one wants to sharpen one's political judgment, one should read the newspapers. That is why political philosophers have rarely managed to combine penetrating theoretical vision with reliable practical wisdom. And that, in turn, is why philosophers and theorists should hold no special privileges in the domain of

---

29. "Preface to *A Contribution to the Critique of Political Economy*," in *The Marx-Engels Reader*, p. 6. Although Marx seems to present this as a distraction and detour from his real theoretical interests, I think this "detour" marks Marx's real strength as a political thinker, displayed most brilliantly in his writings on the French politics of his day.

30. For Aristotle's doctrine of phronesis, with its emphasis on the judging of particulars, see *Nicomachean Ethics*, trans. Martin Ostwald (Indianapolis: Bobbs-Merrill, 1962), pp. 14, 35, 44, 51, 157–158, 165–166, 298–302.

common deliberation and decision. For in the matters of day-to-day practical choice we are all schooled, as citizens, when we open up the pages of our morning newspaper. Reciting this daily prayer is, even for philosophers, the token, and the condition, of responsible citizenship.

Nowhere in the above argument is it required of theorists that they abstain from political action; on the contrary, my assumption is that they ought to assume political responsibilities equal to those of everyone else. And nowhere do I demand that they forget that they are theorists, or forget what they know as theorists, when they act as citizens. Finally, nowhere do I deny that there are circumstances in which theory *can* change the world—but those circumstances are not ours. What I do argue is that theorists should never presume that what they do as theorists gives them special advantages in arriving at concrete decisions, or privileges them in their deliberations with their fellows. My position is, I would say, animated by the egalitarianism of Rousseau. If the view of those who uphold the unity of theory and practice were pursued to its logical conclusion, we would arrive at the unpalatable position, which Plato perhaps embraced, that only theorists ought to act politically.[31] I can well imagine that there are ways in which one can separate theory and practice without being a democrat or affirming democracy, but I fail to see how one can hope to unify theory and practice without positing, by intention or not, an aristocracy of theory.[32]

31. For a powerful defense of the unity of theory and practice (really, the subordination of practice to theory) in reply to Burke's thoroughgoing critique of theory on behalf of practice, see Harvey C. Mansfield, Jr.'s introduction to his edition of *Selected Letters of Edmund Burke* (Chicago: University of Chicago Press, 1984), pp. 1–27. However, Mansfield's argument entails the Platonic assumption that practical actors who lack theoretical understanding are at some level politically incompetent.

32. Bakunin, for one, faced up to this problem squarely: "The terms educated socialists and scientific socialism, which are encountered continuously in the writings of the Lasalleans and the Marxists, themselves demonstrate that the alleged popular state will be nothing more than the despotic rule of the popular masses by a new and numerically small aristocracy of real or imagined scholars." Mikhail Bakunin, *Statism and Anarchy*, ed. J. F. Harrison (New York: Revisionist Press, 1976), p. 270. For commentary, see Bernard Yack, *The Longing for Total Revolution* (Princeton: Princeton University Press, 1986), pp. 287–288; more generally, see Yack's very illuminating analysis of the theory-practice problem on pp. 285–287.

To all of this it may well be objected that recent experience in Eastern Europe demonstrates the political efficacy of intellectual cadres. Indeed, the moral authority of writers and philosophers in the East is undeniable; yet the lessons to be drawn from that very different cultural experience are less easy to discern. The point is that there is a real difference of experience, and this has to be taken into account in measuring the force of the counterargument. In the West, intellectuals as a class are impotent and irrelevant—or at least the good ones are, the ones who are not easily utilizable for immediate ideological purposes. It is simply honest for members of this class, both Right and Left, to acknowledge this fact.[33] Why is it that this judgment is clearly inapplicable to societies on the Eastern side of what is now being called Central Europe? Philip Roth remarked about his first visit to Czechoslovakia: "It occurred to me that I work in a society where as a writer everything goes and nothing matters, while for the Czech writers I met in Prague, nothing goes and everything matters."[34] To my way of thinking, this confirms the primacy of ethos; so, for instance, poets and philosophers in the East can exercise spiritual influence not because theory shapes the ethos of their society, but because there already exists the necessary ethos (the receptivity to intellectual impulses, including poetry) that no theory could itself conjure into existence.

Again, ethos cannot be legislated. One must proceed on the basis of what is given. Liberal theorists cannot resummon a dedication to liberal morality merely by appealing to theoretically designed liberal principles, any more than communitarians can conjure up a desired communitarian reality simply by a feat of theory. One encounters the same problem, for instance, within Marxism: working-class solidarity cannot be conjured up by a theoretical coup; it must either well up naturally, through spontaneous solidarities, or

33. For an instructive exchange on the theory-practice issue, see "Hannah Arendt on Hannah Arendt," in *Hannah Arendt: The Recovery of the Public World*, ed. Melvyn A. Hill (New York: St. Martin's Press, 1979), pp. 303–310. It seems to me that Arendt evinces greater honesty than her critics (and not just false modesty) when she says: "I don't believe that something very tangible comes out of anything which people like me are doing, but what I am after is [simply] to think about these things" (ibid., p. 331).

34. Philip Roth, "Interview with *The Paris Review*," in *Reading Myself and Others* (New York: Farrar, Straus & Giroux, 1975), p. 167.

be imposed through bureaucratic fiat—in which case, real workers' solidarity expresses itself in suppressed resistance to the official regime. And here, plainly, a strict and impassable limit to theory is demarcated. Here we would do well to echo Hannah Arendt's unyielding vindication of theory: "To these preoccupations and perplexities, this book does not offer an answer. Such answers are given every day, and they are matters of practical politics, subject to the agreement of many; they can never lie in theoretical considerations or the opinion of one person, as though we dealt here with problems for which only one solution is possible."[35] So we are back to the conception of theory as unapologetically critical in purpose. To borrow Schumpeter's phrase, intellectuals, to be true to themselves as intellectuals, "cannot help nibbling" at the foundations of the society they inhabit.[36]

Naturally, liberals will tend to see all these disclaimers about the limits of theory as merely a way for critics of liberalism to excuse their own indulgence in denigrating a political order for which they have little to offer in the way of practicable alternatives. But why should it necessarily be the business of social theorists to design a set of feasible institutions to supplant those of political liberalism? Isn't this rather like the case of the dejected playwright who complains that theater critics should desist from writing critical reviews until the critics themselves are capable of composing a better play? Theorists qua theorists are not politicians (though some first-rate theorists have been second-rate politicians). Nor is a text in political theory a political manifesto; if that is what it is intended to be, it is sure to be poor political theory and an even poorer political manifesto. (We are not at a loss to think of important works of theory

---

35. Hannah Arendt, *The Human Condition* (Chicago: University of Chicago Press, 1958), p. 5. Cf. Judith Shklar, "Rethinking the Past," *Social Research* 44, no. 1 (Spring 1977): 81: Philosophy "does not tell people how to behave but how to think. . . . It does not try 'to offer solutions or to give advice.' [Philosophy commands reflection,] not exhorting, preaching, or directing conduct." And George Armstrong Kelly, *Hegel's Retreat from Eleusis* (Princeton: Princeton University Press, 1978), p. 155: "The function of political philosophy is not to 'contribute' to a muddy cascade of subsequent political acts; it is to clarify."

36. Joseph A. Schumpeter, *Capitalism, Socialism and Democracy* (New York: Harper & Row, 1976), p. 151.

that have been dreadful manifestos.) The duty of the theorist is to make judgments about the life of a society; confronted with styles of living that are unseemly, it is least of all the theorist who should be fearful of the presumption of saying they are unseemly. But neither logically nor pragmatically does it follow from this that the theorist is automatically committed to a change of regime in order to impose a new mode of living at all costs; just as, by analogy, in private life one can quite appropriately make judgments about how friends and family members live without being obliged to intervene in how they live. Nor on the other hand does it follow, as it does for the liberal, that because one is not committed to a Jacobin or Leninist politics to coerce people into adopting a different set of practices, therefore one should not enter into the extravagant occupation of making these judgments in the first place. There is a logical and existential breach between the luxuries of reflection and the demands of life that theory should respect. Accordingly, I do not see how, for instance, a mere theory of citizenship can offer a blueprint for a radically redesigned practice of citizenship; what it can help to articulate is why contemporary societies will be in serious trouble unless the practice of citizenship *is* somehow reshaped, practically and concretely, in response to the unique realities of the present age. This is where theory leaves off and political practice begins.

Theory is necessarily an exercise not only in criticism but in self-criticism. For a member of a liberal society, that means self-criticism of the shared way of life of liberal society. The most blatant delusion of liberal philosophy is that there is no such way of life, and therefore no object of self-critical reflection here. It can hardly be doubted by someone who inhabits a liberal society that there are many reasons to prefer it to the illiberal societies throughout history. Nor can it be doubted that even the most strenuous critic of life in a contemporary liberal society will recognize much that is deeply attractive in the aspirations of liberal theory, whether in its Kantian, Humboldtian, Tocquevillean, Millian, or Rawlsian formulations. But it may still be asked whether these acknowledgments exhaust the responsibility of the theorist. The real question for theory, as I understand it, is whether the articulation of liberal ideals makes us more complacent about practices in a liberal society or whether these ideals prod us to be more critical of those practices.[37] Does liberalism fulfill or does it betray the age-old vocation of theory, which is not to give reassurance to the self-understanding of our community, but to be relentlessly critical of the communal self-understanding? Reading the writings of liberals today, are we encouraged to pat ourselves on the back, or are we instead roused by the gadfly's sting?

37. Plato in the *Menexenus* (235d, 236a) has Socrates declare that the orators of repute have made things too easy for themselves by undertaking to praise Athens before an audience of Athenians. A true mastery of the art of rhetoric, by contrast, would consist in being able to praise the Athenians before an audience of Spartans, or to praise the Spartans before an audience of Athenians. Socrates' gibe at Pericles expresses very well, I think, an accusation that can be made against contemporary liberal political philosophers as well: that they "praise the Athenians among the Athenians."

Index

Abortion, 65n.51, 66, 84–86, 87
Ackerman, Bruce A., 70n.64, 99–104, 131
AIDS, 77, 120
Andrew, Edward, 88n.16, 94n.28, 97n.32
Aquinas, St. Thomas, 47, 53, 56
Arendt, Hannah, 10–12, 35, 136, 139–40, 143n.2, 152, 189n.33, 190
Aristotelian and neo-Aristotelian ethics, 3–5, 17, 44–59, 61–63, 65, 70, 71–76, 79, 137–39, 141, 173, 179, 187; ethos in, 5, 22, 44, 75n.74, 173, 179; summum bonum in, 45–48, 52–54, 57–59. *See also* Human telos; Prudence; Teleology; Virtues, theory of the
Aristotle, 3–4, 6, 13, 17, 20, 22, 38, 39–41, 44–59, 61–63, 70–76, 89–90, 113–14, 115, 117–19, 128, 130, 138–39, 141, 148–49, 151, 173, 175–79, 183, 187
Arnold, Matthew, 27n.24
Autonomy, 8, 16, 17, 18–19, 25–27, 28, 31–32, 35–37, 39, 42–43, 51–52, 60–61, 67, 69, 72, 78, 82, 130n.81

Bacon, Francis, 138, 171
Bakunin, Mikhail, 188n.32
Barbalet, J. M., 112n.39, 161n.29
Barber, Benjamin, 107, 117n.52, 119n.55, 127, 157n.21
Bayle, Pierre, 64
Bell, Daniel, 162n.34, 164
Bellah, Robert N., 23n.17
Benjamin, Walter, 10–12
Benn, Tony, 146
Bentham, Jeremy, 89
Berlin, Isaiah, 50, 59
Bloom, Allan, 23n.17, 30n.29, 36
Bodin, Jean, 64

Bond, E. J., 41n.2
Burckhardt, Jacob, 8n.4, 37, 122, 184n.26
Bureaucracy, 34, 66, 112n.38, 118, 120, 190
Burke, Edmund, 122–23, 134, 135, 177, 178, 180, 188n.31
Burnheim, John, 104n.23
Bush, George, 8n.4, 174n.4

Calvino, Italo, 5
Capitalism, 64n.49, 76, 118, 127, 131n.83, 142, 156, 161, 162–65, 166
Carens, Joseph, 90n.22, 102n.16, 103, 113
Castro, Fidel, 153n.13
Chamberlain, Neville, 103n.21
Character formation, 14, 16, 22, 36–37, 39, 43, 49, 63, 75, 78, 126, 164. *See also* Aristotelian and neo-Aristotelian ethics, ethos in
Churchill, Winston, 103n.21
Citizenship, 34–35, 68, 80n.1, 98–141, 143–54, 156–57, 158n.23, 159–60, 162, 164, 167, 168–69, 175, 176, 185, 188, 191; and civic identity, 105, 107–9, 114–15, 119–20, 169; and class, 124; competence for, 105–7, 120–21, 125–29; crisis of, 103, 112n.38, 118; and culture, 125–27, 133–35; defined, 104, 105; and democracy, 34–35, 51, 104–7, 110, 120–21, 127–28, 129–30, 146n.5, 175; and equality, 133, 150, 159–60, 162–63; global (versus national), 102, 110, 117n.51, 120, 121; liberal theories of, 99–104, 108–9, 112–14, 128–29; local (versus national), 110, 121–22; and military conscription, 114n.44; as one among other roles (versus citizenship as privileged),

Designer: Barbara Jellow
Compositor: Maryland Composition
Text: 10/13 Palatino
Display Palatino
Printer: Maple-Vail Book Mfg. Group
Binder: Maple-Vail Book Mfg. Group